Phenomenology

Phenomenology

An Introduction

Michael Lewis and
Tanja Staehler

continuum

Continuum International Publishing Group

The Tower Building   80 Maiden Lane
11 York Road   Suite 704
London SE1 7NX   New York, NY 10038

www.continuumbooks.com

British Library Cataloguing-in-Publication Data
A catalogue record for this book is available from the British Library.

ISBN: HB: 978-0-8264-3143-1
       PB: 978-0-8264-3999-4

Library of Congress Cataloging-in-Publication Data
Lewis, Michael, 1977-
Phenomenology : an introduction / Michael Lewis and Tanja Staehler.
   p. cm.
ISBN-13: 978-0-8264-3143-1
ISBN-10: 0-8264-3143-7
ISBN-13: 978-0-8264-3999-4 (pbk.)
ISBN-10: 0-8264-3999-3 (pbk.)
1. Phenomenology. I. Staehler, Tanja. II. Title.

B829.5.L398 2010
142'.7–dc22   2010010413

Typeset by Newgen Imaging Systems Pvt Ltd, Chennai, India
Printed and bound in Great Britain by the MPG Books Group

Contents

Acknowledgements

I would like to thank my students and colleagues at the University of Sussex for helpful discussions and questions. Special thanks go to a number of people who have provided helpful feedback on individual chapters: Charlotte Fawcett, Alexander Kozin, David Lauer, Timothy Mooney, and Céline Surprenant.

T.S.

I would like to dedicate my work on this book to my Sussex students and friends (2007–2009), and particularly to those who followed the Phenomenology course in the Spring and Summer of 2008.

M.L.

Introduction

What is phenomenology? Phenomenology is, literally, a 'science of the phenomenon', but not 'phenomenon' in the usual sense of a brief, dazzling coruscation. More literally, a phenomenon is something that *appears*; strictly speaking, it is the *appearance* itself. Phenomenology does not attempt to speak about things, but only about the way they manifest themselves, and hence it tries to describe the nature of *appearance as such*. It asks the question of whether or not it is possible to say anything with absolute *certainty* about the nature of appearance in general. When something appears, does that appearing have any general features which we can identify? Does manifestation have an essence? Thus phenomenology focuses not on *what* appears, but on *how* it appears.

For phenomenology, appearances cannot simply appear in splendid isolation: they must appear *to* something, and that something is usually taken to be 'consciousness'. Appearance is thus understood as a form of *giving*. Appearances are *given* to consciousness. In this case, phenomenology asks, how must consciousness be constituted if it is able to *receive* such a gift? What sort of entity is capable of receptivity? At the same time, even if phenomenology finds that it cannot say anything more about *all* phenomena in general, it can nevertheless attempt an exhaustive study of the different *ways* in which phenomena are *given* to us. It can provide a detailed description of all the multifarious forms of 'givenness'.

The word 'givenness' attempts to describe the way in which things appear to consciousness in the most basic and immediate way, prior to any explicit interpretation, before any judgement as to the nature of the thing that is here presenting itself to us, a judgement in which we could always be mistaken. 'Givenness' describes the way in which an entity appears insofar as it is *certain beyond doubt* that the appearance has not in any way been distorted by our experience of it.

Nietzsche

Phenomenology as we know it today was first given a systematic form by Edmund Husserl at the beginning of the twentieth century. It is an attempt to go beyond the 'metaphysical' approach that has characterized most of Western philosophy since the ancient Greeks. Broadly speaking, metaphysics attempts precisely to say something about the *thing* that appears, rather than the appearance itself. Metaphysical thought, as Nietzsche describes it, makes a rigorous distinction between the intelligible world and the sensible world, or, in other words, between being and appearance, essence and existence, between the timeless essence of a thing, and the contingent, distorted way in which that essence actually appears to us in our sensory experience. Nietzsche attributes the distinction to Plato. The realm of appearance was a realm about which there could be no certain, scientific knowledge (*epistēmē*) but only 'opinion' (*doxa*). The latter could perceive only a *part* of its object, because its view was limited to a particular individual *perspective*. Only *thought* was capable of counteracting the limitations inherent in sensory experience, and so only thought could enter the realm of essence, and hence produce a knowledge that was both certain and necessary.

Nietzsche, a crucial forerunner of phenomenology, wished to 'overturn' this Platonism and restore to the *doxa* its dignity, to bestow a new value upon the way things 'seem' to me, which could have been devalued only by the presupposition that things really did exist independently of any perspective in which they might appear. For Nietzsche there simply was no pure 'essence' that existed apart from the multiplicity of its appearances. If there was a 'thing in itself' then appearances were a part of it, and these appearances were a direct presentation of what really existed. In other words, 'perspective' as such was an essential part of reality itself.

A century before Nietzsche, something had already happened in the history of philosophy that had caused it to turn its attention back to the phenomenon: *Kant.*

Kant

With Kant, philosophy makes a radical turn, and in the process, the purely intelligible essence of things becomes unknowable, and hence the very idea of metaphysics becomes problematic. Kant was in his own way attempting to overcome the dogmatism that beset traditional metaphysics in its assertions about the thing-in-itself beyond appearance. He described the distinction between the intelligible and the sensible with the words 'noumenon' and 'phenomenon', two expressions of Greek and indeed Platonic origin: they mean quite simply that which is accessible only to the intellect (*nous*), and what is given to the senses (*aisthēsis*). According to Kant, in our experience, we have no access to the noumenon, the 'thing-in-itself' (*das Ding an sich*), but only to the phenomenon, the various ways in which an entity appears or is 'given' to us.

So, although we can *think* that there might be something in-itself, apart from how it appears *to* us, although we can think (*noein*) the noumenon, we cannot *know* it. It is precisely this distinction between thought and knowledge that traditional metaphysics has forgotten. The thing in itself is cut off from us, unknowable, always beyond our grasp. All we can *know* is now the phenomenon. What metaphysics has said about the noumenon invokes categories that are in fact only applicable to the phenomena that we can actually *experience*. It is as if, after Kant, philosophy had been taught a certain modesty, to restrict the greater part of its attention to the phenomenal half of the metaphysical opposition, which was formerly cast outside of philosophy as the realm of appearance, opinion, and sophistic persuasion.

Our experience of things is always finite, limited because confined to a certain perspective. It can know nothing of what exists apart from all experience, that exists beyond the *conditions* of possible experience, that is therefore 'unconditioned' and so exists 'unconditionally' or 'absolutely'. It can only experience things in space and time, and by ordering the flux of sensuous experience in terms of a series of categories, which assure the unity of a field of experience and the intelligibility of that experience.

Thus with Kant, we find a revolution in the history of thought that is crucial if we are to understand what 'phenomenology' is and how it can be said to assume the task of philosophy. Kant denies that we can know anything of the noumenal thing which does not appear in experience, but at the same time this does not leave us with a merely subjective experience that is purely contingent and individual and about which no general, necessary, *a priori* statements can be made. On the contrary, Kant's task in his *Critique of Pure Reason* (1781/1787) is precisely to show that there are certain features which must of necessity characterize *all possible experience*. His aim is to discover what an 'experience' must involve if it is indeed to count as an 'experience' at all, and that means an experience of an *object*. In other words, his question is as follows: what allows a subjective appearance to be *more* than just subjective, to give us access to an enduring *object* that others besides ourselves could experience?

There are certain necessary conditions that must apply to experiences if they are to count as 'objective', and these conditions are described as *transcendental* conditions. They all describe certain features of the experiencing *subject*: the subject must have certain faculties, certain abilities, a certain constitution in order for knowledge to be possible. Thus, the subject makes knowledge possible; indeed, for Kant, this subject even makes the *object* of knowledge possible: the thing that we know and experience is *constructed* by the subject. Of course, things exist before we are around to experience them: there are 'entities', but they are not 'objects', – objects are always objects *for* a subject, they are experienced by a subject – things in themselves do not have the form that our perception attributes to them.

The subject who constructs the object is the *'transcendental* subject' and it is transcendental in the sense that it comprises the conditions of possibility for objective knowledge (knowledge of the object). The word 'transcendental', after Kant, may be taken to mean 'the conditions of possibility for knowledge', those things which must be in place in order for an *objective* appearance to be possible. This means that with the help of the transcendental subject, appearance is no longer 'merely subjective' – it is the appearance of a real object that exists independently of the individual subject. Thus, if phenomenology studies appearances, it is not confined to a merely arbitrary set of statements about its own opinions and impressions. For, thanks to Kant, we now have a rigorous concept of the phenomenon and of the nature of experience, in which there are necessary structures. There can thus be a genuine *science* of the phenomenon, which metaphysics from Plato onwards would never have thought possible.

Husserl

After the Kantian revolution, and after Nietzsche, Husserl begins his own unique attempt to understand consciousness and the way that it constitutes an objective experience. He begins by bracketing any ontological questions we might have about what exists beyond consciousness. In other words, phenomenology begins with another reinvention of 'scepticism', akin to the ancient kind known as 'Pyrrhonian scepticism', which rather than simply denying that we can have any knowledge beyond our subjective impressions, merely insists that we remain 'agnostic' about this, and suspend judgement. In Greek, this suspension was called *epochē*, and Husserl himself employs this word for the very first element of his phenomenological method. In other words, Husserl believes that we do not need to decide on the reality or otherwise of what is beyond our experiences, the nature of the noumenon: this is precisely what metaphysics believed it could do, to speak of what really existed in itself, independently of all experience of it – what was 'absolute' rather than 'relative' (to us). Ultimately, for Husserl, we can say that everything that *is*, *appears*. The thing in itself appears to us. So there is no distinction between the thing that hides in itself and the thing that appears to me. There is no secluded noumenon hiding behind the mask of the phenomenon. Things *show themselves to me*, they 'announce' or 'express' themselves.

What Husserl shows is that the nature of experience can be properly understood without reference to the real existence of the world beyond consciousness. In other words, the bracketing of any assumptions about the world, which in our naive 'natural attitude' we ordinarily make, can be carried out without affecting the nature of our experience at all. Descartes, one of Husserl's inspirations in this regard, had already shown that even if we presuppose that all of our supposedly 'real experiences' are a product of the deceptions of a malevolent demon, we are still able to discover certain things *internal to consciousness*, that are self-evidently true.

So, things present themselves to consciousness straightforwardly, truly, but they do so only if we learn to look at them in the right way. This is why the motto of phenomenology is, 'Back to the things themselves! (*Zu den Sachen selbst!*)' And these things are the *phenomena*. This in itself testifies to the novelty of Husserl's thought. For Plato or Kant, to say this would have meant to go back to the thing *in* itself, *behind* or *beyond* the phenomena. For Husserl, to say that we must go 'back to the thing itself' means that we must go back to the *phenomena*, to how things *do* and *must* appear.

6 Phenomenology

Husserl has a higher opinion of experience than his predecessors: things *can* show themselves to us as they really are, to our perspectival perception. The reason why they often do *not* is because we think too much: we try to interpret what we see using concepts that we have uncritically inherited, and which implicate us in traditional prejudices about *what* we see. Thus we fail to allow what we are experiencing to come towards us, appear to us, and give itself to us as it really is. We simply believe what we have been told about things and do not scrutinize them for ourselves.

This is why Husserl places such a stress on 'intuition': intuition is ultimately the *method* of phenomenology. 'Intuition' here does not have a mystical sense, but is meant in a more or less Kantian way, which is to say, a direct, non-conceptual access to things, one which receives them purely, without any interpretation. It is a *direct* contact with the thing itself.

Husserl calls this the 'principle of principles', the ultimate principle that governs phenomenology: nothing is certain unless we access it directly in intuition. We can certainly *know* something only if we can verify that we are experiencing each of its aspects correctly in a direct *intuition*, because in this intuition the thing as it is in itself is *given* to us, 'in the flesh'. The principle of principles states that the only adequate source of knowledge is intuition, the direct bodily presence of the thing we are seeking to know.

Phenomenology insists that we should not accept anything we have learnt, any particular ways of thinking we might have inherited from our culture and upbringing – we are to verify everything for ourselves, individually, with our own intuition.

So, the aim of phenomenology, in very simple terms, is to do away with interpretation and to let the things themselves speak for themselves. Once we have learnt to do this, we will have a firm foundation for a science of the phenomenal.

* * *

Plato had – according to Nietzsche – devalued appearance, reduced it to a mere *seeming*. The real thing was somewhere else, behind its many, deceptive appearances. Appearances were things about which one could not acquire certain knowledge, one could only have opinions, points of view. In opposition to this, and even without the reference to the noumenon that Kant retains, Husserl returns to appearances their philosophical dignity. One can make scientific statements about the nature of appearance, its necessary structures and character.

We have known since Descartes that, in fact, appearance – that which we are conscious of – is what exists *most certainly of all*. Descartes founded the whole of science on the fact that there is one thing that cannot be doubted, and that is that I am indeed experiencing my own experiences, and that I and my representations exist: that at least I can be certain of.

Thus, beginning with Plato and going by way of Kant, to Husserl, Nietzsche's anti-Platonic dream of a rehabilitation of the phenomenon – the apparent world – is achieved. We find in Husserl an attempt to realize the dream that the phenomenal realm may no longer be the subject merely of *doxa*, of imperfect subjective opinions, but of a genuine *science*.

Husserl entitled this science, 'phenomenology'.

The word

Literally, 'phenomenology' is the *logos* of the *phenomenon*. *Logos* can be translated in this context as science, doctrine or account, as bio-logy is the *logos* of life and psycho-logy the *logos* of the psyche. *Phenomenon* is derived from the Greek word, *phainomenon*, which is the present participle of the verb *phainesthai*, to appear, and thus designates what appears to us or the *appearing* as such. The *phenomenon* is *what* appears, together with its appear*ing*, or rather, it designates that which appears *in* its very appearing.

The text

The bulk of the present book attempts to describe the nature of phenomenology as it is developed by four thinkers, Edmund Husserl, Martin Heidegger, Jean-Paul Sartre and Maurice Merleau-Ponty. The remainder attempts to describe in concise terms the powerful and sometimes critical responses to the entire movement made by Jacques Derrida and Emmanuel Levinas, before providing two examples of the way in which, despite the force of these objections, phenomenology remains a viable and vital school of thought: Michel Henry and Jean-Luc Marion.

Parts I and IV were written by Tanja Staehler, along with Chapter 18 of Part V; Parts II, III and the remaining chapters of Part V were written by Michael Lewis.

Tanja Staehler
Michael Lewis

Sussex
February 2010

Part I
Edmund Husserl (Prossnitz, Moravia 1859—Freiburg, Germany 1938)

Husserl was born in 1859 in Prossnitz, Moravia (now in the Czech Republic). At university, he studied philosophy and mathematics. In 1900/01, he published his *Logical Investigations*[1] which is famous for its refutation of psychologism. While psychologism claims that logical laws can be reduced to psychological laws, Husserl argued that the laws of logic are valid necessarily and a priori. In the final *Logical Investigation*, the sixth, Husserl develops the concept of 'categorial intuition' to describe the fact that we can have an intuition not just of individual items, but of entire states-of-affairs (such as 'the cat is black').

In 1911, he started introducing phenomenology systematically with the publication of the first volume of his *Ideas Pertaining to a Pure Phenomenology and to a Phenomenological Philosophy*, usually referred to as *Ideas I*. This book develops the main ideas and concepts of Husserl's phenomenology, especially the phenomenological *epochē*. Further introductions to phenomenology follow, such as *Cartesian Meditations* (1931) and *The Crisis of European Sciences and Transcendental Phenomenology* (1936), usually referred to as *Crisis*.

After a long and illustrious career, because of his Jewish origins, Husserl was no longer allowed to enter the University of Freiburg after 1933 when the National Socialists came to power in Germany, yet he continued writing until he died in 1938. To make sure that his manuscripts and notes would not be destroyed by the Nazis, a Belgian Franciscan monk named H. L. Van Breda secretly brought them to Leuven, Belgium, where he founded the Husserl Archive. Up to this day, Husserl's writings are still being studied and edited there. In addition to his various published works, of which only a few have been mentioned in this short introduction, Husserl left over 38,000 pages of working notes written in an old-fashioned short hand.

The Phenomenological *Epochē*

Main primary literature: 'Considerations Fundamental to Phenomenology' in *Ideas I*, pp. 51–119/56–113.
Note on citations: A list of abbreviations is given at the beginning of the bibliography (p. 242).

In this chapter, we will discuss Husserl's notion of *epochē* which is a central component of his phenomenological method and perhaps the single most important aspect of his phenomenology. At the same time, several problems emerge in relation to the *epochē* which forced Husserl to develop and redefine this concept continuously. One of the reasons why Husserl wrote several works of an introductory character or 'introductions to phenomenology' is that he felt the need to explain better what the *epochē* consists in, how misunderstandings about it can be avoided, and how the need for conducting the *epochē* can be justified.

In order to explain the *epochē*, Husserl needs to examine where we find ourselves before undertaking the *epochē*, which is where we always already find ourselves. Husserl calls this common state the 'natural attitude', that is, the attitude towards the world which we have prior to and outside of philosophy. It could also be called 'common sense'. Accordingly, the *epochē* is a shift in attitude which opens up a different perspective on the world. Introducing the natural attitude is important also because phenomenology holds a complex relation to it; rather than moving away from the natural attitude, phenomenology reflects on it and investigates it. In that sense, phenomenology can be said to move more deeply into the natural attitude in order to explore its previously hidden layers and facets.

(a) The natural attitude

The opening words of the central section of *Ideas I* (the 'Considerations Fundamental to Phenomenology') read as follows: 'We begin our considerations as human beings who are living naturally, objectivating, judging, feeling, willing *"in the natural attitude"'* (*Ideas I*, 51/56). The analysis of the natural attitude shows that it has two basic characteristics. First, it is directed in a straightforward manner towards its objects, and second, it is convinced that these objects are not only there when we turn to them, but exist independently of our attention.

The first aspect, the talk of a 'straightforward attitude' is meant to express that in the natural attitude we concentrate entirely on the object. For the most part, we encounter objects in the light of specific goals and interests, as 'practical objects of every sort: streets with street lights, dwellings, furniture, works of art, books, tools, and so forth' (*Ideas I*, 78/77). We are only directed towards *what* we perceive, or as Husserl puts it, towards the 'what' of our perception (or memory, or imagination), and not towards the 'how', the way or mode in which this 'what' comes to appearance. Phenomenology will attempt to step back from this straightforward directedness towards the object in order to see just *how* the object is given to us, and how different objects are given differently.[2]

The second characteristic is the natural attitude's firm belief that objects exist and endure, even if we turn our backs on them or fall asleep. We 'take it for granted that mental processes do not exist only when we advert to them' (*Ideas I*, 175/178). The natural attitude attributes to things an existence independent of our consciousness; positing the existence of things is the main feature of the natural attitude. Yet do we not constantly undergo the experiences in which this conviction is disappointed, that is, when an object turns out to be different than we assumed it to be, or that something which we believed to exist turns out to be an illusion, a shadow or reflection of light, such that we need to take back our initial judgement? Indeed, we may be mistaken about the existence or the 'being' of individual objects, but the natural attitude is only shaken for a moment by such incidents; it immediately replaces the wrong assumption with a new one. The important point is that the nexus of objects remains valid throughout. We may be mistaken about something specific, but we are not deceived about the whole. That the world remains in existence is our fundamental conviction. 'The world is there for me', 'The world *is*' – such is the basic claim, the general thesis (*Generalthesis*), of natural consciousness. This thesis is obviously not an explicit thesis expressed by natural consciousness; it always remains in the background without becoming 'thematic' – in other words, the explicitly considered 'theme' of an investigation or thought. If the basic conviction of natural consciousness were expressed from the standpoint of philosophical consciousness, however, that thesis would result. To move from the natural to the philosophical or phenomenological attitude, according to Husserl, means precisely to bracket this general thesis.

(b) The phenomenological *epochē*

A preliminary explanation of the idea of the *epochē* may start with the problem of scepticism: how do we know that there is an outside world there at all? Might we not just be dreaming about it or simply imagining it? Can we have any certainty that the world continues to exist when we stop perceiving it, and that it has an existence independently of us? These questions have troubled ancient as well as modern sceptics. Philosophers who wanted to remain true to the ancient Greek ideal of philosophy as a universal science have often felt the need to find a solution to the sceptic's problem before philosophy proper could begin. However, no solution to the problem of scepticism has been found which would be truly flawless and generally convincing.[3] Yet if the problem is so complex that it has not yet been resolved, and if at the same time it seems to present a fundamental problem for philosophy which cannot be avoided or circumvented, should philosophy persist in confronting this problem? Husserl suggests that we should in fact suspend the problem altogether; this means to remain in some sense agnostic about it: if we neither confirm that the world has an existence independently of our conceiving it nor deny such an existence, we manage to avoid basing philosophy on an untenable foundation. But can philosophy ever rightly begin if it suspends this crucial issue? Husserl wants to show that this is indeed possible – if we understand what the suspension consists in and what remains after the suspending.

> The **epochē** is a suspension of judgement; the Greek *epechein* means to suspend, refrain, bracket. Specifically, the phenomenological *epochē* means a suspension of judgement regarding the being of the world which is neither affirmed nor denied.

Husserl modified his response to the question of how we can enter into phenomenology several times. Throughout his work, he considered the *epochē* to be a necessary component of an introduction to phenomenology; yet he altered the concept of the *epochē* repeatedly, attributing different systematic positions and roles to it. The main idea of the *epochē* will be presented here in roughly the shape which Husserl gave it in his *Ideas I*.

Husserl requests that we perform a radical change and break with the natural attitude. The way in which he introduces this change of attitude is in the literal sense unmotivated: 'Instead of remaining in this attitude, we propose to alter it radically. What we now must do is to convince ourselves of the essential *possibility* of the alteration in question' (*Ideas I*, 57/53, my italics). *Why* we would perform this change of attitude is thus not thematized by Husserl in this text; he is merely concerned with demonstrating the possibility of such a change. It will turn out that Husserl criticizes this aspect of his *Ideas I* later on, discussing in particular the question of how to motivate the *epochē*.

Yet Husserl's 'Introduction' to *Ideas I* and his procedure in the 'Fundamental Considerations' already show why the universal thesis of the natural attitude cannot remain active and must become questionable. Since Husserl conceives of his philosophy as a science, several conditions need to be fulfilled. Philosophy as a science needs to be universal, that is, it must not exclude anything from consideration. Furthermore, it must not accept any presuppositions without examining them. The existence of the world can be doubted, as Descartes has shown; it is no secure basis on which a science might be founded. We can thus no longer take our natural certainty of the world for granted but must place it in doubt. The universal *epochē* is a specific kind of doubt; it refrains from positing the being of the world. Husserl states that we thereby 'bracket' (*einklammern*) or 'put out of action' (*ausschalten*) the general thesis of the natural attitude (*Ideas I*, 54/65).

If we no longer pass judgements about the being of objects and of the world, we are still left with objects and the world as they appear to us – and this is, on closer consideration, all that we have access to anyway. Husserl thus rightfully states that 'we have not lost anything' (*Ideas I*, 119/113). Rather, we are left with the world as it appears to consciousness, and this is the main focus for phenomenology.

> **World** in the phenomenological sense is not a totality of entities, but designates the relations or references between them; it is a *context of references*. We find ourselves in this context; we do not bring it about, but we do give meaning to it.

The judgements about an independent being of the world do not directly concern any particular thing which appears to us; they are judgements which we pass (or rather, have always already passed) on the basis of what appears to us. In the phenomenological attitude, we are no longer directed 'straight-forwardly' towards objects but towards their appearance in consciousness, to 'how' they appear. The motivation for the *epochē* is thus not a turning away from the world but a turn towards it; world and objects shall be considered in an untainted fashion. For this reason, all prejudices and ready-made opinions are bracketed, and we focus entirely on the way in which world and objects appear to us.[4] This reflection on appearances is the phenomenological reduction which amounts to the continuation and completion of the *epochē*.

> Husserl often employs the concepts '**reduction**' and '*epochē*' interchangeably; they belong very closely together. Where he differentiates them in his terminology, the *epochē* refers to the moment of bracketing, of suspending the thesis about the world's existence, whereas the reduction designates the redirecting of our attention towards the ways in which the phenomena appear to consciousness.

For the remainder of this section, *epochē* will designate the whole of *epochē* and reduction while emphasizing specifically the aspect of refraining or suspending.

It is important to note that the focus on how the world and objects appear to us does not mean that phenomenology describes merely subjective experiences. Rather, phenomenology strives to determine the structures of our experience which can be considered 'transcendental': they are the conditions for the possibility of all experience. We will encounter several such structures, of consciousness and of the world, in subsequent chapters. For example, it is not a particularly interesting observation for phenomenology that I see a chair from the back rather than the front, but it *is* interesting that we never see the object from every side at once. Before examining such structures, the procedure and problems of the *epoché* need to be discussed further.

(c) The Cartesian way

Husserl pursues his 'Considerations Fundamental to Phenomenology' beginning from the natural attitude, and he pursues them in the form of statements in the first person, by way of 'simple meditations' (*Ideas I*, 51/48). A first point of contact with Descartes' *Meditations* is thereby established. But Husserl performs only the first step in Descartes' method of doubt, the 'refraining from opinion'.[5] He does not carry it out to the very end, which is the explicit negation of the existence of the world. Descartes negates the world in order to combat the habitual tendency on the part of natural consciousness to affirm the being of the world. Yet if we carry out the phenomenological *epoché*, we pass no judgement whatsoever on the world's being and consider the world entirely in its appearance.

Yet due to Descartes, we know that we can be indubitably certain of the existence of one area which we can turn to for our phenomenological analyses: the *ego cogito* or pure consciousness. At the same time, Husserl criticizes Descartes for misconceiving the essence of consciousness. According to Husserl, Descartes saved 'a little tag-end (*Endchen*) of the world' in the form of the 'apodictic' (the absolutely certain) pure ego (*CM*, 63/24). In other words, Descartes does not properly recognize the qualitative difference between consciousness and the world. We will not examine here whether this critique does justice to Descartes. A decisive difference is established by Husserl when he asserts that his principle brings nothing to expression which 'we ourselves do not "see"' (*CM*, 64/24). Husserl takes Descartes to have failed in this respect, yet he does not elaborate further on this failure. What Descartes brings into play, even though it cannot actually be verified by intuition, is the existence of God which guarantees that the *ego* can connect to an (existent) outer world.[6] Husserl's philosophy does not require a God in this respect because he leaves the question regarding the world's existence open and because he finds the entire wealth of the world in pure consciousness, albeit as phenomenon.

What mode of being does pure consciousness have if it is not affected by the universal *epoché* but 'remains' as the field of examination? The decisive point is that consciousness's mode of being is different from that of the world. Pure consciousness is not 'mundane' (world-like) but has a necessary, absolute being; the being of the world is contingent and relative, always limited by a certain horizon, and thus incompletely and inadequately given (*Ideas I*, § 49). In order to strengthen and elucidate the claim that the being of consciousness is substantially different from that of the world, Husserl introduces the problematic thought experiment of an annihilation of the world. According to Husserl, it is plausible that 'while the being of consciousness, of any stream of mental process whatever, would indeed be necessarily modified by an annihilation of the world of physical things, its own existence would not be touched' (*Ideas I*, 110/91f.). Husserl thus does not claim that it makes no difference to consciousness whether the world exists or not. Consciousness would necessarily be modified; yet even if the world no longer existed, the existence of consciousness might continue. This idea has been strongly criticized since it gives the impression of an extreme form of idealism, while Husserl, in fact, proposes a specific form of transcendental idealism, which he even claims to be a realism of sorts, if properly understood: a turn to the things themselves (as they appear). Several further problems with the *epochē*, especially in its Cartesian form, will be briefly sketched out in the next section.

(d) Problems with the *epochē*

(i) The problem of consciousness

One of the problems emerging from the Cartesian way lies in the fact that Husserl here designates consciousness as a necessary and absolute being, thus passing judgement on the being of consciousness. In order to be consistent, Husserl would need to leave the question concerning the being of consciousness open and restrict his examinations to the way in which consciousness appears to us. In examining the appearance of consciousness, it would then be necessary to ask how it is that consciousness appears to us as an absolute and necessary being, that is, how the apodictic being of consciousness is constituted.

However, Husserl wants to found phenomenology as a science, and transcendental consciousness is meant to serve as the foundation for this new science. Fortunately, it is not necessary for phenomenology to affirm the absolute being of consciousness. It is sufficient to show that transcendental consciousness appears in a fundamentally different way than the world. The universal *epochē* refers explicitly to the universal thesis of natural consciousness about the being of the *world*. The turn to transcendental consciousness and the investigation of the world's constitution within it is possible only if transcendental consciousness is not itself an object in the world. Transcendental consciousness is the flipside of the world, as if consciousness and world were two sides of the same coin. Consciousness and world together form an encompassing whole. There cannot be two separate totalities here but only one, considered from two different perspectives.

This does not mean that consciousness and world are collapsed into one. It is an essential component of our consciousness of world that the latter appears as something which transcends consciousness. The phenomenological task consists in clarifying the meaning of this transcendence by returning to examine *consciousness*. We will see below how the problem of consciousness gets resolved when Husserl develops an introduction to phenomenology that starts out from the lifeworld (Chapter 3 (f)). The status of consciousness will turn out to be more complicated than it first appeared; once phenomenological analysis takes history into consideration, it has to realize that consciousness is also historical and cannot acquire a standpoint 'above' the world.

(ii) The paradox of subjectivity

Husserl himself criticizes in retrospect his talk of pure consciousness as a 'residue' (*Residuum*) which remains after the 'annihilation of the world' (Hua VIII, 432). The problematic expression 'annihilation of the world' is unnecessary as well; the purpose of this thought experiment consisted in showing that pure consciousness has a fundamentally different mode of givenness to the world and is also different from the empirical ego. It is sufficient to bear this distinction in mind as a difference in the respective modes of givenness. In Husserl's later texts, this distinction occurs under the heading of a 'circle' or 'paradox' which can, however, be resolved. In the *Crisis*, Husserl formulates the problem as follows: 'How can a component part of the world, its human subjectivity, constitute the whole world [...]?' (*Crisis*, 183/179).

The apparent paradox is resolved by conceding that the human being is a subject that experiences the world and yet also an object in the world – the latter, the human being as embodied, as person, etc., is itself considered as a phenomenon once the former has carried out the *epochē*. The question is how the human being as object is constituted by the transcendental subject, 'considered purely as the ego-pole of his acts, habitualities, and capacities' (*Crisis*, 187/183). The empirical ego with its own character and name is thus substantially different from the transcendental ego, and when we usually speak of the 'I', we mean the empirical ego. The transcendental ego can only be accessed indirectly, as the correlate of objects and the world; when we try to reflect on it, we always arrive a little too late.'

(iii) Partial and universal *epochē*

In the *Crisis*, Husserl explains a decisive disadvantage of the Cartesian introduction to the *epochē*. The Cartesian way is short, but 'while it leads to the transcendental ego in one leap, as it were, it brings this ego into view as apparently empty of content, since there can be no preparatory explication; so one is at a loss, at first, to know what has been gained by it' (*Crisis*, 158/155). If we bracket the world as a whole, this empties consciousness of content, an emptiness which must be filled in by phenomenological analyses.

An alternative procedure which Husserl employs especially in the lectures on *First Philosophy* replaces the universal *epochē* initially with a partial *epochē*, relating to specific acts of consciousness. Husserl maintains that the request of abandoning all prejudices is 'a reasonable and necessary request, but as an initial request, necessarily also entirely vague' (Hua VIII, 165). By undertaking individual *epochaí* – such as suspending judgement about the being of a particular perceptual object in order to focus on how it appears, or the examination of past and future consciousness – the potential achievements of the *epochē* become obvious.

Why is the universal *epochē* even needed? Would it not be less problematic and easier to perform an *epochē* with respect to the specific area or region which is to be investigated, such as the region of spatiotemporal objects, artworks, natural objects? Husserl would support such a possibility as an intermediate stage. In the end, however, he aims to found a science which is concerned with everything there is, and which would be capable of universal statements. The universal *epochē* remains necessary in order to engage in transcendental phenomenology in the genuine sense; otherwise, phenomenology cannot relate to the world as a whole. The world as the horizon from which objects come to appear provides the connection between objects, and thus accounts for the unified and not fragmented character of our experience.

(iv) The problem of motivation

It is an essential feature of the natural attitude that it is self-sufficient and does not by itself call for a change. Husserl thus has difficulties in accounting for the motivation of the phenomenological *epochē*, particularly in light of the fact that the benefits of phenomenological analyses are hard to explain to one who remains within the natural attitude. While this is a problem which all philosophy faces, phenomenology needs to take the issue particularly seriously because it wishes to begin philosophizing without presuppositions and without basing itself on other philosophical theories.

In his late philosophy, Husserl engages in historical reflections which allow him to confront the problem of motivation. He asks how philosophy originated in Ancient Greece and is led back to the response which Plato and Aristotle gave regarding the beginning of philosophy: wonder. Husserl expands on this response by linking it to the encounter with the alien which may have aroused wonder for the Greeks and may also do so for us today (Chapter 4 (e) below).

Furthermore, he develops a new introduction to phenomenology that starts from the lifeworld and therefore allows him to seek a motivation for the *epochē* within the world. One important reason for entering phenomenology can be found in an experience of crisis which arises as a crisis of the sciences but turns out to permeate the lifeworld as a whole (Chapter 3 (d) & (e)). Husserl also acknowledges that the *epochē* might not necessarily be the first step of phenomenology, but might be prepared for by reflections on history or the lifeworld; phenomenology might accordingly proceed in a 'zigzag' fashion.

Further reading

Bernet, R., Kern, I. and Marbach, E. (eds) (1989), *An Introduction to Husserlian Phenomenology.* Evanston, IL: Northwestern University Press, chapter 2.

Carr, D. (1999), *The Paradox of Subjectivity. The Self in the Transcendental Tradition.* Oxford: New York, part III.

Held, K. (2003), 'Husserl's phenomenological method' in Welton, D. (ed.), *The New Husserl. A Critical Reader.* Bloomington, IN: Indiana University Press, pp. 3–31.

Landgrebe, I. (1981), 'Husserl's departure from Cartesianism' in Welton, D. (ed.), *The Phenomenology of Edmund Husserl: Six Essays,* Ithaca, NY: Cornell UP, pp. 66–121.

Intentionality and Perception

2

Chapter Outline

Main primary literature: 'Introduction' to *Analyses Concerning Passive and Active Synthesis*, pp. 39–62/3–24.

In this chapter, we shall explore Husserl's account of the way in which we come to perceive an object. First, we will examine the nature of consciousness more generally; here, the key concept of intentionality will be introduced to designate the dynamic character of consciousness. 'Intentional' consciousness is responsible for constituting the appearance of objects as we experience them. This process of constitution involves a series of levels. The most primitive level is one in which consciousness is basically passive; it is here that one finds the most fundamental form of 'time-consciousness': here the very flowing of time is constructed; this level is followed by other forms of passive synthesis such as association. The next level is active synthesis, which involves remembering: such memory is necessary in order for the object we are constituting to remain identical over time, and thus to count as 'one and the same' object from one moment to the next. Beyond these syntheses, in order to constitute an object in the full sense, we need intersubjectivity: there needs to be a potential plurality of subjects each of whom is capable of experiencing the object as the same object. Husserl thus calls into question our usual conviction that perception is from the beginning a matter of a subject facing an object, and investigates the various dimensions involved in perception, from the more fundamental levels of passivity to the higher, more active levels.

(a) Intentionality

> **Intentionality** designates the realization that consciousness is never empty, but is always consciousness *of* something. Furthermore, consciousness is directed towards its object in a dynamic fashion, in the sense that it wants to get an ever closer grasp of this object ('object' taken here in the broadest sense).

Husserl describes the character of intentionality as follows: 'The intention is directed toward its object; it does not want to be a merely empty intending toward it; it wants to go to the object itself – to the object itself, that is, to an intuition that gives the object itself, to an intuition that is in itself the consciousness of having the object itself' (*ACPAS*, 83/126). 'Intention' does not here have the usual meaning of a purpose or a plan, but of an attitude that we take towards an object that we are experiencing: it expresses the fact that in each of our experiences, we tacitly expect the object to appear and to behave in a certain way. These expectations can be 'fulfilled' by the course of experience, or refuted, or they can simply remain unfulfilled. The intention is not satisfied with an initial and superficial fulfilment, for example, touching the object, but strives for an ever more complete determination of its nature. The striving continues until all dissatisfaction is eliminated – and this in turn depends on the circumstances and aims of the subject in question, which are very different if the subject is a natural scientist rather than an artist or a phenomenologist. If the object is given to me in such a way that it does not point beyond its present givenness any more, indicating elements of its nature as yet unilluminated, then it is given to me 'originarily' or 'self-evidently'. Every conscious act is characterized by intentionality, and this means that it strives for fulfilment in the form of self-evidence.

Intentionality thus designates consciousness's continuous striving for the fulfilment of its intentions; yet this also means that we permanently face the risk of disappointment. An example which Husserl takes up repeatedly concerns a red ball which turns out to be green and dented on the rear side. This example will be presented at some length here since Husserl claims that the example serves to trace 'the original phenomenon of negation'. This means that 'negation is not first the business of the act of predicative judgement but that in its original form it already appears in the prepredicative sphere of receptive experience' (*EJ*, 97/90). I see an object which I take to be a uniformly red ball. My expectation is thus that no matter how I turn and twist the ball, I will find the quality of being red and ballshaped everywhere. Yet instead, I realize that the reverse side of the object is green and dented. My intention has been disappointed – but something even more fundamental has taken place. I know that the object has not just now changed its shape and colour, but was green and dented even before I found out about it. Hence a 'retroactive crossing-out' occurs: During the entire preceding time, I was (without knowing it) dealing with an object that was not uniformly red and ball shaped.[8] At the same time, I am still aware of my original intention, only now in the mode of being crossed-out. Husserl says that we are 'still conscious of the previous sense, but as "painted over", and where the corresponding moments are concerned, crossed out' (*ACPAS*, 31/69).

In order to describe in more detail how consciousness is always consciousness *of* something and to designate what it is conscious of (without falling back to a stage prior to the phenomenological *epochē* and assuming a being-in-itself of the object), Husserl distinguishes between two components within intentional consciousness: the *noema* and the *noesis*.

Noema is the object as it is intended by consciousness or the object-side of intentionality. It is that which is perceived, intended or conceived (Greek *noein* = to perceive, intend, conceive).

  Noesis is the intentional process of intending or the act-side of intentionality. It describes the perceiving, intending or conceiving.

When I remember seeing an apple tree in a garden, the noetic side to be investigated is the remembering (of the apple tree), whereas the noematic side is the apple tree as it is given to me in my memory. Concerning our perception of a spatio-temporal object, Husserl describes the noetic side by pointing out that I perceive an object from one perspective at a time; on the noematic side, the same insight can be described in terms of the object's 'horizons', in other words, the way in which our experience of an object is always *limited* in various ways.

(b) Horizons and passivity

One peculiarity of perception is that we perceive a unitary object while at the same time perceiving manifold aspects and properties of this object. The realization that a spatio-temporal object is never given from all sides, at once but only in a one-sided fashion, leads us to ask the most crucial questions regarding the nature of perception. Hence the first sentence of Husserl's *Analyses Concerning Passive and Active Synthesis*: 'External perception is a constant pretension to accomplish something that, by its very nature, it is not in a position to accomplish' (*ACPAS*, 3/39).

How do we perceive a unified object even though it is always only partially given to us? How are the manifold modes of appearance connected to the unity of the object? These questions preoccupied Husserl again and again; they are decisive for his phenomenology since perception for him represents the paradigm example of all experience. All memories, expectations, idealizations, point back to perception. The realizations that perception is necessarily perspectival and that the object is always given inadequately are among Husserl's most significant insights. How fundamental these insights are becomes obvious, for example, in Husserl's famous remark that even God can only see an object in a one-sided fashion (*Ideas I*, §§ 43 and 44).

In order to approach this mystery, Husserl first points out that the sides of the object which we do not currently perceive are nevertheless in some sense present for us. They are present indirectly, by way of the actually present sides; a phenomenon which Husserl designates as 'co-presence'. Such co-presence is possible because the different sides are connected by way of references. The front side of the table 'refers' to its rear side, and so on. Husserl describes the pull of these references by imagining what the object would say if it could speak; the object 'calls out to us, as it were, in these referential implications: "There is still more to see here, turn me so you can see all my sides, let your gaze run through me, draw closer to me, open me up [. . .]"' (*ACPAS*, 41/5). This peculiar mode of description is used, first, to show that the sides refer to each other in such a way that I do not need to become actively involved and judge that there somehow should or has to be a rear side; our perception indeed runs its course without such judgements being necessary. Second, making the object 'speak' serves to show that perception is not just my doing, but the object calls on me and draws my attention to it. To explore the phenomenon of attention, something like an 'allure' from the side of the object needs to be considered; the object calls me to itself, as it were.[9]

Everything which comes to appearance is surrounded and permeated by an empty intentional horizon, by a void which 'is not a nothingness, but an emptiness to be filled-out; it is a determinable indeterminacy' (*ACPAS*, 42/6).

> **Horizon** designates a context of references that opens up around an object beginning from what is currently present. We can distinguish between an inner horizon which provides further aspects of one and the same object, and an outer horizon which contains references from the current object to further objects and everything in the immediate or more distant environs.

For our current purposes, we will abide with the example of a single object and investigate further how it happens that we naturally follow the references that populate the object's 'inner' horizon. The unity of an object is then constituted in and through the connections between the object's modes of appearance, connections that come about through associative links. Mostly by way of similarity and contrast, associative links help us to imagine the object as a whole. For example, I do not turn towards the reverse side of my cup in a mechanical manner, but because the front of the cup points to it and prefigures it by means of uniformity and similarity. The referential implications are what connects the object's various modes of appearance – a connection that can be described in terms of a question and an affirmative or negative answer, or in terms of intention and its fulfilment or disappointment.

We are able to follow these references in a passive way; in Husserl's terms, we are capable of making *passive* syntheses. The expression 'passive' is used, as Husserl himself explains, for want of a more appropriate expression for the phenomena in question (*ACPAS*, 76/118). It is important to understand what belongs to this level since it is the very foundation of the genuine *activity* of the ego. In his *Analyses Concerning Passive and Active Synthesis*, Husserl analyses everything that enables us to perceive things – such as associations, doubts, disappointments or fulfilments of expectations, and modifications. On the level of passivity, what is being constituted is not yet an object, but an object-like formation (*Gegenständlichkeit*), a prefiguration of an object. An object in the full and genuine sense has to remain identical with itself such that we can return to it in remembrance and anticipate it. An object thus has to be constituted by way of the ego's activity.[10]

Another important dimension of passivity lies in the role of 'kinaestheses'.[11] My movement (Greek: *kinēsis*) in the form of bodily movements is always involved in my perception (Greek: *aisthēsis*). Natural consciousness does not recognize this involvement since it normally takes place habitually, without my actively taking part in it. But when this normal course of events is inhibited or disturbed, I become aware of my involvement. For example, if I hurt my neck, I realize to what extent my vision is restricted all of a sudden – even though I previously would have thought that I do not move my neck very much in perceiving things, but almost always look at what is right in front of me. Natural consciousness tends to attribute the essential role in the perceptual process to the object; yet perception is an interplay of subject and object, and an intertwinement of passivity and activity.

All passive syntheses are grounded in the structure of intentionality and presuppose the most fundamental passive syntheses: those of time-consciousness.

(c) Time-consciousness

The most basic dimensions of passive synthesis are the syntheses of time-consciousness, and it is already on the level of time-consciousness that a primordial shaping of intention and its potential fulfilment or disappointment occurs. The syntheses of time-consciousness, 'retention' and 'protention',[12] are the most fundamental and, at the same time, the most abstract elements of passivity.

> **Retention** is the holding-on to a 'now' as the 'now' is slipping away from actual presence, **protention** is directed towards the coming 'now'. Thus they amount to Husserl's attempt to explain how we always have an elementary experience of the past and the future, respectively.

Without retention and protention, we would not be able to follow a sentence or the course of a melody. As we listen to the current tone of a melody, we still retain the previous note and anticipate the following one; otherwise, we would not hear a melody, but rather a series of disconnected tones or sounds.

It is precisely within time-consciousness that we experience an inevitable disappointment: if we grasp a 'now' and want to focus our attention on it, this 'now' has already passed by and is not 'now' any longer. Retentionality is this primordial tendency of holding onto what is slipping away; but it always comes too late. Of course, disappointment in all these contexts has a neutral connotation and should not cause frustration on our part, unless it is our goal to bring the 'now' to complete presence (as one might, for instance, in a philosophical analysis).

Remembering is connected to retentionality in the following fashion: Since every retention brings with it a further retention, a chain of retentions stretches into the past like a 'comet's tail' (*PCT*, 35/30). We are thus capable of representing past moments which are implicitly connected with the present moment through this chain of retentions, and we are able to do so without being aware of all the retentions that lie in between. In order to perceive an object as an object in the true sense, remembering is necessary. Only by virtue of rememberance is there an 'again and again', in the sense that we are able to repeatedly identify a single object as remaining the *same* across time (*ACPAS*, 370).

Already on the passive level, we synthesize the different sides or aspects of the object and come to perceive it as unified. Similarities and contrasts as well as references between the different sides guide this process, and we keep track of and connect the fulfilments and disappointments with the help of time-consciousness as the most fundamental passive synthesis and pre-condition for all association. Nevertheless, the precise relation between unity and multiplicity remains enigmatic and constitutes the primary problem of perception.

(d) The unity of the object

What is the relation between the manifold modes of appearance and the unity of the object? It is essential to perception, as Husserl points out, 'that in the sense of concordantly and synthetically progressing perception, we can always distinguish between an unceasingly changing sense and an identical sense running through the changing sense' (*ACPAS*, 58/20). A particular sense belongs to each phase of the perception; the perceptual object is given in a particular way. However, running through this constantly 'new' flowing sense, there is 'the unity of the substrate X, which holds sway in a steady coinciding, and which is determined ever more richly' (ibid.). Namely, the object remains the same despite the passing away of each of its temporary phases. When I smell and taste my favourite dish, it is given to me in a different way as when I remember having eaten it with a friend or when I go shopping (recalling the ingredients in order to be able to cook the same dish) – and yet it is the same identical dish in all three cases. And even when the dish is intuitively given to me, it is given to me from a certain perspective.

What is it that runs through the flow of perceptions? Is it one identical point that is left when one abstracts from all the object's perishable and accidental properties? Husserl seems to hold this view in *Ideas I* when he says that what remains identical is 'the pure X in abstraction from all predicates' (Hua III, 321/313). However, Husserl is conscious of the fact that an X of this kind is indeed an abstraction, an abstraction in the literal sense – namely, that which remains when all properties of the object are removed from consideration. What remains in this case is merely an idea and therefore nothing real. One problem with such an idea is that it lacks any of the determinacy which is required for the constitution of an object, for example, its spatiality and materiality. Such an idea is not very helpful if we wish to analyse the nature of perception. Another, even more important problem is the fact that the X that results from the withdrawing of all properties does not offer any clues that would let us distinguish one particular thing from another. Yet perception is precisely the ability to distinguish between a multiplicity of different things.

The manner in which Husserl determines the identical X in his *Analyses Concerning Passive and Active Synthesis* overcomes these problems. Husserl transforms the conception of the X and replaces it with a new idea that takes all determinations into account instead of abstracting from them. The substrate X, the object itself is 'everything that the process of perception and all further possible perceptual processes determine in it and would determine in it' (*ACPAS*, 20/58). This identical objective sense is described by Husserl as an 'idea', an idea that lies in infinity, 'the idea of the completely determined object, of the object that would be determined through and through, known through and through, [...] and where the full determination itself would be devoid of any *plus ultra* with respect to what is still to be determined' (ibid.). This is an 'infinite' idea because the object is never absolutely given in perception; the perception of spatio-temporal objects is necessarily inadequate. In actual perception, there is always a *plus ultra*; a more accurate determination of the object is always possible. Moreover, there always exists the possibility of deception and re-determination through 'crossing out'. However, the idea of a completely determined object plays an essential role in the process of perception: it guides the perceptual process. In order to avoid misunderstandings on this point, one has to examine how such an idea can be constituted and how it can function as a guide throughout the process of perception.

Husserl's conception of the 'teleologically anticipated adequate givenness of the object' can be described as the solution to a certain paradox.[13] The paradox is to be found in the fact that on the one hand, an adequate givenness of the object is essentially impossible, and on the other hand, every appearance anticipates this adequate givenness or the substrate X as the ultimate aim of perception. The goal of the perceptual process thus cannot be the adequate givenness of the object but the fuller determination of the thing in the process itself. Yet this process does not unfold in a blind way; we want to perceive the object ever more completely, and the adequate givenness or the substrate X functions as a guiding idea for perception. Husserl writes in *Ideas I* that the adequate givenness of the thing is present in the form of an idea, namely, as an idea that can be 'intellectually seen'. The idea of an infinite continuum of appearances is 'not itself an infinity', and the 'intellectually seen givenness of the *idea* of this infinity' is not only possible but even necessary (Hua III, 351/343). Without this idea, the unity of the object that persists throughout the perceptual process could not be explained.

The substrate X must not be misconstrued as something ready-made existing prior to the perceptual process; rather, it is constructed during the process of perceiving. In and through the multiplicity of appearances and by returning to the multiplicity, the substrate X is determined; yet it is not identical with this multiplicity since it is a unified idea. In perception, we anticipate the ideal of an adequately given object despite the fact that we never reach it; this object provides the perceptual process with implicit guidelines according to which appearances point to other appearances, all converging towards the construction of a single unified object. The fundamental structure of this process is the interplay of intention and fulfilment or disappointment.

How is this substrate X constituted? This question is addressed by Husserl in the fourth section of his *Analyses Concerning Passive and Active Synthesis*. A motivation for positing such a unified object can be found in the fact that there is an excess or surplus of modes through which the object can be given. Our experience has shown that the stream of appearances does not come to an end; one mode of givenness always points to another. An object does not come to fulfilment in a single mode of appearance, but confronts me with the request to study it more and more closely, to turn and twist it, and so on. Since the object constantly promises further modes of givenness to come and persists throughout the respective modes of givenness, natural consciousness goes so far as to attribute a being-in-itself to the object, a being beyond its actual givenness for consciousness.

(e) Genetic phenomenology

The investigations discussed here are part of a new kind of phenomenology: 'genetic phenomenology'. In a manuscript from 1921, Husserl describes the methodological distinctions between static and genetic phenomenology:

> In a certain way, we can therefore distinguish 'explanatory' phenomenology as a phenomenology of regulated genesis, and 'descriptive' phenomenology as a phenomenology of the possible, essential shapes (no matter how they have come to pass) in pure consciousness [. . .]. In my lectures, I did not say 'descriptive', but rather 'static' phenomenology. (*ACPAS*, 340/629)

Genetic phenomenology is characterized here as 'explanatory' phenomenology, in contrast to static phenomenology which is merely 'descriptive'. Explanation here does not primarily answer the question 'why', but rather asks 'how' a certain phenomenon has come about. This question is based on the idea that specific laws or regulated structures can be discerned in the genesis of consciousness; genetic phenomenology aims to find these laws. Such a quest must not be conflated with a developmental history of consciousness as it is investigated by developmental psychology. Yet in a different way, the history of consciousness's development is indeed at stake, provided we are able to understand these concepts in a new and literal fashion. It is an essential insight of Husserl's analysis of perception that we always perceive objects in certain contexts. These contexts are not just the horizons or referential contexts in which we encounter an object, but also contexts on the side of consciousness. We have already seen objects that are similar or different to the one we are currently perceiving, and we relate what we currently perceive to what we have perceived earlier, that is, to our perceptual acquisitions.

Every perceptual act is thus historical; hence Husserl's talk of a '"history" of consciousness' (*ACPAS*, 339/627). There is good reason for Husserl to place 'history' in quotation marks, since we are not yet dealing with history in the genuine sense which has to include intersubjectivity, including its intergenerational sense. What genetic phenomenology takes into consideration, in contrast to static phenomenology, is the temporality of consciousness. Temporality is understood here in the concrete sense which includes all the contents of time-consciousness. Husserl states in *Ideas I* that time is 'a name for a completely *delimited sphere of problems* and one of exceptional difficulty' which we can 'leave out of account [. . .] in our preliminary analyses' without endangering their analytic 'rigor' (*Strenge*) (*Ideas I*, § 81). When Husserl examines time and temporality in his static phenomenology, he takes them as structures, and not as processes or geneses.

The fundamental structures of passive synthesis form the basis of all egoic activity. In turn, the results of our activity become sedimented in the ego: they become *habitual*. Once habitualized, we can always return to them. The accomplishments of active reason flow into passivity, and in this sense, Husserl is justified in claiming that passivity partly precedes activity – in and through the laws of inner time-consciousness, association, and so on – and partly integrates activity (*CM*, 113/79). Active and passive realms can be distinguished, but not separated. Without the occurrences of passive synthesis, the ego would not be capable of active accomplishments. The results of active genesis, in turn, feed back into the passive realm; passivity is always already interspersed with activity. The prefiguring of passive synthesis is 'not a blind and fundamentally senseless prefiguring coming from the outside; rather it is one that is accessible to ego-consciousness in the form of knowledge' (*ACPAS*, 215/267 f.). Without the mutual infiltration of activity and passivity, an analysis of passive synthesis would not be possible; passivity would remain inaccessible and closed to philosophical investigation.

At the same time, habituation does not imply that we would be aware of such sedimentations. Husserl purposefully treats such occurrences under the heading of passivity, and where he examines association and reproductive memory, he states: 'I do not need to say that the entirety of these observations that we are undertaking can also be given the famed title of the "unconscious" (*Unbewußten*)'. And immediately afterwards, he states explicitly: 'Thus, our considerations concern a phenomenology of the so-called unconscious' (*ACPAS*, 154/201). Husserl wishes to elucidate the laws which govern this 'so-called unconscious';[14] the stream of consciousness does not come about as a mere 'series' (*Nacheinander*), but as a 'development' (*Auseinander*), that is, 'a process of becoming according to laws of necessary succession' (*ACPAS*, 339/628). If the stream of consciousness were a mere succession of arbitrary experiences, the undertaking of genetic phenomenology would be non-sensical. There are certain features which the 'history' of consciousness shares with history in the genuine sense as conceived by Husserl: in both cases, the progression is goal-directed, we have certain expectations, and our experiences are connected in a lawful or ordered fashion (e.g. through laws of association).

The analyses of genetic phenomenology concern not the ego in the abstract sense (including the structures of consciousness which emerge when we try to abstract from conscious contents), but the concrete ego. In examining the genesis of egoic consciousness, the ego as individualized and different from others comes into view and is designated by the concept of the 'monad': 'Finally, we have reached the phenomenology of monadic individuality, including the phenomenology of a connecting genesis in which the unity of the monad emerges and in which the monad exists through the process of becoming' (Hua XIV, 38).[15] However, the concept of the monad should not lead us to believe that perception can take place in an isolated subject without any relation to others. In order for perception to be objective, it has to be intersubjective. In addition to remembering, which is the first condition for the possibility of objectivity, we need intersubjectivity since an object is only an object insofar as it is *both* an object given to me and an object shared with others (see Chapter 4).

Although the community of monads is intersubjective, the framework of Husserl's genetic phenomenology ultimately only allows for a community of contemporaries, that is, of contemporary monads. This is due to the fact that his analysis in the *Fifth Cartesian Meditation* is based on empathy rather than linguistic communication. Empathy presupposes that the bodies of others are given in the flesh; it can thus not involve past and future generations. In the *Fifth Cartesian Meditation*, Husserl states explicitly that the 'generative problems of birth and death and the generative nexus of psychophysical being have not yet been touched' (*CM*, 169/142). Only this higher dimension, which is to say, the dimension of generative phenomenology,[16] allows us to understand history in the genuine sense. Husserl's reflections on history will lead him to suggest a different way into phenomenology that will be examined in the following chapter.

Further reading

Held, K. (2003), 'Husserl's phenomenology of the life-world' in Welton, D. (ed.), *The New Husserl. A Critical Reader*. Bloomington, IN: Indiana University Press, pp. 32–62 (esp. pp. 40–48).

Steinbock, A. J. (2001), 'Translator's Introduction to Husserl's *Analyses Concerning Active and Passive Synthesis*' in Husserl, E., *Analyses Concerning Active and Passive Synthesis*, Dordrecht: Kluwer, 2001.

Concerning the unity of the object:

Bernet, R. (1979), 'Perception as a teleological process of cognition' in *The Teleologies in Husserlian Phenomenology. Analecta Husserliana*, vol. IX. Reidel, Dordrecht: Kluwer, pp. 119–32.

For a more general discussion of perception:

Drummond, J. (1979), 'On seeing a material thing in space: the role of "kinaesthesis" in visual perception' in *Philosophy and Phenomenological Research*, vol. 40, no. 1, pp. 19–32.

Mulligan, K. (1995), 'Perception' in Smith B. and Smith D. W. (eds), *The Cambridge Companion to Husserl*. Cambridge: Cambridge University Press, pp. 168–238.

The Lifeworld

Main primary literature: *The Crisis of European Sciences and Transcendental Phenomenology*, esp. § 9 and §§ 33–43.

The concept of the lifeworld – probably the most widely used Husserlian concept – is introduced by Husserl in order to elucidate a crisis which was afflicting the European sciences, but also, due to the enormous influence of these sciences, European humanity as a whole.[17] Husserl maintains that the crisis of the sciences is caused by a forgetfulness: a forgetfulness of the lifeworld. This forgetfulness, as we will see in the current chapter, amounts to a loss of the basis on which the sciences were built: the natural world in which we live and upon which all activity rests.

(a) Introducing the lifeworld

The concept of the lifeworld poses some problems because Husserl proposes several such concepts. Rather than contradicting each other, the different concepts of the lifeworld develop out of each other, reflecting different stages in Husserl's reflections on the sciences and their crisis. The lifeworld in the narrow, preliminary sense is defined in contrast to the scientific world of ideal objects; the lifeworld in the broad sense, however, encompasses the results and accomplishments of the sciences and will be discussed once we have examined the mathematization of nature which leads to the establishment of the world of ideal objects.

In order to examine what the sciences are and how they change our life, Husserl asks about the pre- and non-scientific world (since the sciences have not always existed). Ultimately, the important question concerns the way in which the sciences came to be, that is, how they were instituted and the sense or meaning they were meant to have. Since we have long been taking the sciences for granted, it is only by abstraction that we can access a world without science.[18]

> The **lifeworld** in the **narrow** sense, as it is introduced in the *Crisis*, emerges as the *pre- and non-scientific world* as it is encountered in simple sensuous intuition (*Crisis*, 108/106 & 113/111).

Already in the 1920s, Husserl designates the world of straightforward intuition as the lifeworld.[19] This world of intuition is pre-theoretical, pre-cultural, and a-historical; therefore, Husserl is confronted with the question of whether this world actually exists. Indeed, he had already stated in his lectures on *Phenomenological Psychology*: 'That which is given to us in simple intuition as something seen, heard, or somehow experienced, exhibits upon closer consideration traces of earlier spiritual accomplishments (*Geistestätigkeiten*). It is thus doubtful as to where we can ever find a truly pre-theoretical world in pure experience, devoid of the sense sedimentations (*Sinnesniederschlägen*) of previous thought' (*PhPsy*, 56). Although the world of pure intuition is a product of abstraction, it plays an important role in the examination of the emergence of the sciences.

The lifeworld in the narrow sense is fundamentally determined by the fact that it is 'merely subjective-relative' (*Crisis*, 125/127), that is, given to the specific subject which has these intuitions. In contrast to this subject-relativity, the modern natural sciences present their ideal of subject-independence or object-ivity. Husserl follows the process by which the sciences construct a world of exact ideal objects against which the lifeworld will then be measured, as if the former were quite simply the 'true world'. How is the ideal world formed? The key concepts which Husserl uses to describe this process are 'mathematization' and 'idealization'.

(b) The mathematization of nature

Section IX of the *Crisis* is entitled 'Galileo's Mathematization of Nature'; it opens with the important question: '*What is the meaning of this mathematization of nature*? How do we reconstruct the train of thought which motivated it?' (*Crisis*, 23/20). By posing this question, Husserl already implies that the motivation for this process is accessible to us. As it will turn out, there are tendencies in our everyday life which resemble this idealization and can serve to prepare for it. In order to see more clearly how idealization originates in lifeworldly experience and is nevertheless fundamentally different from it, it is helpful to recall the main features of our perception of an object as they were exposed in the previous chapter.

In perception, an object is always given in a one-sided fashion, yet we constitute an in-itself of the object that guides our perceptual process as an idea. This unattainable idea of the completely given object is formed in the perceptual process and is transformed again and again as this process continues. Now, the natural sciences also deal with ideas or, as Husserl calls them, 'idealities' (*Idealitäten*). Hence the question arises as to how the perceptual idea of the object in-itself and the scientific idea are related. The most significant difference consists in the fact that the perceptual idea always harbours indeterminacy and flexibility whereas the sciences want to exclude this indeterminacy and achieve complete exactitude. The natural sciences intend to determine the idea of the object which guides the perceptual process. Yet since the perceived object necessarily includes indeterminacy, this intention of the sciences already shows that their object cannot be a perceivable one.

How is idealization possible, that is, how can an idea of the object be accomplished in which its essential indeterminacy is eliminated? As the sciences idealize their object, they develop the tendency inherent in pre-scientific consciousness that brings the object to an ever more exact givenness. This tendency, which could be called a 'tendency toward perfection', is shaped and controlled by practical purposes. Even though we never attain the complete givenness of the object, there exists a point of termination in the practical realm, 'in the sense that it fully satisfies special practical interests' (*Crisis*, 25/22). Perfection in the practical sense is accomplished when our practical goals and purposes have been satisfied such that there is no incentive to pursue the exploration of the object any further. For example, the carpenter assesses whether the bed he builds is long enough and whether its sides and legs are fixed at right angles. But there is no need for the carpenter to theorize about precise ninety degree angles, and the goniometer which he uses does not show any exact right angles. Exact right angles are not to be found in the lifeworld at all. As Husserl puts it, the objects of intuition 'fluctuate [...] in the sphere of the merely typical' (ibid.). The indeterminacy of the object will be diminished, but never eliminated. As technology progresses, 'the ideal of perfection is pushed further and further' (*Crisis*, 25/23); this formulation emphasizes once again that the idea of the fully determined object is fashioned and modified in the process of closer determination.

By way of practical perfection, we never attain scientific idealities free from any indeterminacy. Such idealities are 'limit-shapes', that is, 'invariant and never attainable poles' of the particular 'series of perfectings' (*Crisis*, 26/23). In the context of describing the mathematization of nature, Husserl reverts to formulations from the domain of mathematics, a domain very familiar to him. A limit (*limes*) can, for example, be the limit of a series of numbers shaped in accordance with a specific law. If we start from the number '1' and apply the law of dividing it into equal halves, we yield a series of ever smaller numbers (1/2, 1/4, 1/8, 1/16, 1/32, ...). These numbers approach '0' without ever reaching it; '0' is thus the limit of this series. If we transfer this law to objects of perception, we learn that the object's limit shape belongs to a different level than the intuitive object and can only be reached through a transgression. Furthermore, the example of the number-series indicates how the transgression is supposed to be thought, namely, as following a series of shapes which develop in a particular direction, and finally as an accomplishment of thought which prolongs the series to infinity, thus leading to a limit shape as its conclusion. In an appendix to the section on Galileo, Husserl designates idealization as a 'general attitude of thought, in which, departing from an exemplary individual object as exemplar for "any object whatsoever", this object is imagined to have passed through an open endless manifold of its ever incomplete, but to be completed subjective presentations' (*Crisis*, 359, appendix not included in English translation). The 'open endless' infinite manifold of 'presentations' is a specifically modern idea since only the modern mind tackles infinite tasks and attempts to describe the infinite universe of beings with the help of a mathematics which does not fear the step to infinity. Pre-modern mathematics 'knows only finite tasks', as Husserl points out (*Crisis*, 21/19).

It will turn out that idealization is necessarily restricted to a limited number of the object's features whereas certain other qualities of the object can only be mathematized in an indirect fashion. The qualities of the object which lend themselves particularly well to idealization are its 'spatio-temporal' qualities: the spatial extension of the object and its situatedness in time, as well as the correlation between space and time in change. To be sure, this is an abstraction since the objects exhibit many other qualities such as colour, consistency and flavour (*Crisis*, 29/27), but the sciences strive to mathematize such qualities as well since they want to be universal sciences. Furthermore, the qualities of the object are connected by way of its inner horizon and so point to each other; it would become apparent as a lack or limitation if the sciences were to focus on just one quality and ignored all the others.

(c) Mathematizing the sense-qualities

Husserl designates the non-spatio-temporal qualities of the object as 'specific sense-qualities' or as 'plena' or 'fullnesses' (*Füllen*) (*Crisis*, 30/27ff.). These plena can only be mathematized in an indirect fashion. It is even possible to determine the reason why a direct mathematization is impossible, and 'impossible in principle:' there is just *one* mathematics of space, just *one* geometry. Husserl explains: 'We have not two but only *one* universal form of the world: not two but only *one geometry*, i.e., one of these shapes, without a second for plena' (*Crisis*, 34/33). A quantitative description of the world is only possible in a single and unified way. Geometry is a science which was originally based on the empirical craft of measuring. For Galileo, geometry was already fully established; Galileo's special contribution to the development of modern science is the hypothesis that an encompassing, universal mathematization of the world is possible. Husserl recommends that we reflect on the 'strangeness' inherent in the idea of universal mathematization, especially since nowadays we take this idea for granted.

How is the indirect mathematization of the plena brought about? Husserl approaches this process by pointing out that the plena are 'closely related in a quite peculiar and *regulated* way' with the spatio-temporal shapes (*Crisis*, 35/33).

Husserl gives the example of the causal relation between the pitch of a tone and the length of the vibrating string as noted by the Pythagoreans (*Crisis*, 37/36), or more generally, the connection between the sensible quality, 'sound' and the geometric quality, 'length of string'. Several further examples come to mind, and Husserl simply chooses one of the historically earliest. The important point is that plena exist in gradations; there are various degrees of warmth, various pitches of sounds. These gradations motivate the idea of a description in terms of numbers; this possibility has to be explored and confirmed with respect to each quality. Once it has turned out, for example, that liquids expand in a regular fashion when its temperature increases, the invention of a thermometer is only a small step away.

Nevertheless, it is a huge leap from such individual examples to the idea of the universal mathematization of the world. According to Husserl, this idea is founded on the conviction that every change occurs in line with the laws of causality and that every change of the plena is connected to some change of shape. However, 'we do not have an a priori insight that every change of the specific qualities of intuited bodies [. . .] refers causally to occurrences in the abstract shape-stratum of the world' (*Crisis*, 36/34). Here lies the audacity of Galileo's thesis or of the thesis of modern natural science – even though we now take this idea for granted. 'Thanks to our earlier scientific schooling' (36/35), we imagine sound as a wave that travels between a source and our ear. Yet the fact that it is difficult to understand the 'referring' between spatio-temporal shapes and plena, and thus the possibility of an indirect mathematization of plena might be an important indication that there is something in the plena which evades all mathematization or which gets lost in the reduction of sense-qualities to spatio-temporal qualities.[20] Husserl therefore describes Galileo as 'at once a discovering and a concealing genius' (*Crisis*, 52/50). The idea of a universal mathematization is daring and has contributed to the sciences' progress, but it also meant the loss of a direct, concrete relation to sense-qualities and objects, and, as a consequence, to the lifeworld in its indeterminacy and richness.

The sciences, striving to be universal, aim at a mathematization of the entire object and, subsequently, a mathematization of all objects. The possibility of moving from one object to the next is based on the connectedness of objects, designated by phenomenological analysis as the outer horizon of referential implications. When Husserl states that idealizing thought expands 'also outwards toward the infinity of the world' (*Crisis*, 360), he is pointing to the outer horizon. In a supplementary text to the *Crisis*, Husserl describes idealization as a two stage process in which, first, ideas are formed on the basis of appearances and, second, ideas are combined to form a 'configuration of ideas' (*Crisis*, 361). In this fashion, a 'realm' or 'world' of pure limit shapes emerges (*Crisis*, 26 ff./23ff.). This ideal world consists of ideas which can be fully determined and stand in a causal relation to each other; these relations can be described unequivocally and infallibly by mathematical laws. Such ideal objects move from one point in an ideal space to an other, with a specific, uniform or uniformly increased speed such that an exact determination of their location can be made.

The indirect mathematization of the plena made it possible for the natural sciences precisely to mathematize the world in its entirety. As a result, the sciences presume that they have left the naïve attitude of everyday consciousness far behind.

(d) The lifeworld in the genuine sense

The subsequent decisive step consists in relating the world of idealities to the pre- and non-scientific lifeworld: the lifeworld is subordinated to and measured against the ideal world. There is a 'surreptitious substitution of the mathematically substructed world of idealities for the only real world, the one that is actually given through perception, that is ever experienced and experienceable – our everyday lifeworld' (*Crisis*, 49/49). If it were possible to relate the intuitable lifeworld and the world of idealities in this fashion, then the indeterminacy and subject-relativity of the lifeworld would simply point to the exactness of the scientific world and would rightfully be measured against the latter. However, something essential is disregarded in the subordination of the intuitive lifeworld. This oversight is the reason why the contrast between the lifeworld and the world of idealities cannot be sustained and the lifeworld cannot be restricted to its narrow sense (the sense in which it is opposed to the natural scientific world). Overlooked is the fact that the natural sciences are not simply grounded in the lifeworld, but even belong to it.

Concerning the first point, the sciences presuppose the lifeworld not only because they have historically emerged from the lifeworld, but also because the lifeworld 'continuously' supplies the ground for the sciences because the scientists examine lifeworldly objects, work in laboratories, and use measuring instruments that are given to intuition (*Crisis*, 123f./121f.). Secondly, the sciences themselves are encompassed by the lifeworld. In order to explain how this is the case, Husserl coins the expression 'flowing into' (*Einströmen*). The results of scientific research flow into the lifeworld and become sedimented here, such that we often handle them without awareness (*Crisis*, 113/115). Husserl explains that the phenomenon of 'flowing into' lets the opposition between the lifeworld and the world of idealities collapse (*Crisis*, 462).

> The **lifeworld** in the **wide** sense is much more than a mere pre- and non-scientific world; as the all-encompassing, concrete world of our life or our universal horizon, it includes the sciences as well. The lifeworld in the encompassing and genuine sense is the historical world which contains nature as well as culture.

However, the narrow sense of the lifeworld is not hereby rendered superfluous; rather, the encompassing lifeworld is *based* on the intuitive world. For disclosing the ideal world of the sciences and the way in which it is founded in the pre- and non-scientific world of mere intuition, the narrow concept of lifeworld is necessary to provide a contrast between the scientific world and another kind of world. However, the lifeworld in the genuine sense encompasses the intuitive world as well as the accomplishments of the sciences, including even scientific theories and the world of idealities.

The lifeworld in this inclusive sense is thus no 'partial problem' but 'a universal problem for philosophy' (*Crisis*, § 34 f). But if the lifeworld is supposed to become a theme for philosophy, a difficulty arises: how can the lifeworld be investigated philosophically? Husserl deems the project of an 'ontology of the lifeworld' important (cf. *Crisis*, § 37), but he never executes it in any comprehensive fashion. Apart from indications for an ontology of the lifeworld in his late manuscripts,[21] Husserl sketches in the *Crisis* what direction such an ontology might take and what would be its presuppositions. One important presupposition concerns the lifeworld as having 'in all its relative features, a *general structure*' which is 'not itself relative' (*Crisis*, 139/142). This general structure gives rise to the idea of a 'lifeworld a priori' (140/143). The talk of invariant structures does not mean that these would be given in an unchanging fashion: invariant structures are always concretely given in a historically mediated form, yet the structure as such persists through these changes. Examples of such structures are the transcendental forms of the lifeworld as horizon (*Horizont*) and ground (*Boden*).[22]

Horizon and ground are two complementary modalities of the lifeworld. The first emphasizes the temporal, and the second the spatial aspects of the lifeworld. Husserl characterizes the horizon in the *Crisis* as a 'vital horizon' which includes 'old acquisitions' and old values which are presupposed in an unquestioning fashion (*Crisis*, 149/152). These 'acquisitions' structure our life, often without us being aware of them as such. The lifeworld provides the (forgotten) ground for the modern natural sciences; however, this concept of ground presupposes mostly the narrow, preliminary concept of lifeworld in contrast to the world of the sciences. Husserl suggests a closer examination of the lifeworld in its function as ground (*Crisis*, 154/158), yet undertakes this examination elsewhere, especially in the manuscripts entitled 'Notes on the Constitution of Space' and 'Fundamental Investigations into the Phenomenological Origin of the Spatiality of Nature'. The titles of these manuscripts already imply that ground, here more specifically named the 'earth-ground' (*Erdboden*) designates the way in which the spatiality of the lifeworld is constituted. In order to examine the nature of the earth-ground, Husserl returns to his reflections on the lived body (*Leib*). Just as the lived body is a zero point, an absolute 'here' which gives meaning to movement and rest,[23] the same holds on the 'macro-level' also for the earth: 'In the original shape of its presentation the earth itself does not move itself and does not rest; only in relation to it do rest and motion first have sense';[24] in this way, the earth is a ground.[25] The function of the earth as ground can serve as an example for the way in which the modern natural sciences conceal the nature of the lifeworld. In scientific research, the role of the earth as ground is negated, and the earth turns into a mere body, one of many aerial bodies which move in relation to each other. Yet if we were not first and foremost grounded on the earth, we would not even know what movement means.

These brief indications concerning the invariant structures of the lifeworld must suffice at this point.[26] Generally speaking, the modern natural sciences regard the world as an object or totality, and this is a fundamental misapprehension because there 'exists a fundamental difference between the way we are conscious of the world and the way we are conscious of things or objects' (*Crisis*, 143/146). Objects can only be given as objects in the world, and the world is not given, but always already pregiven. The 'questioning concerning the world's pregivenness' (*Crisis*, 154/156ff.) is a basic phenomenological question which lies entirely beyond the scientific perspective.

(e) The crisis

The way in which the sciences conceive of the world as an object provides evidence for Husserl's thesis that the sciences basically remain caught in the natural attitude. The attitude of the modern sciences could be described as a 'natural attitude of a second order'[27] or, as Husserl describes it in *Ideas II*, a 'naturalistic attitude'. The scientific attitude shares several characteristics with the natural attitude; it strictly separates subject and object, attributes a being to the object which would be independent of its being-for-consciousness, and considers the object as the essential component (in comparison to the inessential subject). These features hold for the modern sciences even more than for the everyday, pre- and non-scientific attitude. This intensification is not confined to an emphasis on the object of research, but implies a conscious exclusion of the researching subject. This is the meaning of the sciences' quest for objectivity and subject-irrelativity.

The modern natural sciences are thus characterized by a twofold forgetfulness. They forget the researching subject (and thus human subjectivity as a whole), on the one hand, and the lifeworld, on the other. This twofold forgetfulness makes the natural scientific attitude almost entirely insusceptible to philosophical critique. In his historical reflections in the *Crisis*, Husserl shows how this quest for absolute objectivity cannot be fulfilled. Scientific research is always founded on the lifeworldly praxis of the researcher, it remains tied to it and flows back into the lifeworld. Once these connections are elucidated, the natural scientific attitude can be transformed into the philosophical attitude. The necessity of philosophical questioning emerges from the crisis which Husserl diagnoses. We experience this crisis because we come to realize that science provides no answers to the questions that concern who we are as human beings. Science consciously abandons any questions that deal with the subject in order to achieve an objective account of the world. However, the crisis is not only a crisis of the sciences, for in our present time, sciences determine the nature of our existence as a whole. The sciences tell us who we are or, as Husserl tersely remarks, 'merely fact-minded sciences make merely fact-minded people' (*Crisis*, 4/6). The twofold forgetfulness of the sciences is perpetuated by the way in which we adopt the sciences' quest for objectivism and expect the sciences to provide us with *the* truth in the shape of scientific facts.

Yet the objective responses which we receive do not seem to reach deep enough to have existential significance or to satisfy our quest for meaning. Furthermore, scientific results appear strangely disconnected because they disregard the lifeworld as a context of references. In order to investigate the origins of the current crisis, we have to reflect on the emergence of philosophy and science and on the meaning they had at the moment of their origin, their 'primordial institution' (*Urstiftung*).

Urstiftung is a term which is difficult to translate into English. 'Ur-' means 'original', 'primal' or 'primordial', and 'Stiftung' can be translated as 'institution', 'establishment' or 'foundation'. Husserl uses the term in his historical reflections to refer to those ideas or theories which became a lasting acquisition or heritage (e.g. science), and which we can understand better by asking how they were first instituted, and what their original sense or meaning was.

According to Husserl, the ancient Greeks originally understood philosophy and science to be united and believed them to constitute a single universal science that was absolutely justified. This is precisely the sense that Husserl wishes to capture in his phenomenological philosophy. It is Husserl's thesis that philosophy has not remained true to its primordial institution, and the meaning of philosophy has been concealed by a certain privileging of the search for objectivity. Historical reflection thus intends both to disclose the original meaning of philosophy and to find out why philosophy has been led astray.

However, the quest for the original sense of philosophy and the sciences at the moment of their institution should not blind us to the fact that already the original sense was determined by a duality which *prepared* for the current crisis. According to Husserl, science emerged from the realization that there is a distinction between the multiple ways in which an object appears to us and the one unified object which presents itself in those multiple ways. From the beginning, science focused more on objectivity than on subjective multiplicity, on the unified object rather than its multiple subject-relative appearances. This one-sided tendency turned into objectivism when the mathematization of nature allowed for an apparently truly objective description of nature by means of numbers and ideal geometric shapes. Yet the tendency as such was already prepared for in the original sense of philosophy and science, and did not just emerge in the modern era. Phenomenology wants to create a balance by focusing both on the unified object and its structures and their multiple appearances or manners of givenness.

(f) The way into phenomenology through the lifeworld

In the wake of his historical reflections on the lifeworld and its crisis, Husserl also proposes a new way into phenomenology. This way has the advantage of allowing Husserl to provide a response to one of the problems concerning the epochē which we outlined at the end of Chapter 1: the problem of motivation. One significant motivation for phenomenology would be the current crisis, which calls for a diagnosis and examination. Furthermore, the new intro-duction circumvents the problems that beset the Cartesian way which proved difficult to enact since it required us to reflect on transcendental conscious-ness from the beginning. One of the main disadvantages of the Cartesian way was the impression it gave of turning us away from the world; although the analyses following the epochē show that nothing of the world (which appears to us) was lost, it is more helpful to start our phenomenological investigation from the *world*.

The introduction developed in the *Crisis* takes its departure from the lifeworld. It is usually designated as the 'ontological way' into phenomenology because one of the phenomenological ways of reflecting on the lifeworld is to be found in Husserl's project of an 'ontology of the lifeworld'. The ontology of the lifeworld needs to relate to the whole world and investigate its structures. Husserl states that the task of a lifeworld ontology consists in undertaking a 'concretely general doctrine of essences' of all beings in the lifeworld (*Crisis*, 142/145).

A third possibility of introducing phenomenology is also suggested in the *Crisis*, namely, the way that leads through psychology (*Crisis*, Part III B). Phenomenological psychology attends purely to subjectivity, and objects are considered merely in their 'how' of appearance. However, consciousness is at first merely understood as a worldly or 'mundane' entity. When the researcher realizes that such a conception concerning the mode of being of consciousness leads to contradictions, he or she is motivated to undertake the transition to transcendental philosophy and recognize that consciousness is itself trans-cendental. Phenomenological psychology, when thought through to the end, leads into transcendental phenomenology, according to Husserl.[28] The advantage of the psychological way consists in the fact that the two main difficulties that haunt the introduction to phenomenology are split into two steps. These two steps concern, first, the comprehension of 'inner experience' and, second, the insight into the transcendental nature of consciousness.

However, the psychological way proves somewhat problematic because psychology is an individual science whereas phenomenology strives for universality (it is not just concerned with the soul, but with the entire world). Furthermore, psychology is a positive science and should therefore be submitted to the same criticism which Husserl advocates in the *Crisis* with respect to all science, and which ultimately leads him to broach the ontological way into phenomenology. The ontological way thus proves to be the more fundamental and encompassing one.

All positive or objective sciences can be shown to be lacking in a certain way, according to Husserl, and it is this lack which causes the current crisis of the sciences. This lack consists in forgetting subjectivity. But the subjective dimension is crucial since the relation to subjectivity is that which 'could procure meaning and validity for the theoretical constructs of objective knowledge and thus first gives them the dignity of a knowledge which is ultimately grounded' (*Crisis*, 121/119). Because they ignore this ground, the sciences remain 'on the "plane"' and disregard the 'infinitely richer dimension of depth' (121/119).

The image of the plane with its hidden dimension of depth reveals a crucial strength of the ontological approach in comparison with the Cartesian procedure. The ontological way departs from the richness of the world and encounters subjectivity as a fundamental dimension that is nevertheless ignored. Consciousness thus does not emerge here as 'residual' or as that which remains when everything doubtful has been eliminated, but as that which comes to the fore when phenomenology thoroughly questions what is given, thereby inquiring more and more deeply into it.

Husserl characterizes this procedure as a reversal of the Cartesian approach since the lifeworld is now the beginning and point of departure for the analysis (*Crisis*, 175/169). This reversal of procedure illuminates more clearly the way in which the ontological way involves an intersubjective dimension. The objectivity of the world is scrutinized rather than established. Husserl expresses this concisely when he states that 'the point is not to secure objectivity but to understand it' (*Crisis*, 193/189). This also means that intersubjectivity is always already in play and remains in play; objectivity presupposes the possibility of communicating with others about what is given.

The ontological way includes the universal *epoché* as an essential moment. But the *epoché* is now better prepared for and motivated, and its sense becomes clearer. At stake is a '*total change* of the natural attitude' (*Crisis*, 151/148) which allows us to question the world's depth. The given is examined with regard to its modes of givenness; it is considered as a correlate of the subjectivity which constitutes it. Since the attitude of the positive sciences is so deeply ingrained in us, it proves extremely difficult to assume and maintain the new attitude. The phenomenological attitude is thus an attitude in continuous tension which needs constantly to examine itself, the natural attitude, and the relation between both. The point cannot be to abandon the natural attitude, but to examine it and reveal its dimension of depth, which is to say, transcendental subjectivity, which will turn out to be transcendental intersubjectivity. We shall examine the topic of intersubjectivity in the following chapter.

Further reading

Carr, D. (1974), *Phenomenology and the Problem of History*. Evanston: Northwestern University Press.

—(1977), 'Husserl's problematic concept of the life-world' in Elliston, F. A. and McCormick, P., *Husserl: Expositions and Appraisals*. Notre Dame: University of Notre Dame Press, pp. 202–12.

Dodd, J. (2004), *Crisis and Reflection. An Essay on Husserl's Crisis of the European Sciences*. The Hague: Kluwer.

Held, K. (2003), 'Husserl's phenomenology of the life-world' in Welton, D. (ed.), *The New Husserl. A Critical Reader*. Bloomington, IN: Indiana University Press, pp. 32–62.

Intersubjectivity 4

Main primary literature: *Cartesian Meditations*, meditation V.

The *Fifth Cartesian Meditation* has often been taken to represent Husserl's final position on the question of intersubjectivity, and it has been heavily criticized, leading to the common conclusion that Husserl's account of intersubjectivity is for the most part unsuccessful. In this chapter, we shall examine the principal ideas contained within the *Fifth Cartesian Meditation*, and this will lead us to the insight that the goal of the text is more modest than is often assumed, and that this less ambitious task is indeed an achievable one. Following this, Husserl's later accounts of transcendental intersubjectivity, 'homeworlds' and 'alienworlds' will be investigated.

(a) The question of the *Fifth Cartesian Meditation*

It can be instructive to think about philosophical texts in terms of the question to which they aspire to provide an answer.[29] Husserl's *Fifth Cartesian Meditation* is a text which has been subject to a great deal of criticism, and interpreters tend to agree that the text fails to accomplish its task as they perceive it. But do interpreters actually agree on the task, or on the question that Husserl poses? This does not seem to be the case. At first, it might seem that the *Fifth Cartesian Meditation* strives to answer the general philosophical question, 'How can the existence of other minds be proved?' This is presumed even by prominent philosophers such as Sartre, Ricoeur and Habermas.[30] Yet an intention to establish the certain existence of other minds would run counter to Husserl's phenomenological project as a whole, and indeed the text of the *Cartesian Meditations* does not explicitly raise this question. True to his phenomenological method, Husserl investigates *how* the Other is given to me, not *whether* the Other exists. The fact that we live in an intersubjective world is taken as a principle which guides the investigation; this fact re-emerges at the end of the text as a 'reconstruction' that follows a methodological abstraction.

It thus seems that the *Fifth Cartesian Meditation* has a more modest goal than is often assumed, a goal which follows from the phenomenological method and has in fact influenced phenomenological accounts of intersubjectivity ever since – and especially those phenomenologists who criticize Husserl vehemently. The most succinct formulation of the question of the *Fifth Cartesian Meditation* would be: '*How is the Other given to me on the most basic level?*' The response which the text gives to this question would then be as follows: The Other is accessible as inaccessible. Or in Husserl's more careful rendition: 'The character of the existent "other" has its basis in this kind of verifiable accessibility of what is not originally accessible' (*CM*, 114/144). This response has – in direct and indirect ways – influenced every subsequent phenomenological analysis of the Other. Derrida is thus entirely correct when he states that 'it is still a very profound lesson that Husserl taught us', the lesson being that 'I have no originary access to the alter-ego *as such*'.[31] The Other is accessible in the mode of inaccessibility, or to put the same paradox in a different way, the Other's mode of accessibility consists in his or her inaccessibility.

The inaccessibility of the Other manifests itself on an everyday level in the experience of my inability to really know what the other person is thinking. The phenomenological analysis reveals a deeper level to this mundane experience: the inaccessibility of the Other's internal world or 'sphere' (a concept which will be explored below). Due to this inaccessibility, I can never fully understand the Other or anticipate their behaviour. On the other hand, the fact that we are able to communicate relatively successfully suggests that the Other must be to some extent accessible. It is only because of this accessibility that the inaccessibility of the Other can come to appear.

Formulating the question of the *Fifth Cartesian Meditation* as concerned with the way in which the Other is given to me is not to deny that Husserl in this text repeatedly asks about the objectivity of the world. Yet the issues of otherness and objectivity are intertwined; Husserl takes as his point of departure our experience of the world as intersubjective and objective and strives to elucidate its givenness in this fashion. As Husserl puts it very clearly in the concluding sentence of the *Fifth Cartesian Meditation*: 'phenomenological explication does nothing but *explicate the sense this world has for us, prior to any philosophizing*, and obviously gets solely from our experience – *a sense which philosophy can uncover but never alter*' (*CM*, 151/177). Phenomenology can explain how it is a necessary part of our perception of the world that it be a shared world, experienced by other subjects, but it cannot alter this sense; nor can it establish the certain existence of others and of the world. When phenomenology examines the world, it turns out that the sense of world includes the property of being objective and intersubjectively shared. Furthermore, a phenomenological analysis shows that the Other is given in such a way that he or she is essential for my sense of the world, without the world of the Other ever being entirely accessible to me.

(b) The solipsistic reduction

But why has it proved so easy to misunderstand the goal of the *Fifth Cartesian Meditation*? David Carr has pointed out, that a major reason for misunderstandings can be found in Husserl's slightly misleading use of the notion of solipsism.[32] Husserl uses the term 'solipsism' even though he is not at all concerned with the problem of solipsism in any traditional sense.

Solipsism in the traditional (non-phenomenological) sense is the suspicion that others might only be a product of my imagination; the solution to such traditional solipsism would take the form of a proof of the existence of others (or other minds).

Husserl does not want to prove that others exist; his ambition is a different one: he wishes to show that it is possible to make sense, phenomenologically speaking, of the Other in his or her otherness. Although Husserl is not concerned with the problem of solipsism in the traditional sense, he does at certain moments of criticism use the term in a traditional way. This is the case especially at the end of the text, where he states that 'the illusion [*Schein*] of a solipsism is dissolved' (*CM*, 150/176). This does not just mean that the problem has been resolved, but that the problem was an illusion in the first place.

The reason solipsism in the traditional sense can be nothing but an illusion is clearly described by Merleau-Ponty in his essay, 'The Philosopher and his Shadow'. Thus, he points out that, for Husserl, solipsism is not an original experience but a thought experiment. The philosophical problem of solipsism is always posed by abstracting others from a world in which they are already supposed to exist, and this abstraction presupposes that the world is already given to us as a shared world. True solipsism would require that I do not experience myself as an individual self in distinction from other selves, but as the only self that there is (Latin: *solus ipse*, the etymological source of 'solipsism'). In this case, however, there would not be a self in the true sense. 'We are truly alone only on the condition that we do not know we are; it is this very ignorance which is our solitude' (*PS*, 174). Such might be the situation of an infant before it experiences itself as separate from its original other. But it is not the position of the philosopher who reflects on the possibilities and dangers of solipsism.

When Husserl in the *Fifth Cartesian Meditation* suggests performing a 'solipsistic reduction', he indeed suggests a thought experiment, and more precisely, an abstraction. Husserl uses the terms 'abstract' and 'abstraction' relatively frequently throughout the text to emphasize this aspect of his analysis. If I perform the peculiar thematic reduction that Husserl calls the solipsistic reduction, I am required to abstract from everything which the Other contributes to my sense of the world. As a result, I am left with a certain kind of nature and with my own body, but I also experience the bodies of others – as mere physical bodies. However, the nature that belongs to the solipsistic sphere would not be the kind of nature studied by the sciences because it would be lacking in objectivity. It would consist of trees and rocks, but I would not really know them in their full sense as trees and rocks because the Other usually contributes to these concepts of mine, and in the solipsistic reduction I imagine a world without any contribution from the Other. Similarly, a strange experience of the Other's body is part of my solipsistic sphere, as a mere physical body which is neither objective nor inhabited by an alien subjectivity. Even though my experience of what is other belongs to my solipsistic sphere, this is not truly an experience of the other *as other*, but of the other as reduced to a mere physicality, devoid of the Other's consciousness, contributions and conceptions.

(c) The sphere of ownness

The sphere to which the thought experiment of the solipsistic reduction leads me is designated by Husserl as the **sphere of ownness**. It involves an abstraction from everything which the Other contributes to my sense of the world.

The 'sphere of ownness' appears enigmatic as well as problematic for at least two reasons: First, how could it even be possible to perform an 'abstraction from everything that transcendental constitution gives me as Other' (*CM*, 93/125)? Secondly, how would it be useful, that is, how can such an abstraction help to elucidate the sense of the Other? The same response can be given to both of these concerns: the exploration of the sphere of ownness is indeed questionable where *my* sphere of ownness is concerned since the reduction to the sphere of ownness is always artificial. Such a sphere must be isolated through an act of abstraction, and this abstraction is only interesting because it helps to elucidate the sphere of ownness which belongs to the *Other*. But when it comes to the Other, the abstraction is indeed legitimate and methodologically helpful, since the alien sphere of ownness designates that which is inaccessible to me.

This methodological step corresponds to the way in which the natural attitude would approach the problem of solipsism. For the natural attitude, thought experiments about solipsism usually involve scenarios of a child growing up in the forest, a person being stranded on an island, and suchlike. Alluding to common sense, Husserl mentions 'humans in a cave or a box' in a manuscript on solipsism (Hua XV, 562). Yet this example is merely an illustration for Husserl, complementing his thought experiment involving abstraction. The solipsistic sphere of ownness is a methodological and provisional concept because Husserl is not ultimately interested in an abstractive sphere that does not actually exist. In the solipsistic sphere, we do not consider others as others but only as physical objects within my sphere. Bodies of others, cultural products, and so on, are in that sense part of my solipsistic sphere – but not as human bodies, nor as cultural products. However, when I consider this sphere thoroughly, I find that it points to the sense of the Other. The sense of the Other's body is missed if it is limited to a physical body which can move without the help of conscious directions and intentions. In the thought experiment, I would still perceive the body of the Other with arms, hands, legs, etc., but these would seem to move around arbitrarily. Yet no matter how hard I try to take the Other as a mere abstraction, that is, as a mere physical object, the Other will alert me to the fact that it is not merely a physical body, but a lived body (*Leib*) which resembles my own, with its own alien sphere of ownness.

How, then, is the Other constituted? How is he or she given to me as another person? Husserl explains the relation between the mere physical body which appears to me in the solipsistic reduction and the 'full' sense of the Other with the help of the concepts of 'pairing' and 'appresentation'.

> **Pairing** designates the way in which I group two or more items together because of their likeness, in this case: my body and that of the Other, which are connected through similarities in demeanour, gestures, postures, and so on.

This concept operates on the level of passive synthesis (see Chapter 2 above) since it relies on association as the main principle of this kind of synthesis which does not require the active engagement of the ego. Merely by way of similarity and contrast, there is a connection established between my body and that of the other without any specific judgements being passed.

Yet in order for this body which reminds me of my own to be given as a lived body, as the body of the Other, an additional step is necessary. As with 'pairing', Husserl uses a term which is not confined to the realm of intersubjectivity, but describes a general process of perception, especially from the genetic perspective.

> **Appresentation** means that I bring something to presence in addition to what is actually given to me as present: I make it 'co-present'. In this case, what is actually present is the body of the Other, and I ap-present what is missing in order to turn the body of the Other into the full sense of the Other.

To make matters worse, Husserl fluctuates in the *Fifth Cartesian Meditation* between 'appresentation' and '(analogizing) apperception', where apperception designates what I grasp: my perception and what is added to it as 'ap-perceived'. Both terms – appresentation and apperception – include the prefix 'ap-' (originally the Latin *'ad'*) which means 'to', designating my 'full' presentation or perception, inclusive of that which passive synthesis has added 'to' it by way of association.

My appresentation of the Other is determined by an intriguing dynamic between 'here' and 'there'. I am here, and the Other is over there. Yet by way of appresentation, I could be over there – in real terms, because I could move to the place of the Other at some later point, and in fictive terms, because I can imagine myself over there right now; I can conceive of myself 'as if' I were over there.[33] However, I can never really be over there right now, and in that sense, the inescapable otherness of the Other is confirmed on the level of bodily perspectives. The Other is the being which is 'there' in such a way that I can be there at some later point, and I can even imagine myself over there right now, but I cannot actually be 'there' right now, because 'there' is where the Other is (while I am 'here').

Pairing and appresentation are then complemented by empathy (*Einfüh-lung*) where I literally 'feel' myself 'into' the other person and establish that the perceived body is a lived body and not a mere physical body which brings about this comportment that is similar to my own. Empathy does not diminish the inaccessibility of the Other; it does not mean that the Other's sphere of ownness becomes transparent to me, but it means that I feel myself into the Other and intuit that there is indeed a sphere of ownness there.

It is important to bear in mind that Husserl does not claim that we run through the processes of pairing, appresentation and empathy when we encounter other people. In a certain sense, the introduction of these processes becomes necessary only because of the thought experiment of the solipsistic reduction which serves to disentangle and examine our complex intersubjec-tive lifeworld by trying to determine what exactly the Other contributes to it. As we have seen, the procedure of abstraction leaves us with a layer which can be distinguished, but not separated in our experience.

Husserl therefore comes to introduce another, more encompassing version of the sphere of ownness: the 'primordinal sphere of ownness'.[34] This is the sphere that includes 'my actual and possible experience *of* what is other' (*CM*, 98/129); it is the sphere of everything that is part of my stream of consciousness and immediately accessible to me. The concept of the sphere of ownness creates problems which are not coincidental, especially now that we have encountered two such concepts. The problems result from the way in which Husserl attempts to take apart an experience that is always more complex than the abstract picture he uses to consider it. Our full sphere of ownness includes all our experiences as immediately accessible to us. The Other's sphere of ownness which Husserl is striving to illuminate is not limited to the experience of a solipsistic world, abstracted from other subjects, cultural objects, and so on, but involves an experience of the world in its entirety, and yet remains inaccessible to me. The initial, solipsistic sphere of ownness which tries to abstract from everything that the Other contributes to my experience thus plays a methodological role, but is a merely provisional concept, to be replaced by the notion of a more encompassing primordinal sphere of ownness. Otherwise, the Other's sphere of ownness would not even be of interest to me because it would be entirely inaccessible, while the challenge is to conceive of the real paradox which serves as our guiding thread throughout this chapter: to be accessible in the mode of inaccessibility.

(d) Transcendental intersubjectivity

Although solipsism indeed serves a methodological function as a thought experiment, exploring how the already existent Other is given, rather than proving his or her existence, some problems still remain. First, even if the solipsistic reduction is a methodological step and does not refer to solipsism in the traditional sense, it is still questionable whether Husserl can withstand the charge of a solipsism which is sometimes raised against his phenomenological method. Secondly, the claim that the Other is accessible in the mode of inaccessibility remains a rather paradoxical response to the question concerning the Other's givenness. It will turn out that these two issues are closely related to one another.

Husserl's response to the first problem involves his notion of transcendental intersubjectivity. Ultimately, the world is not constituted by transcendental subjectivity but by transcendental intersubjectivity; more precisely, transcendental subjectivity turns out to be transcendental intersubjectivity. The objectivity of the world which Husserl aims to elucidate in the *Fifth Cartesian Meditation* is a product of transcendental intersubjectivity. At the same time, my transcendental consciousness is the place where intersubjectivity and the intersubjective world come to appearance. The transcendental ego, 'starting from itself and in itself, [. . .] constitutes transcendental intersubjectivity, to which it then adds itself as a merely privileged member' (*Crisis*, 188/185). To be sure, 'constitution' means that the ego endows the Other with sense or meaning, not with existence. But do I myself not owe just as much to the sense-giving acts of others? Not only did Husserl leave this possibility open, but, in some texts, even seems to find it persuasive. Yet he emphasizes that even if I owe my own ego to others, the transcendental ego is still the place where this state of affairs comes to the fore. 'Only by starting from the ego and the system of its transcendental functions and accomplishments can we methodically exhibit transcendental intersubjectivity and its transcendental communalization' (*Crisis*, 189/185f.); everything that can be said about me and my dependence on the Other will need to be said from the perspective of the ego.

The transcendental ego is thus merely the place where transcendental intersubjectivity comes to appear. Yet in order for us to experience the world as we do, which is to say as objective, transcendental intersubjectivity must be presupposed. Furthermore, it has to be kept in mind that the transcendental ego is itself not entirely accessible to me. Interestingly, the frequently criticized analogy between alien experience (*Fremderfahrung*) and remembering, which Husserl uses in the *Fifth Cartesian Meditation* can serve to illustrate this point (*CM*, §55). The commonality consists in the fact that both remembering and intersubjectivity involve a plurality of experiences of the same object – in one instance as a temporal succession, in the other as simultaneity. In the first case, I remember seeing the cup yesterday, and this adds to my current perception of it; in the second case, I realize that my perception of the cup is complemented by the Other's perspective on the cup. The point of connection is the object's identity. I encounter the Other's ego as another *ego* because I experience the commonly experienced and constituted world; I thus experience the other as a functioning, constituting ego.

To be sure, there are significant differences between remembering and the alien experience. The experiences of Others are in principle only accessible to me in the mode of inaccessibility, whereas my own past experiences belong to the same stream of consciousness as my present ones. Nevertheless, it is conceivable that the very inaccessibility of the other ego might reveal something about the sense in which even my own past ego is alien to me. Thus the familiar occurrence of remembering 'in me' would then not only reveal something about the supposedly incomprehensible experience of the other ego but would also elucidate how intersubjective experience discloses something about the nature of my own transcendental ego. Husserl speaks of the 'community' of the present with the past ego, thus borrowing a concept from the intersubjective realm: 'In empathy [*Einfühlung*], in originally understanding them and having them as persons in co-presence, I am in contact [*in Fühlung*] as I with the Thou, with the other ego, similarly to the way in which I am in contact with myself in the difference of remembering, in a community of consciousness with the past ego'.[35]

This passage points to the intriguing concept of the 'living present' as the elusive core of the ego. The field of what is presently given to me exhibits a certain extension or breadth, and the late Husserl designates this whole – of retention, original impression and protention – as the 'living present' (*lebendige Gegenwart*).[36] In order to reach the centre or core of this living present, the horizons of past and future need to be bracketed so that the 'pure there' (*reine Da*) of the present remains. Within this radicalized reduction we encounter an enduring core, yet we also see that this core is perpetually flowing and withdrawing.[37] When I reflect on the ego as it is functioning – engaged in perceiving, remembering, and so on – I always arrive too late. At the same time, reflection is only possible because the 'living present' has a certain extension and because there is a primordial distance between the ego as reflecting and the ego as the object of reflection. In this sense, it would be possible to say that there is already some inaccessibility at the core of the transcendental ego. Strangely, its accessibility depends on this fundamental inaccessibility; if the ego were not flowing and elusive, but static and self- identical, it would not be accessible to itself at all.

The preceding considerations already provide a partial response to the second question, namely, the paradoxical accessibility of the other ego. We have just seen that a paradoxical combination of accessibility and inaccessibility also occurs at the heart of my own transcendental ego. I can never access my transcendental ego as it functions, and at the same time, if there were no flow but only a static unity at the centre of the ego, the ego would not be accessible at all, not even as inaccessible. Since the ego as it is engaged cannot be made an object of reflection, it is characterized by a peculiar anonymity. Similarly, the other ego is only accessible to me as fundamentally different from myself and ultimately inaccessible.

Husserl describes the way this problem entails its own solution. 'These two primordial spheres – mine which is for me as ego the original sphere, and his which is for me an appresented sphere – are they not separated by an abyss I cannot actually cross [. . .]?' He continues to find an enigma in the fact that I experience the perceived body as the body of the other and not merely as an *indication* of such otherness. But in the end the enigma is not so enigmatic;

'the enigma appears only if the two original spheres have already been distinguished – a distinction that already presupposes that experience of someone else has done its work' (*CM*, 121/150). The accessibility of the Other as inaccessible is a fact that can be elucidated but neither proved nor disproved, neither confirmed nor altered. The task is simply to understand this inaccessibility and its various dimensions more fully, a task that has been taken up by many philosophers after Husserl.

(e) Homeworld and alienworld

In one of his manuscripts on intersubjectivity, Husserl tells us that, 'transcendental subjectivity expands to intersubjectivity or rather, strictly speaking, it does not expand but merely understands itself better' (Hua XV, 17). Once subjectivity has gained an understanding of itself as intersubjectivity, it becomes obvious that there are unities of subjects which are more than the mere sum of their members. Here, it is necessary to distinguish between 'loose communities' for which an encompassing personality is lacking (e.g. groups of people who merely happen to be in the same place, be it by chance or by force) and such unities which can be said to exhibit the characteristics of an individual person, albeit by analogy. Husserl mentions families, clubs and nations as examples, and he explains that the will of a state is different from the will of a citizen belonging to that state. In this sense, it is justified to speak of 'personalities of a higher order' (*Personalitäten höherer Ordnung*) (e.g. *Crisis*, 191f.; *CM*, § 58) and to attribute a 'supra-personal consciousness' to them.[38]

In order for a supra-individual consciousness to take shape, there have to be 'communal memories'. These joint memories usually come about through communal actions and practices. By pursuing a common purpose – be it a specific purpose like a joint project, or a more general one like living together in a state – the group is constituted as a group through its common directedness. Although the original purpose of the group may no longer be present after a certain period of time, it can still function but only in the form of a habit.

As his thoughts on intersubjectivity progress even further, Husserl replaces the term 'personalities of a higher order' with the concepts of homeworlds and alienworlds. This terminology has the advantage of leading us back to the concept of a world which makes it possible for us to explore such communal worlds in phenomenological terms; as we shall see, such phenomenological

58 Phenomenology

examinations of home and alienworlds are quite fruitful. The term, 'personality of a higher order' had the disadvantage of having metaphysical rather than phenomenological connotations. At the same time, there might appear to be disadvantages to the term 'alienworld' since it would seem to refer exclusively to nations or cultural worlds, and not to other groups united by a communal history. However, Husserl's concept of the alien is general enough to accommodate other modalities, and even though Husserl mostly employs the term alienworld for a cultural world, the term could be expanded to include other modalities of the alien as Husserl introduces them (e.g. children, animals).

As history acquires a renewed significance for Husserl and the concept of the lifeworld becomes central to his thought, the terms 'homeworld' and 'alienworld' become appropriate designations for such historical, co-constitutive worlds. Husserl calls alienness a 'fundamental category of all historicity' (*Crisis*, 320/275). The concept of the alienworld allows us to develop a response to the question of what an alien object is: the special feature of an alien object is that it is not only an object unfamiliar and incomprehensible to us, but an object that seems to belong to a context that is alien to us. The alien object appears to have a meaning that is unfamiliar to us, but familiar to others; it vaguely points to other objects that are also more or less alien to us. An alien tool is still recognized by us as a kind of tool that supposedly fulfils a certain function, that is not a work of art, and so on. This means that it belongs to an alienworld.

> The **homeworld (*Heimwelt*)** is the world familiar to us, the world in which we are at home in the broadest sense of the term. It is a world historically generated and steadily evolving.

The homeworld can only be grasped by a historical approach, as a process which encompasses our ancestors and descendants and is thus generative. Our homeworld has developed its 'historical face', its 'cultural face' over time, and the same holds for the alienworld (Hua XV, 233, fn. 1). Since I have not participated in the history of the alienworld and have not grown up with it, this world presents my understanding with severe obstacles. Homeworld and alienworld undergo modifications; my homeworld can become alien to me, or I can become more and more at home in the alienworld. Yet the contrast between home and alien as such is never eliminated; rather, it belongs to the structure of every world.

The rupture of my familiar surroundings by the alien makes me aware that all beings in general appear in contexts, in horizons, that they belong to a coherent world. Since the encounter with the alien can alert me to the world in the phenomenological sense, as a context of references which I usually take for granted, it can play a methodological role for phenomenology. In his historical reflections, Husserl examines the primordial institution (*Urstiftung*) of philosophy and science in ancient Greece. In his Vienna lecture, the text in which Husserl first introduces the ideas which he then develops in the *Crisis*, he refers back to Plato and Aristotle, who regarded wonder, *thaumazein*, as the origin of philosophy (*Crisis*, 331/285). According to Husserl, the particular significance of wonder lies in the fact that it is entirely unpractical. It is a mood (*pathos*), something we are overcome by, which is not at our disposal. Because of this character, wonder bears a particular affinity to the beginning of philosophy: we can never fully explain how philosophy comes about or what motivates us to start philosophizing. We are intrigued, overcome by a mood to which we respond but which we did not bring about.

Why is it that philosophy originated in ancient Greece? What distinguishes the situation of the ancient Greeks from that of other peoples and other times? Husserl investigates the factual motivation for the emergence of philosophy in the concrete historical situation of the Greeks. What is important about these historical considerations is the claim that the encounter with the alien, with alien nations, led to the institution of philosophy. As a trading nation, the Greeks were particularly exposed to alienworlds.

Normally, our experience is 'undisturbed by any noticeable disagreement'. But when we encounter the alien, 'when we are thrown into an alien social sphere [. . .], we discover that their truths, the facts that for them are fixed, generally verified or verifiable, are by no means the same as ours' (*Crisis*, 141/138ff). According to Husserl, in the encounter with alien nations an essential distinction comes to fore: on the one hand, there are different conceptions, interpretations and mythologies; and on the other hand, there is a core of identity which relates to all these conceptions and remains the same throughout. As Husserl puts it in a manuscript related to the *Crisis*: 'It is the same sun, the same moon, the same earth, the same sea, etc. that are so differently mythologized by the different peoples according to their particular traditionality' (Hua XXIX, 387). Traditional philosophy resembles the sciences in placing an emphasis on the identical being-in-itself of a thing in contrast to the various subjective ways of grasping it. Phenomenology, by contrast, strives to examine both the relative ways of givenness and the non-relative core, as well as the difference between them. Such invariant structures exist, even in relation to the lifeworld, as we have seen (Chapter 3 (d)). They always appear in a culturally relative form, but since every culture in some shape or form relies on them, it is correct to identify the structure itself as invariant. In addition to the previous examples of earth-as-ground and world-as-horizon, we have now encountered the structure of the home and the alien as a structure which can undergo changes, but which cannot be eliminated.

(f) Phenomenology of culture

Husserl's considerations on home and alienworlds open up various possibilities for phenomenological examinations of culture; at the same time, a number of questions and problems emerge. Because his own writings on the alien are not very systematic (and Husserl's death occurred before he had a chance to develop them), other phenomenologists have taken these ideas further. Three issues will be briefly sketched here.

(i) Ethical issues

One of the main difficulties for a phenomenology of the alien is how to examine the alien without eliminating its alienness, or how to thematize it *as alien*. Bernhard Waldenfels has repeatedly stressed this difficulty, pointing out that it is impossible ever to resolve the initial paradox of the Other as accessible in the mode of inaccessibility; otherwise, the otherness of the Other would be lost. And yet, despite the paradox, we interact with each other. This interaction needs to be described in appropriate terms; Waldenfels suggests 'pathos' and 'response'. The interplay of *pathos* and response describes different dimensions of the alien. *Pathos* or passivity describes the way in which we experience the alien as being beyond our control and categorization. Response designates our most basic reaction to the alien, which can take a variety of forms (ranging from indifference to violation).

On the level of culture, this issue translates into the difficulty of responding to other cultures without eliminating their otherness. Important issues that are discussed in this context include the character of the boundaries between cultures (since these usually take a more subtle form than literal checkpoints or border controls). Where are these boundaries located, and what character do they have? How do we describe the fact that they can be transformed, but not as such eliminated or resolved? How can the movement between homeworld and alienworld best be characterized? We always have to start from the home when we encounter the alien, this starting point cannot be surpassed (Hua XV, 624). 'Crossing over from within' has been suggested as a name for this kind of movement which can only come from the home, and excludes us from taking either the perspective of the alien in a direct way, or an encompassing view from outside of both.[39] However, the expression 'crossing' might still be misleading since it implies that we must leave the home perspective behind and make a transition into the alienworld, whereas a description of the actual experience shows that we continue to remain tied to the home and are suspended between the two worlds. The term 'transgressing (from within)' might be more apt since the element 'trans-', also involved in 'translation', signifies a movement 'across' that never fully arrives, but remains a movement 'between' two worlds.

The relationship of homeworld and alienworld is of necessity asymmetrical; I can never integrate the alienworld into the homeworld. It cannot be our goal to achieve an encompassing synthesis or to integrate the alien into the home (or the home into the alien) but rather, to respond to the alien from the perspective of the home. All other approaches are a violation of the limits between homeworld and alienworld.[40] Respecting these limits means that the points of view of home and alien are not interchangeable, and that there is no higher standpoint which unites them.

(ii) The problem of the one world

In light of the relativity between homeworld and alienworld, the question of *one* encompassing, non-relative world arises.[41] Husserl speaks often of 'the common objective world', the 'world in itself' (Hua XV, 436f.), or the 'true world' as the topic of transcendental phenomenology (Hua XV, 215 fn.). At the same time, he says explicitly: 'The world in itself [. . .] is never given' (Hua XV, 614). Is Husserl here contradicting himself? Even if he might use misleading formulations at times, his position seems to be the following, non-contradictory one: The world in itself is indeed never given in experience. However, phenomenology searches for 'invariant' structures of the lifeworld, which belong to the project of a lifeworld ontology, such as the structure of earth-as-ground.

Although every world has in one way or another the character of earth-as-ground, the 'one' earth-as-ground, the earth-as-ground in itself is never given to us. What is given is always one specific earth-as-ground, as it comes to appear in the context of a homeworld. Nevertheless is it legitimate for phenomenology to search for those structures if we bear in mind that they are 'ideas' and not something given in experience. Likewise, we have a 'right to the idea of a complete understanding' (Hua XV, 625), even though there are always factual limits to our understanding, due to the limits of the homeworld and the alienworld.

(iii) Language and narrativity

As the significance of history and of the alien for Husserl's phenomenology increases, language also becomes more and more important. Intersubjectivity is now described as that which extends 'through the open chains of genera-tions' (Hua XV, 219), and this is only possible because 'linguistic communi-cation is always involved in creating the experiential sense of the world' (Hua XV, 220). As far as Husserl's phenomenological project is concerned, we need linguistic expressions in order to understand the sense of philosophy and science when they were originally instituted (their *Urstiftungssinn*); otherwise, we will never be able to illuminate the crisis which Husserl has diagnosed.

Furthermore, the transformation and renewal of our world presupposes language. I myself can make some changes in my life, but changing and renewing the world requires me to be able to communicate with others (cf. Hua XV, 465). Husserl therefore claims that language is the 'basis of all sociality' (Hua XV, 475). Language is an essential extension of my horizon, such that not only present but also past and future worlds open up for me. By way of stories, myths and narratives, language connects me with my ancestors and predecessors.

Language and history are thus interconnected, and narrativity becomes a significant topic for phenomenology.[42] Narrativity gains additional importance for an understanding of the lifeworld as the phenomenological analysis shows that our experience is itself structured in narrative terms. We experience time as divided up into sequences with a beginning, middle, and some kind of open or closed, satisfying or disappointing ending. However, are not these pheno-menological analyses of narrativity and language influenced by the way in which they take Western languages and narratives as their starting point? Yes, but this is only an argument in favour of expanding the project and pursuing further such analyses. For example, some cultures appear to have more of a cyclical than a narratively linear understanding of time and history; this would also be reflected in their literature and structures of communication.[43]

Translation in the widest sense thus emerges as a central topic for phenomenological explorations of culture. From a phenomenological perspective, language reveals itself as a world in which we learn to dwell, rather than a body of words to be accumulated. Translation thus has to negotiate between two different worlds; the translator emerges in this process as a guide who bears ethical responsibilities towards both sides rather than just striving for correctness or fluency.[44] Furthermore, it turns out that there is translation within one and the same language as well as between linguistic and non-linguistic languages such as gestures or artistic expressions. Merleau-Ponty has taken several important steps towards the construction of such a phenomenology of translation and of cultures (see Chapters 14 and 15 below).

Further reading

Carr, D. (1973), 'The "Fifth Meditation" and Husserl's Cartesianism' in *Philosophy and Phenomenological Research*, vol. 34, no. 1, pp. 14–35 (still the best article on the *Fifth Cartesian Meditation*).

Smith, A. D. (2003), *Husserl and the Cartesian Meditations*. London: Routledge.

Zahavi, D. (2001), *Husserl and Transcendental Intersubjectivity. A Response to the Linguistic-Pragmatic Critique*. Athens: Ohio University Press.

On home- and alienworlds:

Steinbock, A. J. (1995), *Home and Beyond. Generative Phenomenology after Husserl*. Evanston: Northwestern University Press.

Waldenfels, B. (1990), 'Experience of the alien in Husserl's phenomenology', in *Research in Phenomenology* 20 (1990), pp. 19–33.

—(1998), 'Homeworld and alienworld' in E. W. Orth, Chan-Fai Cheung (eds), *Phenomenology and Life-world*. Freiburg/München: Alber 1998 (reprinted Moran and Embree (2004)).

Part II
Martin Heidegger (Messkirch, Germany 1889–Freiburg, Germany 1976)

Heidegger after Husserl

Main primary literature

History of the Concept of Time, pp. 102–34.
Being and Time, Introduction.

(a) Existence and being-in-the-world

Martin Heidegger was the most influential, and perhaps the greatest student of Edmund Husserl. His conception of phenomenology seeks to correct certain misunderstandings which he perceives in Husserl.[1] Broadly speaking, for Heidegger, Husserl inherits a certain mistaken way of thinking about consciousness from the history of philosophy, but without realizing it. A crucial part of Heidegger's innovation in phenomenology is his attention to history. This attention is crucial, not least for the reason that our concepts, particularly after long usage, come to seem self-evident. Thus they seem not to involve any sort of interpretation at all, or any possible bias. Only by attending to the history of a concept can we reveal that in fact this appearance of self-evidence is just a facade, and has been built up from a series of layers, an accumulation of different discourses on the same subject, which have 'hardened', and which now seem to be timeless facts. In fact, they are the product of history. For Heidegger, Husserl stands at the summit of the history of philosophy, which means that he shows the way down, after philosophy has exhausted all of its possibilities, but also that he has inherited certain ways of thinking from the past, and brought them to their highest development. These ways of thinking, these concepts, remain unquestioned since they seem so obviously true. Heidegger however deems it necessary for phenomenology to 'deconstruct' (*abbauen*) these notions, which means precisely to demonstrate the many different historical layers that have constructed them, as well as the core of truth which they contain.

For Husserl, the meaning of a phenomenon can only become self-evidently present to us when it is immediately given to our intuition. And fundamentally, the intuiting consciousness is the primary source of meaning for all phenomena. For Heidegger, phenomena are rather more like signs, in need of interpretation, and the process of bestowing meaning is not done by a human subject in the present moment of intuition, but by a historical process, which gradually deposits new layers of significance on top of a certain original bedrock, that is then covered over.

Thus, for Heidegger, we are more passive with respect to meaning than the Husserlian subject — which he largely inherited from the tradition — would have us think, and at the same time, a phenomenology which attempts to give us unhindered access to the phenomenon needs to do a great deal more work to secure this access. First of all we must attend to history, and perform a certain deconstruction; these signs must be *interpreted*: the ancient name for interpretation was *hermeneuein*, – from the name of the god, Hermes, 'the messenger' – and the science of interpretation, 'hermeneutics'.

Husserl had in truth already seen that phenomenology did require a number of special procedures in order to reach the phenomenon as it gives itself, free of any particular interpretation that would distort it. First, there is a process of bracketing which removes us from our 'natural attitude' of common sense belief in the existence of things as they appear outside of consciousness, and then there are various reductions, which all intervene between consciousness and its own experiences: indeed the world and its contingency, language and history, are precisely part of the problem for Husserl, since they obstruct our access to the meaning of phenomena. For Heidegger, however, this process is not one of bracketing the world, for the world itself, which is the repository and product of history, and hence many different successive, even contradictory interpretations, is one of the chief *sources* of meaning. What things are is partly a product of their place in the world. This does not render phenomena fundamentally opaque to a consciousness that would be ultimately trapped in its own sphere, able only to understand the meanings that it itself has attributed to things, since, for Heidegger, human beings are essentially a *part* of this world: 'The world is therefore something "wherein" Dasein [Heidegger's word for the human being] as an entity already *was*' (*BT*, 106/76). Hence any attempt to bracket the world, as Husserl does, will not do justice to man's specific mode of existence, and will at the same time, paradoxically, prevent us from ever having a genuine experience of phenomena.

The worldly provenance of meaning leads Heidegger to revise Husserl's understanding of the human subject as an active entity which constitutes the world, and to think of it as nothing beyond an entity that is itself in the world, a 'being-in-the-world', but one that is distinguished from all others by the especial capacity to be *open* or responsive to the meaningfulness that is already inherent in factual, empirical things, To this capacity Heidegger gives the name 'Dasein'.

In large part, Heidegger is opposed to two features of the transcendental subject: its activity and its reflexivity. For Heidegger, meaning is already constituted, and forms an 'objective' world which – to a certain degree – Dasein only inherits and does *not* constitute; secondly, this meaning is not accessed by means of a withdrawal from one's natural, everyday, practical activity, and a reflection on one's own experiences of that world. It is just such a reflective attitude that has led philosophers since Plato to misunderstand what things are. For Heidegger it is only through a certain immersion in the world that we have a genuine experience of things. But at the same time, we are not explicitly aware of what it is we are experiencing: it remains hidden from us, and to become aware does indeed require a break from work. However, this break itself inherently misunderstands the essence of things by failing to take account of this prior hiddenness, and the way in which ultimately the very capacity to reflect and bring things into the light exists in a complex relation of dependence *with* this hiddenness or 'concealment'.

All of this leads Heidegger to rethink the very method of phenomenology. His most basic gesture is to refuse the bracketing of the world and the transcendental reduction that reduces consciousness to a pure reflection upon its own contents, and to suspend judgement as to the existence of the factual, contingent, world beyond it. For Heidegger, while it is true that strictly speaking there would be no 'world' without Dasein, the balance shifts towards the contrary statement, that without world there would be no Dasein. At the same time the accent shifts from the activity of constitution to the passivity of reception, and the phenomenologist is advised to remember that the subject does not have sole responsibility for the meaning of his experiences, and that there are certain sources of meaning which are essentially mysterious to him.

This is due to the contingent situation of Dasein at a certain point in history and geography, and within a certain culture and language. For Heidegger, to presume in any way that consciousness can experience itself in the absence of the world is false, because it would cut phenomena off from the context that ultimately determines their meaning. This context is called 'world'. It is only an entity's place in a world that defines *what* that entity *is*.

Husserl's ultimate stress on the activity and indeed the voluntary free will of consciousness as it bestows meaning through 'intending' shows that he did not truly interrogate the traditional answer to the question of what consciousness was. It was ultimately modelled, as the name suggests (con-sciousness, *con-scientia*), on a disinterested, disengaged subject, knowing the world, and hence rendering it fully visible and meaningful before its own (metaphorical) gaze. He accepted the modern, Cartesian answer that the truest kind of experience belonged to a consciousness cut off from the world in its most basic dimension and for whom the world exists only as its own representation *of* that world. In other words, he understood consciousness as a *subject*. And as a result he understood the 'being' of whatever remained outside consciousness as an *object*. Subjectivity and objectivity thus constitute the traditional modern philosophical answers to the question that was Heidegger's ultimate concern: the question of being. This is the question of what it means simply to *be*, and Husserl's answer, which ultimately he took to be self-evident, was subjectivity (in the case of the human being) and objectivity (in the case of everything else).

Heidegger, by investigating the historical provenance of these two answers, demonstrates them to be prejudices inherited from certain philosophical traditions, and hence not the obvious, unhistorical, simple 'truths' they are taken to be; and by means of this 'deconstruction' of concepts, he reaches his own renewed thinking of *what* the human subject is. But because this discovery demonstrated the falsity of the opposition of subject and object, this meant that the world in its factual existence could no longer be understood in a way that was fundamentally opposed to the consciousness of the transcendental subject. Initially, Heidegger understands the phenomenal realm to be co-extensive with the 'world', a space of illumination and meaningfulness, with a certain obscurity at the source of that world's signification, but one which can nevertheless be illuminated by deconstruction. He realized that he himself was still caught in a traditional way of thinking about the phenomena, as ultimately submitting to the enlightening powers of a consciousness unencumbered by the opacity that results from one's situation in a factual world. Later he therefore came to make this notion of situatedness more fundamentally a part of the experiencing subject and the phenomenon which it experienced, and by developing it into a certain underside which remains resolutely in excess of the world, which Heidegger calls the 'earth'. Heidegger, from the very beginning, was attempting to understand experience not as something that could ever belong to anything that remains distinct from the world, but as a passively received revelation that occurs to a certain special kind of entity *within* the world (hence his ultimate use of the word 'event' to describe manifestation).

The consequences for phenomenology as a method result from Heidegger's rethinking of what it is to be a *phenomenon*, what the nature of *appearance* actually is. Ultimately this will mean that the phenomenon does *not* at first show itself. And in fact, in different ways throughout his long career, Heidegger will show that a certain invisibility or hiddenness is actually an inherent part of the phenomenon. Due to the essentially worldly nature of phenomenon and the consequent necessity of contingency and historical depth, the ultimate meaning of phenomena may *never* be fully revealed to consciousness, since it will always involve certain mere 'givens', facts whose provenance is intrinsically inapparent and unavailable to us. More precisely, if phenomenology is interested in the meaning of the phenomenon, it must be interested in what attributes meaning, the origin of the signification of phenomena, and if this is no longer just the finite human being but also the world, which is the product of a history whose ultimate depths disappear into the obscurity of the past, the full conditions of possibility of phenomena will never appear to us.

The conditions of possibility for a phenomenon, what allows it to appear to us as it does, constitute the 'being' of that phenomenon, and if these conditions are the ultimate *meaning* of the word 'phenomena', then the ultimate phenomenon studied by phenomenology is something that remains *hidden*, that does *not* show itself, and the task of philosophy, by means of a process of interpretation and direct intuition, will be to determine the *limits* of our ability to determine the meaning of phenomena, and the extent to which they really can be 'given' to us. So while the phenomenon is defined by Heidegger as what 'shows itself', the very fact that we are not the ones who *make* it appear, means that not all of that phenomenon – to be precise, its very conditions of possibility – will ever become apparent to us. The condition of an entity's appearance, that which allows it be what it uniquely is, is its 'being'. Thus the ultimate target of phenomenology is precisely 'being'. Ultimately, phenomenology will attempt to determine the extent of the phenomenon's intelligibility, and how much of it will remain forever beyond our ken. This effectively amounts to understanding the dividing line that runs between 'being' and 'beings', which Heidegger calls the 'ontological difference'. We shall attempt to trace the way in which Heidegger's understanding of this boundary shifted from his early works to his late, in order to give some sense of what he understood to be the basic task and nature of phenomenology.

To begin to approach this, we need to investigate his initial innovations, 'Dasein' and 'world', and the intimate relation between them that is expressed by Heidegger's curious compound phrase, 'being-in-the-world' (*Inderwelt-sein*). This will reveal the necessity for rethinking the method of phenomenology, beyond the bracketing of the world and its associated reductions. If anything, far from bracketing and reducing, phenomenology demands that we attempt to return ever more fully to the experience of *living* in our 'everyday' attitude.

The intimate relation that is being-*in*-the-world may be taken to be Heidegger's rewriting of Husserl's crucial concept of 'intentionality', which always opens consciousness onto something beyond itself. Thus we have three elements: Dasein, being-in-the-world, and the world itself.

Let us take these three notions in turn, first consciousness, understood as Dasein (in section (i)), then the relation to the world (ii), and then the world itself (iii).

(i) From the transcendental subject to Dasein

Heidegger, then, is dissatisfied with the notion of a transcendental consciousness which is capable of detaching itself from all of the empirical contingency of the world and reflecting on itself and its experiences to achieve a fully adequate intuition of the meaning of things. This for Heidegger embodies the traditional philosophical standpoint of *theoria*, a disinterested, contemplative, theoretical attitude, and it affects the way Husserl understands both the subject's relation to the world and its relation to itself. In both cases this is understood as a relation of subject to object. It is this understanding of consciousness that Heidegger thinks must be overcome, for it in fact presupposes a different and more basic relation to the world, one which would better be described as 'practical'.

The subject is not first of all reflective, and it is never separated from the empirical world. Heidegger captures these two characteristics with the words 'existence' and 'being-in-the-world'. The first refers to the non-reflective nature of the subject, its standing outside of itself or being directed beyond itself rather than simply being turned back upon itself; and the second refers to the fact that if we are to understand how a subject can relate to itself in a 'reflective' way, we need to understand what it means to be a 'world'.

With these two notions, Heidegger is attempting to investigate the *being* of Husserl's notion of intentionality, without the historical prejudices that seemed to him to infect the latter's own understanding. For Heidegger, then, Husserl does not pay sufficient attention to *ontology*. While he speaks of consciousness and describes its operations in many different modes, Husserl does not ask the ontological question of *what* consciousness *is*, which is ultimately what makes its intentionality possible (cf. *HCT*, 102ff./139ff.). When we ask what something is, we are pursuing the discipline of ontology.

This attention to ontology is what leads Heidegger to rename Husserlian 'consciousness' as 'Dasein' ('*being*-there'), a notion to which we shall return. Heidegger provides us with what he describes as a 'fundamental ontology', which requires us to investigate precisely what Dasein *is*.

> **Dasein:** Heidegger's word for 'human being' in his early work, which might be said to span the years between 1919 and 1931, but the human being understood in a particular way: it attempts to define what is ontologically specific about the human being, and that is the fact that it has an understanding of being (*Seinsverständnis*), that man *is* ontological, or has a pre-ontological understanding of what things are. '*Da*' means 'there' or 'here', a location, and '*sein*' means 'being' or 'to be'. Dasein is the location where beings come to appear in a significant way. This is to say, where the world as a whole comes together and forms a totality, and as a result the individual entities within it come to take on a sense or meaning.

Before we can do anything in the way of 'general ontology', we first need to examine fundamental ontology, and for Heidegger this takes the form of an analysis of *Dasein*. Why? Because Dasein is that entity whose very essence includes the ability to understanding being. In order to understand being properly, we need to examine the structure of that entity which has an inherent insight into being, and by developing this, we should be able to refine this understanding to the requisite level.

Dasein is defined by Heidegger *in its being* as being-in-the-world. It *is* this relation.

(ii) Being-in-the-world and facticity

Let us show how this notion of being-in-the-world is implicitly an attempt to rewrite the Husserlian notion of intentionality.

The meaning of entities is for Heidegger bestowed upon them by their place in a world, a wider context of interrelating entities which refer to one another and form a system. What is crucial is that the particular world in which we find ourselves at any one time is contingent. *Which* world we are in is a mere fact, and there is simply no explanation as to why it is that we should find ourselves in this one rather than another. For Heidegger this 'factuality' is a crucial part of Dasein's existence, and he describes it with the German word '*Faktizität*' which may be translated as 'factuality', but is generally transliterated as 'facticity' (a *factum*, something which is already done, *facere*). From the very beginning Heidegger was concerned with the notion of contingency, which was a preoccupation of the medieval thinker whose work formed the topic of his post-doctoral thesis, John Duns Scotus.

Thus, the significance of things in the world cannot be simply bestowed upon them within the transparent space of consciousness; it is partly the consequence of a historical process of accretion that, because of our limited – or 'horizonal' – vision, remains a mystery to us. Thus a certain contingency enters consciousness, as well as a certain opacity, whereas for Husserl consciousness, in reflecting on its own experiences, did have the possibility of a fully adequate experience.

Thus Heidegger openly posits the existence of a real, contingent and particular world as essential for the very existence of Dasein: for Heidegger, it is the very existence of the relations which comprise the world's structure that ultimately makes it possible for Dasein to refer to itself reflexively in this way. This is perhaps the ultimate meaning of Heidegger's designation of Dasein as 'existing', which literally means 'standing outside of itself'. We can only understand man's potential self-relation if we first examine the relations that hold between *things*.

At birth we are thrown precisely into *a* world. Heidegger describes this as the essential 'thrownness' of the human being, we are always already thrown into facticity: the fact of the matter as to *which world* we are thrown into is purely contingent, inexplicable: it is simply a fact. There are *facts* about us and our world which we cannot change, with regard to which we are *un*free. The world of course is not just the 'external' environment, for we are ourselves part of the world, in our possession of a body, our physical characteristics: we are also thrown into *ourselves*.

If something is a fact, it means that it has not issued from us, but has rather been *given* to us. There are certain 'givens' with regard to our situation. Heidegger wishes precisely to direct phenomenology's attention to this *givenness* or 'thereness' of phenomena. He speaks throughout his life of the German phrase which has been translated as 'there is . . .', '*es gibt*'. The fact that things exist at all, and more precisely that things exist *in a particular way*. This is simply what it is to exist as a being, an entity, since to exist as a *being* is to exist in a certain limited, determinate fashion. This is what distinguishes *a* being from *being itself (Sein)*, which in German is far closer to the *infinitive verb* 'to be' (*sein*), in other words, a pure event that has not yet been limited by a determinate form. Heidegger wishes to understand precisely this process of giving that transforms this infinitive verb into a definite noun, Being into being*s*. This is precisely to understand the processes whereby manifestation comes about, the *appearing* of phenomena. Hence this givenness, this given factuality is precisely the subject of his *phenomenology*.

Heidegger uses the word 'Dasein' to express the fact that man is not the active constructor of a coherent universe but merely a *place,* a 'there' (*Da*), wherein entities are *revealed* in a meaningful way, in their being (*Sein*). Beings existed before Dasein did, but without meaning, and without being organized into a coherent world. For this, they needed an entity that was sufficiently open to receive them and capable of articulating what it received.

Things, then, are *presented* to us, we do not *make* them present. Thus the world of presence is given to us. It is at least partly our calling to open ourselves to this presence that is passively *disclosed* to us. Heidegger in his early thought speaks of Dasein's *own* 'disclosedness' *to* things, and precisely attempts to think and describe the forms that it takes.

In his early thought, Heidegger performs a similar kind of 'transcendental deduction' to that which one finds in Kant's *Critique of Pure Reason*. He asks: if there is such a thing as appearance, – and obviously there *is* such a thing – how must Dasein be structured, Dasein being the one *to whom* appearances appear? His answer runs along much the same lines as Kant, at a very basic level. Dasein must possess mood and understanding, and something like language, which at this stage Heidegger calls discourse (*Rede*). So man must have an active understanding, a passive ability to be affected, and the capacity to speak. Understanding, mood and language.[2] These are all ways in which the world is opened up, disclosed, revealed, and rendered significantly apparent.

Thus in a move away from Husserl's understanding of consciousness as actively constituting a world, already we can see that Heidegger's renewed understanding of intentionality must be understood as a passive form of disclosure *to* phenomena which manifest *themselves*. This is one reason why the 'voluntarist' overtones of 'intentionality' rule the word out of Heidegger's vocabulary altogether.

To understand more about the way in which the world itself goes to make up Dasein's very being, as being-*in*-the-world, we shall have to rush ahead into the world itself, and understand just what it comprises. Then we shall be able to understand how Dasein *inhabits* it.

(iii) World

The elements of our cultural world (and perhaps also our natural world) already have certain functions and relations. Heidegger's word for these functions and relations is 'significations' (*Bedeutungen*). A signification is different from a meaning (*Sinn*) in that a signification can exist only in a context. It is the result of a relation *between* things, as is implied by its name which involves the notion of 'indicating' or 'pointing' (*deuten*). One thing points at another, it signifies this other. No entity can signify itself, on its own, it needs to differentiate itself from others in order to achieve this kind of individuality. Thus, inherent in the notion of significance is that of *relationality*. But one cannot simply have two things, where one signifies the other, for the first element must also receive its meaning through its references to other things, or strictly speaking through its *differentiation* from them, since the relation of reference can run both ways. The weave of this 'context' is a '*world*'.

The world is effectively made up of things that Heidegger describes as 'ready-to-hand', things that can be used. For Heidegger, beings can appear to Dasein in three different ways: as ready-to-hand (*zuhanden*), as present-at-hand (*vorhanden*), or as Dasein itself.[3] Heidegger's great achievement in *Being and Time* and the surrounding lecture courses is to understand how these three relate, and what their relative priorities are.

Presence-at-hand

Presence-at-hand, or simply presence (*Vorhandenheit*), means the mere existence of something, its pure actuality. In German, the word simply means 'presence', 'existence' or 'subsistence', the mere fact that something is present rather than absent. It is in terms of 'presence' that the whole of philosophy has understood the word 'being'. Particularly today, when the natural sciences so pervade our understanding of the world, it is assumed that being either means nothing at all, or simply refers to the fact that something exists or is 'in being'.

This understanding of being is precisely the understanding that is implicit in the notion of *theory*. Presence-at-hand is the way that an entity presents itself before a theoretical, observational or experimental gaze. It is the way in which a scientist looks at an entity. The Greek word for science or knowledge is '*epistēmē*'. Philosophy has long suffered from an epistemological prejudice: it has believed that *knowledge* or – today – empirical, natural science, provides us with the most accurate picture of how things really are, in their *being*.

It is this that Heidegger wishes to contest.

He shows that this present-at-hand understanding of being *logically presupposes* another kind of being – and indeed, ontologically presupposes it: there must a different way of being that exists *prior* to this being-*present*. This more original way of being is 'readiness-to-hand'. This is the level at which beings are not just physical objects with certain properties that can be intuited by a momentary glance. Here beings have *meaning*. They are not simply isolated from a wider context but are precisely individuated *by* their interrelations with other entities in the same world.

Prior to the universe as the scientist or epistemologist examines it, prior to this place of facts, properties, cause and effect, is the world of significance. A world endowed with meaning, and possibilities: in fact, possible *uses*.

World (*Welt*): The world is the system of signifying references that constitute the being of the ready-to-hand: entities insofar as they have possibilities. In order to have their own individual way of being, beings need to be part of an interrelated totality, and to be differentiated from everything else within the same system. The structure of this system is the world. Thus the world is the context that makes it possible for an individual thing to appear as what it is, as an individual entity.

Since being is also understood by the early Heidegger as signification, at this point in his trajectory, being *is* world, the relations between things that differentiate them from one another.

Readiness-to-hand

Present-at-hand entities are things in their actuality. What are the ready-to-hand? They are not a separate realm of entities, but a different way in which the *present*-at-hand can *appear*.

We can examine something from a distance, disinterestedly, *or* we can take that thing up and *use* it. When we stop *thinking* about something and approach it as an *implement*, that thing becomes *ready-to-hand*, ready for *use*. The ready-to-hand are the entities of the world insofar as they can be used for certain purposes and tasks. And this means that these entities must *refer* to certain functions and ends beyond themselves. They can only do this because Dasein *understands* them to have these possibilities. Thus Dasein's 'being-in-the-world' means something very precise: it means that our own existence is absolutely bound up with the *ready-to-hand*, that there cannot be one without the other.

Tools are things that have *possibilities*. If Dasein did not exist, things would be merely present-at-hand, exhaustively defined by their actuality alone. They would not have possibilities. This is due to the nature of possibility itself. A possibility is something that is not being actualized right now, but could be, or could have been. So to have possibility, an entity must relate to its past and to its future, and for the early Heidegger, one simply cannot say that a pure actuality like a rock really does that. It is *Dasein* and Dasein alone that has this 'temporal' (or 'timely') existence. So *it* has possibilities, and *for it*, other things have possibilities, but in themselves, they should be understood as pure actualities, present-at-hand.

If the possibilities of ready-to-hand things exist only in Dasein's understanding, and if Dasein *is its* possibilities, then Dasein *exists in* the possibilities of ready-to-hand things. It exists outside of itself, outside of its actual body, here, in the present moment, and it exists as all of the possibilities that it has of using things in the world. Dasein is not here, confined to this body, even to this consciousness. It is projected out there, spatially and temporally, cast into the possible things it can do with the ready-to-hand. This projection is what creates the structure that is called 'world'. Dasein *is* the world. Hence its being is quite literally 'being-in-the-world'. The world is 'that wherein concern always dwells' (*BT*, 105/75).

That is what it means to understand something: to understand what it can do, and this is precisely to understand an entity's 'being'. Ultimately Heidegger will have to say that being *is* possibility, it is the appropriate 'uses' that can be made of any particular thing.

(b) Concern and knowing

Heidegger's word for Dasein's relation to the ready-to-hand is 'concern' (*Besorgen*). One is *concerned* with things. One 'deals' with things, and uses them *deftly* (BT, 83/56–7) Heidegger precisely distinguishes this from the perceptual relation that characterizes the theoretical approach: 'The kind of dealing which is closest to us is, as we have shown, not a bare perceptual cognition, but rather that kind of concern which manipulates things and puts them to use' (*BT*, 95/67). Being-in-the-world is our original aptitude for using things.

Dasein has an implicit 'pre-ontological' understanding of being which it is not explicitly aware of but which manifests itself in the way that it acts: it clearly knows what a bottle is because it uses it for drinking water, a window for letting in air: 'that understanding of being which belongs already to Dasein [. . .] "comes alive" in any of its dealings with entities' (*BT*, 96/67).

(c) Four kinds of world-relation, four kinds of cause

We already know something of the nature of the world. It is the context which allows the significance of individual objects to exist, and it is created by Dasein's temporal ability to project possibilities into the future. But Heidegger gives us a much more precise understanding of the nature of signification in his description of the various ways in which items of equipment relate to other items of equipment. This insight is one of the richest in all of Heidegger's thought, and will prove crucial later on when we are trying to understand the technological world and how it works (cf. *BT*, 91–122/63–89).

Heidegger describes the world it as having four elements, which he names in a very strange way: every usable item has an 'in-order-to' (*Um-zu*), a 'towards which' (*Wozu*) a 'whereof' (*Woraus*) and a 'for-the-sake-of-which' (*Worumwillen*).

The four elements of world may be understood to be Heidegger's rewriting of the four kinds of 'cause' (*aitia, causa*) which Aristotle identifies in his *Physics* and *Metaphysics*. These are not just mechanical causes in the modern sense, but include everything that is *responsible* for the way in which a thing appears phenomenally: how it *is*.

The four relations of Heidegger and the four causes of Aristotle

Heidegger	Aristotle
In-order-to [*Umzu*] (action)	efficient (*causa efficiens*)
towards-which [*Wozu*] (product)	formal/essential (*causa formalis*)
whereof [*Woraus*] (constituents)	material (*causa materialis*)
for-the-sake-of-which [*Worumwillen*] (end purpose)	final (*causa finalis*)

The most important relations to consider at first are the 'in-order-to' and the 'for-the-sake-of-which': the 'in-order-to' comprises the possible ways of *using* an item of equipment, and the 'for-the-sake-of-which' is the ultimate *goal* of this use.

Each piece of equipment, or 'furniture', has its own set of possible functions. The hammer is used for hammering, the chair for sitting on, the floor for standing upon. These examples already make it clear that we are using the word 'equipment' (the established and admittedly narrow translation of '*Zeug*') in a very general sense, and when we say it is 'ready-to-hand', we are not just referring to the *physical* hands (the reference to the hand in the German word is much less glaring than it is in the English phrase). Anything that we utilize 'in-order-to' do *anything* is 'equipment'.

When we are using tools, we *see* the possible uses of things. Heidegger describes this sight (*Sicht*) as 'circumspection' (*Umsicht*): this is our non-explicit understanding of what things can do. It is not theoretical, it involves no explicit thought, it is a 'foresight' – and indeed 'hindsight' – that sees *possibilities*, things that could be done or could have been done with items of equipment. These possibilities are not currently being actualized, so we can not see them in the same way that we see actual things. The German word *Um-sicht*, 'seeing around', should be taken literally to mean that our attention focuses on — for instance — the *act* of hammering, rather than the hammer itself, on the act of sitting, rather than the chair itself. We merely focus on the 'in-order-to' (I use the hammer *in order to* hammer, I use the chair *in order to* sit): 'the peculiarity of what is proximally ready-to-hand is that, in its readiness-to-hand, it must, as it were, withdraw in order to be ready-to-hand quite properly. That with which our everyday dealings proximally dwell is not the tools themselves' (*BT*, 99/69).

In fact, our attention strays even further ahead, forming another layer in our experience of practical action, towards the intended product or result of the action. Heidegger calls this the 'towards-which' of the action.

The work is also made *of* something, a certain material, and Heidegger calls this the 'whereof'.

But there has to be a reason why we found it necessary or desirable to make this product in the first place. There must be something 'for-the-sake-of-which' we make it. And that is always ultimately to satisfy some need or desire of a *Dasein*. We also have intermediate ends, as when we put up shelves for the sake of stacking books, but ultimately, this will be *for the sake of* opening up a new possibility for Dasein: we arrange books on the shelves so that we can easily find the volume we want.

To summarize this particularly dense passage of Heidegger's thought with the help of an example of which he was fond: We are using the hammer in order to perform the act of hammering [=in-order-to] so as to produce a cabinet [=towards-which], made out of wood [=whereof], and we do so with a view to letting Dasein store things *in* that cabinet [=for-the-sake-of-which].

All of these compound phrases refer not to isolated things, but to relations *between* things, the different kinds of relation that exist between the various elements of the world. They make up the very *structure* of the world. They constitute every possible kind of signification, the ways in which entities refer to one another. 'The structure of the being of what is ready-to-hand as equipment is determined by references [*Verweisungen*]' (*BT*, 105/74). These strange words, 'in-order-to' and 'for-the-sake-of-which' are not originally nouns or verbs, they are *joining*-words, conjunctions and prepositions, words that *link* things together, but which are made to *function* as nouns. Heidegger finds it necessary to make them into nouns in order to bring to the fore these relations which are normally concealed behind the substances *that* they relate. This unorthodox, revelatory use of language is a *phenomenological* act, it precisely brings to appearance something that is usually hidden.

These references between things are precisely what we are (implicitly) 'thinking' about and understanding when we *act*, when we *use* the ready-to-hand. These references are the *possibilities* that equipment has (possible uses, possible ends, possible materials, possible products). Hammering would simply not make *sense* if there were not some reason for doing it, if there were not some wood there, and some cabinet to be built. What Heidegger is doing here is showing how the present act of hammering *refers* to the past (material) and the future (the product, the user and his ends).

These reference-relations decide what the being of each particular tool *is*: an item of ready-to-hand equipment just *is* its peculiar set of references (to its use, its goal, the materials it can work with). It is the structure of the context that decides on the significance of the equipment within that context, for it is only by differentiating itself *from* other things that a certain item of equipment can be *individuated*. And these differentiating relations, these references *are* the '*world*'. The world is this context of references which gives an individual tool its meaning, and which thereby *individuates* the tool. This differentiation of the tool is what the world carries out. And this explains why the ready-to-hand is *presupposed* by the present-at-hand, because without the world, things are not individuated from one another at all. Thus without a world-context, the *present*-at-hand would not be divided up into individual things, whose distinct properties could then be examined by the contemplative gaze.

The world is not made up of entities, it is the set of references that run from one ready-to-hand entity to another. It lies in the preposition, that which links one word to another. And this world, this cluster of possibilities, is what Dasein understands. These possibilities are the *being* of the ready-to-hand. And this is what *being*-in-the-world is, it is the *understanding* of those possibilities that make equipment what it is: to be in the world literally means to *be* the references that *make up* the world. 'Being-in-the-world, according to our Interpretation hitherto, amounts to a non-thematic circumspective absorption in references constitutive for the readiness-to-hand of a totality of equipment' (*BT*, 107/76).

(d) Problems with the world

The upshot of this analysis of the significance-bestowing world is this: Far from being the product of a constituting consciousness, what entities are is determined by their place in a contingent context with other things, all of which refer to each other and constitute a systematic totality. Now ultimately, it is the fact that *this* is the source of signification that renders an entity's meaning opaque at a certain point, for ultimately it will prove impossible to limit the size of this worldly context that *bestows* its significance. If every element is differentially defined, then even those elements that might have been supposed to mark the perimeter of the world, separating it from other more alien worlds will *refer* to elements from other worlds in order to define themselves. This reference runs 'synchronically' and 'diachronically', in other words, both at the current time and back into history.

At the same time, there seems to be a second problem associated with meaning's dependence on the world: it would appear to make entities absolutely common to all of us, their very being would seem to be defined by their place in a structure which could just as well be taken by another entity of the same type. How does this cohere with our hypothesis that Heidegger wishes to understand being as an entity's *singularity*?

For the early Heidegger, since all entities are disclosed within an essentially public or common world, as replaceable instances of a certain type, or rather as examples of a certain generic *function,* this singularity cannot be a feature of things themselves, so much as a result of our *experience* of them.

For Heidegger, being is the ultimate topic of phenomenology, and phenomenology is thus precisely an attempt to describe the singularity of things, and to drag this singularity out from under the many obscuring layers which cloak it, particularly due a certain attitude that we generally adopt towards the *world*, which is more or less one of total submission, an attitude that is exacerbated by the contemporary world of technological mass-production.

If we experience things *purely* in terms of their place in the world, we shall not be experiencing their true being, and hence not properly carrying out our phenomenology. We must now see just how Heidegger suggests that we can make our way towards the experience of singularity.

The beginnings of this way lie in the fact that, in each case, my experience of this relatively common thing is *mine*. And it is this *mineness* that will allow Heidegger to address the topic of singularity: each experience I have is characterized by certain general features that all experiences of the same thing share, but it is also uniquely *mine*. It is unlike any other experience because it is *mine alone.*

However, this mineness is itself not usually seized upon, and as a result, not just the individuality of things but *my own* individuality is understood in terms of common possibilities gleaned from the world. This is an understanding of ourselves which Heidegger calls 'inauthenticity' (*Uneigentlichkeit*). It is precisely this mineness that we have to make our own, to genuinely 'understand', and this will involve putting an end to the illusion that there is anything in the world that I can do or own that will make me into an 'individual'. Thus, in what follows we shall attempt to show how mineness (*Jemeinigkeit*) emerges from this 'inauthentic', 'disowned' state to become our *authenticity* (*Eigentlichkeit*).

For it is only in this authentic state that we shall be capable of doing phenomenology, for it is only when we become aware of the unique aspect of our experience that we can then have an experience of the singularity of things, and thus an experience of their being, and it is this experience that is the ultimate task of phenomenology.

Further reading

Heidegger, Martin (1962 [1927]) *Being and Time*. Trans. John Macquarrie and Edward Robinson. Oxford: Blackwell, pp. 91–122 (on the 'world').

Harman, Graham (2002), *Tool-Being: Heidegger and the Metaphysics of Objects*. Chicago and La Salle, IL: Open Court, chapter 1.

From Mineness to Authenticity

6

Main primary literature

Being and Time, pp. 149–68 (on 'the they').
The Concept of Time, passim.

One of the crucial aspects of the human being for Heidegger is that it is 'in each case mine' (*jemeinig*) (*BT*, 67ff./41ff.). This is to say, not just that it has the structure of an 'I' but that every instance of human life is someone's *belonging*, and this belonging is absolutely unique: no one else shall ever own this 'life' and I shall never own another. This lends – or should lend – to each and every experience an absolutely unique tint. The task of Heidegger's work is to allow us to appreciate this. Indeed, this is what phenomenology amounts to for Heidegger: a quasi-*ethical* transformation of our ability to *experience*. Heidegger's phenomenology was from beginning to end an attempt to do justice to the potential singularity of phenomena, which is ultimately the meaning of the word 'being'.

We need to take a brief detour through the question of what 'being' means in order to show just how the notion of mineness opens up the possibility of authenticity for each of us. For mineness means that we are a *self*, we relate to ourselves and thus form a genuinely individual entity, which in fact we are *not* for the most part.

This reflexive self-relation is what we *are*: thus to become clearer as the nature of this 'mineness' we need to examine more fully what it means to *be*.

This is related to the problems that we identified with regard to the world, which seems to make individuality possible *and* to stifle it. Being thus appears to be both a set of generic possibilities and a set of singular ones. How can this be so? We obviously need to clarify the notion of 'being' in order to continue with our exposition. What we shall see is that there are only *certain* possibilities which may be said to be *proper* to each kind of entity, and it is only *man* (Dasein) who is capable of recognizing and respecting this propriety.

(a) Being

For an entire lifetime, Heidegger asked himself but one question: What is it to be? Not to be any particular type of thing, but simply *to be*. What is 'being' (*Sein*)?

Heidegger's answer was: possibility. An entity's being – *what* that thing *is* – is comprised of its possibilities. Entities *are* possibilities, but more precisely, they are those particular possibilities which are *appropriate* to that thing.

Heidegger's lifelong task was therefore to understand what it means to be *appropriate*, to be *proper*: when we are referring to human beings we sometimes say 'authentic' (*eigentlich*). What is the proper or 'authentic' way for each thing and each type of thing to *be*? And what is the appropriate way to understand and treat entities?

> **Being (Sein)**: the meaning of the word changes slightly from early to late Heidegger, but broadly speaking it means the condition of possibility for the appearance of things. In the early work, it is effectively synonymous with 'world', which means the context of signification which allows any particular thing to be differentiated from any other and thus take on its own individual meaning.
>
> If beings appear in a significant way, then being (Sein) is *significance*, the significant *way* that beings appear to man. However, appearance involves not only a world but also Dasein, an entity *to* whom things appear. And it is because of man's unique perspective in each case that entities can take on a *unique significance*.
>
> In his later work, it becomes clearer that what Heidegger means by 'being' is *singularity*, the temporal and spatial uniqueness of a particular entity.

Another constant refrain of Heidegger's thought is that the only entity which is concerned with this proper treatment is the *human being*, or rather 'Dasein'. There is something special about man and his understanding which means that, for Heidegger, he is the only entity which has the ability to allow beings to manifest themselves as what they are. The entity most prone to appropriate entities for his own ends is also the only entity which is capable of letting them go, letting them be (*seinlassen*, *Gelassenheit*). This is why Heidegger's most famous work from his early period, *Being and Time* (1927), deals almost exclusively with man, or rather, with 'Dasein'. This is his 'existential analytic' which is also a 'fundamental ontology' since it grounds the very possibility of any more general ontology.

Heidegger argues that it is only because something like Dasein has an 'understanding of being' that being '*is*' at all. In other words, it is only because there is an entity which 'cares' about what something is, that this thing *has* certain possibilities, and not just any old possibilities, but ones that are particularly suited to it. If there could be a world without man, it would be a world in which everything was replaceable, a mere place-holder fulfilling a functional role; but thanks to man, individual things can become more precious than that.

Possibilities do not exist in the present moment but rather in the *future*. Therefore, possibilities can exist *only* if there is an entity which can look ahead into the future, to project and plan. This is what it is to understand the being of an entity: it is to be able to project into the future the *kinds* of things that can be done with that entity, the kinds of things it may properly be expected to do.

Man can have such an awareness of propriety because he is so made as to have a certain concern for his *own*. Mineness is the most basic form of property, or propriety.

This mineness is the most primitive form of the 'self', a reflexive relatedness to oneself, which is the most basic precondition of what the Cartesian tradition calls 'consciousness'. This 'belonging to self' is a loop, a vector that has folded back on itself. Heidegger has a particular way of understanding this folding, which renders it more of a spiral than a loop, for it does not remain static, like a circle, or simply return to the exact same place that it started out from. In fact, Dasein's self-relation *unfolds*, and it does so in two directions, one that runs forward in time and one back: its existence is *temporal*. In order to understand what this means we must examine these two vectors along which Dasein unfolds and through which it relates to itself: they are called 'projection' and 'thrownness'.

(b) Projection and thrownness – understanding and moods

The forward motion is projection (*Entwerfen*). For Heidegger, this is the function of the understanding (*BT*, 184–5/145). To understand something is to project its meaning. Without this, the entity is not comprehensible. So to understand something we have to have a general sense of what that thing means, which is ultimately what it can be used for, what it *is*.

> **Meaning (*Sinn*)**: Meaning is that which allows a phenomenon to be intelligible to us, it is the *ground* of intelligibility. It makes it possible for there to be a significant form of appearance. Since all phenomena are intelligible, meaning amounts to the very condition of the possibility of all beings. Meaning makes possible the 'being' of beings. This does not mean their mere subsistence, which can take place in the absence of meaning, but their 'be-ing' towards an entity which can receive them, their appearance or presentation, the significance that they have for human beings.

Dasein has such a pre-ontological sense of what something is, and this understanding must exist in the future, *anticipating* what something *is*. It is always ahead of any particular encounter that we have, because in advance it knows roughly what any particular thing is, and so it effectively allows that encounter to take place. Heidegger thinks of this ability to project the meaning of things ahead of us as our *freedom*. Through projections, we open up possibilities in the future, and thus we open up a free choice *among* this multitude of possibilities.

However we *are* restricted by something: our past, that world in which we *always already* find ourselves. In other words, there is always something which will have been there before we were, and in which we find ourselves. This Heidegger describes as our thrownness (*Geworfenheit*). However far ahead we stray in our projection of a future which will bestow meaning upon our present, we are always thrown back into a certain world, which constrains that projection by limiting the meanings that we can apply to it. In other words, we are dragged back down to those features of our actual situation that we cannot change.

Heidegger associates this notion of 'finding oneself' not with the *understanding* but with *mood* (*Stimmung*), which is ultimately almost synonymous with 'state-of-mind' (*Befindlichkeit*) which contains the crucial verb, *finden*, to find. In feeling, one encounters the contingency of the world, which includes the body, in the form of meaningless facts about which one can do nothing and with which one's freedom must reckon.

Projection and thrownness are revealed to us through our understanding and our moods respectively. Both mood and understanding are understood by Heidegger as modes of 'disclosure' (*Entschlossenheit*), or ways in which things are revealed to Dasein. Dasein does not first theoretically and explicitly think about things; it has things disclosed to it. What is disclosed to it, or what discloses *itself*, since *we* have as yet *consciously* done nothing, is the *phenomenon*, that which appears, that which shows *itself* or *is shown*.

The phenomenon is thus constituted in two ways, one active and one passive: our projection and our thrownness.

(c) Time

We have associated projection with the future and mood with the past to show that Heidegger thinks that at the bottom of our self-relation, our mineness, what explains the uniqueness of each individual, is *time*.

Being and Time ultimately wishes to show that time is the foundation and support of being, the 'meaning of being': without time, without temporality (*Zeitlichkeit*) (the 'timely' or 'timelike', *zeitlich*), there would be no being. This is precisely a departure from the traditional view according to which the 'essence' of a thing is timeless, absolute and unharmed by its contingent, perishable instantiation, its actual 'existence'.

> **The Meaning of Being (*der Sinn von Sein*)**: The meaning of being is 'temporality' (*Zeitlichkeit*). The form of temporality which is most crucial to Heidegger is Dasein's temporality, which also means its finitude, the *limited* span of time which its existence will take up. It is only because man is finite and hence singular that beings can appear at all, that being *as* appearance can exist, for man's finitude results in his enjoying only a particular, limited perspective on the world, and perspectivity – the characteristic of appearing only to a particular perspective – is a necessary part of the appearance of things.

Phenomena are made possible by *time*. We have already indicated that passivity is a crucial part of the disclosive character of Dasein: *what* is given to us is something that preceded us; it was here before we were, before we had the power to make it. The 'given' therefore arrives from the past. And if we are to project, there must be a future *into which* we project, a futural space that has previously opened up. Time had to be there already in order for us to have a space *in which* to project and *into which* to be thrown, and since Dasein in its mineness is composed of these two vectors, we may say that time has to be there in order for there to be a self, and hence a place in which beings can show themselves.

There must be a time. And this means that there must be limits. The passing of time implies that something is not yet in existence and yet will come to be, which implies that the present moment is itself limited and changeable. Time then implies the notion of a horizon, a *limit* to our vision, beyond which we cannot see. There must be a future that will come to replace the present and that future must as yet be over the horizon, unforeseeable. We must be circumscribed within a present moment and gaze out towards our horizons, – the past and the future – beyond which lie hidden things that are *not* present, and given that the present is the place in which things *are* present, these horizons of the future and the past are the necessary *conditions* of appearance. In this way, temporality is the 'meaning' or 'ground' of being (appearance, 'phenomenality').

This horizonality implies that the Dasein who experiences, who lives through time, cannot see or encompass the whole of time, but is situated at a certain point within it. Horizonality itself is made possible *by* this *situatedness*.

If there were not an entity who was *situated* at a certain moment and thus capable only of a limited experience, there would be no being, there would be no phenomena, no appearance. To be situated is to have limits, and that means most fundamentally perhaps, to be restricted to a certain place in time, which means a place that has horizons.[4]

To be situated is ultimately to be finite, and for the early Heidegger at least, it was the human being who was finite, and thus the human being – when he is *aware* of his limits – is the foundation of being, the condition of possibility for appearance.

(d) Birth and death – authenticity

What are these limits? In what way does an individual man actually experience an absolute past and an absolute future?

The individual Dasein has two experiences which give him access to this pure form of time: his own birth and his own death (*BT*, 425–7/373–4). Here, the future and the past are events which *for us* occur *only* in the future and *only* in the past: we are never *present* when these events occur. They are the pure form of the future and the past, but nevertheless, as we must live, we are aware that we have a limited space in which to project our possibilities, and, however we understand our birth and death, we thus nevertheless relate to them. Even if we exist entirely oblivious to these facts, they are nevertheless a part of our being. Since our projection and our thrownness have limits in this way, Heidegger describes projection and thrownness in their most basic form as our way of existing 'towards' birth and death, our 'being-towards-birth' and 'being-towards-death'. We are unable to project further than our death, and it is ultimately because of our birth that this projection is *thrown* at all, in the sense of returned from the freedom of the future to the constraints of its actual worldly situation.

It is insofar as Dasein properly relates to his absolute limits that he will have a proper understanding of himself and his experience, and will come to appreciate those aspects of it which are unique and those which are common. This would be for Dasein to become 'authentic' or 'properly' itself, to truly *appropriate* its 'mineness'. And since it is in Dasein that being properly appears, it is insofar as Dasein is 'authentic' that being is properly understood, which is why Heidegger is concerned to address this state, and not from any concern for the 'ethics' of the human being.[5]

Hence, while Heidegger's task is to understand being, a necessary precondition of this is to force each individual Dasein properly to understand itself. The task is to lead each individual reader to the point at which he is properly himself, since only thereby can he have some access to the singularity that being *is*. So *Being and Time*, like almost all of Heidegger's works, actively tries to involve its reader in a process of experiencing. It attempts to bring the reader to a proper experience of himself. Why? Because an authentic experience of oneself is an experience of one's singularity, and thus it is an experience of singularity itself.

Authenticity is the proper experience of mineness, it is the possibility that is most appropriate *to* that mineness.

(e) Inauthentic immersion in the world

If Heidegger thinks that man's task is to achieve authenticity, then he must be assuming that we are for the most part in an *in*authentic state. This is a state in which we are immersed in the *world*, which is to say our experience is a purely common experience that limits entities to their function and is not concerned with the singularity of the entity that is actually *performing* that function. At the same time, this is precisely how we experience ourselves: in terms of generic possibilities, places in the world, roles, that anyone could occupy. It does not properly attend to the *uniqueness* of who I am. In this state one cannot say that *I* do something or *I* am something, for I have not truly become an individual, and for this reason Heidegger replaces the personal pronoun I (*ich*) with the impersonal pronoun, 'one' (*man*), sometimes replaced colloquially with the generic pronoun, 'they'. Heidegger substantivizes the pronoun to express the fact that it is an essential part of Dasein's being: *das Man,* the one or the 'they'. This tendency towards inauthentic self-understanding is a consequence of another aspect of man's existence which Heidegger describes as 'falling' (*verfallen*) (*BT,* 219ff./175ff.). This is precisely man's tendency to understand himself in terms of the world in which he currently dwells. It is related to 'thrownness' but to be distinguished from it in that thrownness is our inevitable situation in a certain world, while fallenness is our tendency to *submit* to this world in our self-understanding, at the expense of a free projection.

Now, this is not just an immersion in world as such. There is no 'world' as such. The notion of 'facticity' implies that *world* is always *a* world, some *particular* world. Thus, merely to immerse oneself in that world is to artificially *limit* one's freedom; it limits one's possibilities to those contingently offered by that particular world in which one finds oneself.

To become authentic is to achieve some distance from any one particular world, and perhaps from worlds as such, which are inherently common, inherently public (*BT*, 155/118).

What then, from within this 'immanent' situation calls us to strive for authenticity, what makes it possible and what licenses us to think that it is in some way demanded of us, in the very depths of Dasein's being? What forces us to transform our mineness into 'authenticity'?

(f) Breakdown: the transition between the ready-to-hand and the present-at-hand

Inauthenticity is an immersion in the world which is precisely *unaware* of this immersion or 'fallenness'. If we are to escape from it, this immersion must first be revealed to us. In order to see how this might happen, we need first to understand how Heidegger thinks an individual *element* of the world is revealed to us.

It happens when a node in the network of the world breaks down. We can explicitly access these meanings, the functions and purposes of the entities of the world, when we come to *reflect* on our action. This happens in those moments when a piece of equipment *fails* to fulfil its function. It is only when something stops working that we draw back from our absorption in *acting*, and actually *think* about what we are doing. It is only then that we are forced to consider the nature of our actions, our tools, materials and aim. Only then do we consider them in their *presence-at-hand*, in their actual properties. We look at them as *objects*. This is effectively a decontextualization, the present-at-hand is the ready-to-hand but isolated from its context, which individuated it and gave it its unique meaning. 'The assignments themselves are not observed [when we are using them and they are functioning]; [. . .] But *when an assignment has been disturbed* – when something is unusable for some purpose – then the assignment becomes explicit' (*BT*, 105/74).

The ready-to-hand becomes present before us, present-at-hand: 'what cannot be used just lies there; it shows itself as an equipmental Thing which looks so and so, and which, in its readiness-to-hand as looking that way, has constantly been present-at-hand too' (*BT*, 103/73), 'it seems to lose its character of readiness-to-hand. It reveals itself as something just present-at-hand and no more' (*BT*, 103/73).

Not that the ready-to-hand is then utterly relieved of its functionality. Rather, 'the ready-to-hand shows itself as still ready-to-hand in its unswerving presence-at-hand' (*BT*, 104/74). We would not see something as faulty equipment or as obstructing our work if we did not see it as equipment at the same time. It is equipment, it is just not working at the moment. Indeed, perhaps there is nothing like a pure presence-at-hand utterly independent of the ready-to-hand, for it is only at the level of the ready-to-hand that individual entities are individuated and hence may be said to 'be' at all.

What we can see explicitly here is the *readiness-to-hand* itself. It is as if we here make *readiness*-to-hand *present*-at-hand. We can examine readiness-to-hand, the quality of being a tool, in the way that a scientist investigates a rock.

It is only in a break from practical action that the theoretical attitude is adopted. The philosophical (or 'metaphysical') tradition has however reversed the natural order of things and understood all beings according to the model of the present-at-hand, while understanding the most fundamental relation to beings along the lines of 'theory'.

(g) Unhomeliness

Thus we have seen that it is possible to be roused from one's absorption in the world. But this is not sufficient to force Dasein to understand itself in a way that has *no* reference to the world at all. For that, we need a more universal experience of breakdown, in which *every* tool fails to work. Heidegger does indeed identify just such an experience.

Heidegger wishes to show that Dasein is not absolutely confined by the possibilities that the world offers him. The conviction that he is confined to certain possibilities by his current world is shattered by an exceptional experience in which he sees himself unchained from *any* possible world, and that is the experience of death. Since death will force him to relinquish his hold on any supposedly secure possessions he might have acquired and any achievements he might have made (cf. *BT*, 355–6/307–8), he is never allowed to settle in to whatever home currently shelters him. He is never quite a fixture in any world in which he might become adept at dwelling.

Now, for the most part we are thrown into the world, and this thrownness is revealed to us by the fact that, without our consent, we are always lumbered with a mood. But there is one mood which causes the world to *slip away altogether*, which reveals the insignificance of this world by effectively giving us a foretaste of death: anxiety (*Angst*).

Anxiety reveals a possibility of Dasein's existence which has nothing to do with the world and which hence *cannot* be inauthentic. 'As one of Dasein's possibilities of being, anxiety – together with Dasein itself as disclosed in it – provides the phenomenal basis for explicitly grasping Dasein's primordial totality of being' (*BT*, 227/182).

(h) Anxiety

Anxiety is the opposite of falling. It is to drag us out of inauthenticity *by making it impossible*. It forces us to understand ourselves on our own basis precisely by tearing us away not just from the one particular world in which we are currently immersed, but from the possibility of understanding ourselves in terms of any world at all. Falling is a *fleeing*. We are fleeing from anxiety, from precisely this solitude in which we are unable to glean our possibilities from the world.

But if Dasein is always fleeing from something, it must have caught sight of that which it is running away from. 'Only to the extent that Dasein has been brought before itself in an ontologically essential manner through whatever disclosedness belongs to it, *can* it flee *in the face of* that in the face of which it flees' (*BT*, 229/184–5).

We flee from this authentic possibility *because* it makes us anxious (*BT*, 230/186). For Heidegger the traditional way of referring to that which makes this authentic possibility known to us is the 'call of conscience', the feeling of *guilt*. And for the most part, we do not properly understand this feeling, and do all that we can simply to eradicate it (cf. *BT*, 312ff./267ff.).

Heidegger thinks that if each individual does have this factual tendency to turn away from whatever inflicts it with this angst, the phenomenologist can use this tendency to *investigate* the source of anxiety (*BT*, 229/185). What one is fleeing from in inauthenticity, what one seeks shelter from is oneself, one's proper, authentic possibility, one's *self*.

In anxiety, all beings lose significance for us. This should be taken in a precise technical sense (cf. *BT*, 231/186, *WM*, 90/11). It is as if every tool were broken. We explicitly confront the being of entities within the ready-to-hand world when they *break*. In anxiety, when nothing, no words, no thing, no event can cure us of this feeling, it is as if *every being in the entire world were broken*. Nothing can explain and thus relieve this anxiety, and so nothing 'works'. There is no cure, no remedy for anxiety. And because everything is broken, what we encounter here is the pure being of every one of those worldly beings: 'What oppresses us [in anxiety] is not this or that, nor is it the summation of everything present-at-hand; it is rather the *possibility* of the ready-to-hand in general; that is to say, it is the world itself' (*BT*, 231/187). World is 'being' as we understand it, the being of everything. This makes it clear why, in anxiety, it is not the being of any one ready-to-hand thing that appears, but the being of *everything*, being unchained from any particular being: being itself.

When the beings of the world rush away from us, elude our grasp, slip away, what is revealed is 'nothing': anxiety 'induces the slipping away of beings as a whole' (*WM*, 88/9) and '[t]he nothing [. . .] is encountered "at one with" beings that are slipping away as a whole' (*WM*, 90/11). And what is the nothing? It is what is *not* a being, and yet it is related to beings, because this particular nothing is revealed to us only when *beings* slip away. But this nothing is that aspect of beings which is normally hidden from us when we are dealing with them, when they have significance for us and we tacitly understand how to use them. Now everything is broken, nothing is of any use, and what is revealed to us is the fact that they *had* significance, the very fact of significance. In other words, the world, or being, is what is revealed to us when we suddenly realize that no entity is going to come to our aid: 'the "nothing" – that is, the world as such' (*BT*, 232/187).

It is crucial that the world is revealed in *mood*, and not *understanding*. What is revealed is the wholly *in*significant fact that there *is* significance, that we are thrown into a contingent common world of things that have a definite signification: 'this *insignificance* of what is within-the-world, the world in its world*hood* [my italics] is all that still obtrudes itself' (*BT*, 231/187). What puts us in touch with insignificance is moods.

If inauthentic Dasein understood itself in terms of its world, anxiety takes away that possibility, because in anxiety all the definite possibilities of things in the world slip away. So what anxiety reveals is that Dasein is *not* absolutely determined by its world, by others, by its role in society, indeed by *anything* in any possible world whatsoever. Anxiety shows us that we are not completely governed by the past, into which we have been thrown and on which we constantly fall back. It shows that, fundamentally, as individuals, we are unchained from any world, and from those anonymous others who, with the force of convention, watch over our behaviour.

> The 'world' can offer nothing more, and neither can the Dasein-with of Others. Anxiety thus takes away from Dasein the possibility of understanding itself, as it falls, in terms of the 'world' and the way things have been publicly interpreted. Anxiety throws Dasein back upon that which it is anxious about – its authentic potentiality-for-being-in-the-world. Anxiety individualizes Dasein for its ownmost being-in-the-world. (*BT*, 232/187)

Anxiety draws us away from any determinate world and into the indeterminate. The absolutely universal possibility, which everyone must face – death – but also that which makes each of us unique, for no one can possibly die our death for us, the possibility of dying proves that there is at least one possibility that is not to be gleaned from the world, common to all, and which is ours alone. Hence death, as revealed in anxiety, is the source of the possibility of an authentic self-understanding, it is ultimately the very source of mineness as such, for it alone guarantees the uniqueness of my life and hence the absolute solitude of my self-relation.

This is the sense in which Dasein is 'uncanny' (*unheimlich*, unhomely) (*BT*, 233/188). Not at home in any home he is given, which means not fully determined in what he is by any world. If the world is his home, he is not at home in his home.

Unlike every other animal, his relations with and immersion in his environment do not satisfy him, he must conquer other worlds, constantly shift his world, or at least he will always remain unsatisfied by whatever limited world he finds himself in. It is this constant feeling of being *thwarted* in some way by his circumstances that motivates his *desire*. While animals are entrapped in one sort of environment, man is characterized by a refusal to be anchored to any one specific kind of world, and as a result of this detachment he begins to project possibilities that exceed those offered by his immediate environment. This permanent possibility of moving to another world is a consequence of his being freed by *death* from the one contingent world in which he first finds himself thrown. This is perhaps the ultimate significance of Heidegger's lifelong insistence that 'man alone dies' (cf. *PLT*, 150/152).[6]

We *can* become authentically individual, or at least individualize ourselves more than we are currently doing. That is why we feel anxiety: because, ultimately, who we truly are is *stifled* by the world in which we have ended up, into which we have been thrown. 'Anxiety brings Dasein face to face with its *being free for* [...] the authenticity of its being, and for this authenticity as a possibility which it always is' (*BT*, 232/188).

That said, it is not as if anxiety shows us that we are totally free. After all, moods reveal our *thrownness*, our *un*-freedom. Moods reveal the very general fact that *some* particular world will always be ours, and will always limit the possibilities that we have. But at the same time, it need not be *this particular* world.

What anxiety reveals is perhaps that we are unfree in the following way: we cannot choose *not* to be free. We are not able to disburden ourselves of the responsibility to choose by attributing our situation to the particular world we are in. And precisely because of the *contingency* – as opposed to the necessity – of our being in this particular world.

This is why Heidegger stresses that anxiety, while it individualizes us, does not take us out of the world altogether: 'anxiety brings it back from its absorption in the "world". [...] Dasein has been individualized, but individualized *as* being-in-the-world' (*BT*, 233/189). We may presume that only death removes us absolutely from the world, death as the irreparable departure, but precisely then we are no longer. While we are alive, we are caught in a perpetual *movement* between anxious withdrawal and a falling back into the world. We are never paralysed in a permanent anxiety, nor are we ever entirely free from anxiety, which always remains, 'latent' or 'sleeping' (*WM*, 93/14, *BT*, 234/189).

Anxiety thus shows us that we are fallen, revealing a possibility beyond the inauthentic, and thus the fact that there *is indeed* a choice to be made between inauthenticity and authenticity: 'anxiety individualizes [or rather, individuates]. This individualization brings Dasein back from its falling, and makes manifest to it that authenticity and inauthenticity are possibilities of its being' (*BT*, 235/190–1).

Further reading

Heidegger, Martin (1962 [1927]) *Being and Time*. Trans. John Macquarrie and Edward Robinson. Oxford: Blackwell, pp. 169–209 (on mood and understanding); pp. 279–311 (on death); pp. 312–48 (on conscience).

—(1998), 'What is Metaphysics?' [1929] in *Pathmarks*. Edited by William McNeill. Trans. David Farrell Krell. Cambridge: Cambridge University Press, pp. 82–96 (on anxiety).

Nature and Art

Main primary literature

'The Origin of the Work of Art', *passim*.
Being and Time, pp. 100–101.
Basic Problems of Phenomenology, pp. 116, 169.

(a) Globalization

In his later work Heidegger introduces something novel and extremely important to his notion of the world. It is history.

Heidegger attends very closely to the fact that entire worlds can be born and perish. And precisely what differentiates the various worlds is their attitude to their own world and to other worlds, and indeed to human culture as such in terms of its relation to what lies beyond it: nature, or what Heidegger calls 'the earth'. Since the world provides the framework within which entities can appear, it thus becomes clear that it is not temporality that constitutes the most basic condition for the appearance of entities, but rather *history*. Heidegger thus goes as far as to identify being itself *with* history. Partly as a result of this broader historical vision, Heidegger's work in the 1930s becomes political, for it suggests that certain ways of ordering the world make individual authenticity more or less realizable. For at least one brief period, he saw the National Socialist Party as offering such an opportunity to the German people. In general, in the age of globalization, what we in the West experience is our *own* world encroaching upon every part of the globe, and thus the formation of a world market and a global homogenization. Thus the entire globe becomes part of one 'world' (in French, the word for 'globalization' is '*mondialisation*'). Multiple worlds coalesce into one, and thus the very possibility of *another* world is progressively closed out by this homogenizing process, often attributed to the growth of capitalism, but which Heidegger attributes to technology and more fundamentally to man's very relation to nature, his understanding of beings as a whole, and thus his understanding of *being* – or the lack of it.

 If there is no apparent world to which we might escape, does this not explain the ubiquity of anxiety – along with the desperate therapeutic and pharmaceutic attempts to suppress it – in the contemporary Western world, for one lacks any sense of an alternative source of possibility, and one thus remains *irremediably* inauthentic, and subject to a constant anxiety that one is unable to quell?

 This lack of alternatives is exacerbated by the apparent ease of escaping to 'another world' thanks to the opportunities for long distance travel and the almost immediate presence of distant events by way of the electronic media. But for Heidegger, this precisely amounts to the eradication of real distance and a genuine sense of difference and otherness (*PLT*, 165/167). And at the same time, peoples are being uprooted from worlds that were formerly peculiar to them, and this leads to a feeling of unsettledness and in fact to the sense that this one world in which we are entrapped is not *our* world. Hence we find today a curious mixture of a tranquilized falling back against the world *and* perpetual anxiety, that *feels* its unhomeliness in the world.

 Perhaps this indicates that what needs to change is not just the individual, in terms of the way he experiences himself and his world, as the early Heidegger thought, but the very world itself. Hence Heidegger's ambitions for phenomenology take on a much grander dimension.

Man is *already* overwhelmed by anxiety, and perhaps what is needed is a less reflexive posture, one which does not feel anxiety for itself but terror (*Erschrecken*) for the *world*, or more precisely for the *earth*. And it is the world that needs to change, most of all. For what is being globalized is a peculiarly

Western attitude of indifference and destructiveness towards the earth, which Heidegger reveals to be the outcome of a long history of the understanding of the nature of beings as a whole that originates from the Ancient Greeks. Different attitudes to the one shared earth are being supplanted by a single contemptuous attitude which has issued in the dawning of an unprecedented ecological disaster.

Heidegger's later thought provides us with a historical account of the reasons why this attitude has become so pervasive.

This increased stress on history is also a self-critique on Heidegger's part. It is as if in *Being and Time* there were just one structure shared by all possible worlds for all time, as if the relations of present-at-hand and ready-to-hand were static. History was considered, but more or less in an appendix, and in a way that was ultimately inessential to being. Being itself, in the sense of its differentiation into the three primary kinds of being, remained Platonic, ahistorical, aloof and indifferent to its actual instantiations. Heidegger came to rethink history so radically that we can no longer describe being in its distinctness from history at all.

Let us examine some of the effects of this rethinking, and the entry of history into being. One way to describe these is in terms of the way the ready-to-hand now relates to the present-at-hand, the 'technical' to the 'scientific'. With a proper notion of history, Heidegger was able to address the particular form that human artifice (*technē*) assumes today – technology – along with its role in the very destiny of being, and to think the history of being as a process of its own obliviation (*Vergessenheit*).

Already, in 'The Origin of the Work of Art' in 1934, which marks approximately the beginning of Heidegger's 'later thought', history had entered Heidegger's thought in a new way. Here he describes the world as an '*historical world*' (*OWA*, 42/28), and his first example is of a world that no longer exists, the world of the ancient Greeks. Worlds change, and these changes are precisely what *make* history.

(b) The other sense of nature, the other sense of art

Let us examine the transition to Heidegger's later historical thinking of being more carefully, to understand why it became necessary. One of the most basic changes is the introduction to the world of an *earth*, and this is in fact precisely what allows Heidegger to understand the *historicality* of worlds and of being.

Heidegger quite clearly admits, even in his early work, that there is a certain understanding of nature, a *sublime* understanding, which takes it neither as present-at-hand nor as ready-to-hand (cf. *BT*, 100/71). If there was no category in *Being and Time*'s ontology that could accommodate this entity, then Heidegger had to rethink his ontology in order to make room for this nature: there must be something *beyond* the world. This new 'category' which Heidegger uses to understand sublime nature is 'earth' (*die Erde*).

The only real way to accommodate nature in the early Heidegger's ontology was in the form of the present-at-hand. The other sense was necessarily elided. The fact that Heidegger had to ignore one form of nature is related to another fact: that Heidegger also ignored one of the two forms of *technē* (*ars*).

He focused solely on the work of the craftsman, the technician. But the Greek word, *technē*, means both craft and art. This craft, after the Industrial Revolution, has predominantly come to take the form of *technology*.[7] But where does this leave the other form of *technē* today? *Fine* art.

Art *and* technology were both ignored in an essential way in *Being and Time*. The two go hand in hand for Heidegger as he believes that a focus on the purely technological sense of human activity is ultimately responsible for the devastation of nature, and it is the rehabilitation of a 'poietic' kind of activity[8] that Heidegger believes will help to restrain humanity from the exploitative attitude towards nature embodied by technology.

What the 'poietic' artwork reveals is precisely this unintelligible, sublime *nature*, but it reveals this 'otherness' by way of its *contrast* with intelligibility. This is what Heidegger means by the *strife* (*Streit*) that exists between earth and world, which the artwork captures, or rather, institutes (*OWA*, 49/35).

A different attitude to its 'materials' distinguishes the production of art from the dealings we have with the ready-to-hand. And yet, the work of art nevertheless *reveals* the being of the ready-to-hand. Heidegger's example is that of a Van Gogh painting of some peasant's shoes, in which a relation between the peasant and his particular world, as well as the earthy field and its furrows all come to appearance. Thus the artwork constitutes a *new way* in which to bring the being of things to light, which does *not* require a breakdown or a cessation of activity.

In Heidegger's description, the world issues forth from the opening of the peasant's shoe (*OWA*, 32ff./18ff.). The work of art depicts the very *occurrence* or formation of a *particular* world, a world that has perhaps perished and will certainly be alien to the kind of person who is likely to be visiting a gallery.

What is different here is that this world is not just the everyday world that we all supposedly share, but it is the world of a particular culture at a particular point in history. History determines the way in which the world of Dasein *is*. Why else would Heidegger choose as an example the ancient Greek temple? (*OWA*, 41ff./27ff.) The fact that the work in question here is a piece of architecture makes it clear that for Heidegger art does not *depict* or *represent* the world. It *creates* a world of its own. The work of art opens up a particular world to us, the world of the peasant, the world of the ancient Greeks. . . And Heidegger's truly magnificent descriptions of the work *re*-create this creation of a world before *our* eyes: 'the work opens up a *world* and keeps it abidingly in force' (*OWA*, 44/30).

We are not part of its world, its world has decayed. We are not peasants, we are bourgeois art connoisseurs, and yet these worlds are created for us by works of art. *Another world is created by art works.* Thus they reveal that our specific world *is not the only one.*

By recreating the peasant woman's pre-modern relation not just to her world but to the *earth*, Heidegger reveals that the most fundamental distinction between different historical worlds lies in their respective attitudes to the *earth*. The work of art for Heidegger always brings to light this unintelligibility that remains in excess of the world, but *without* sacrificing its unintelligibility by enclosing it within the horizon of a world that would render it meaningful.

We have suggested that the earth is Heidegger's attempt to incorporate the sublime sense of nature in itself which had found no place in his early ontology. To understand what is meant by 'earth' we need only recall how Heidegger first describes the work of art in *contrast* with the kind of practical activity described in *Being and Time*: the use of the ready-to-hand involves the *dematerializing* of the actual present-at-hand matter from which tools are made and upon which they work, in favour of their functionality and ultimate form. The work of art on the other hand precisely brings this materiality to the fore. The colours of the paint shine, the tone of the music sings, the density of the language shows through the meaningfulness of the word (*OWA*, 46/32). These things are not intelligible, they elude the functional context of any world, but they are what turns a prosaic phrase into poetry, an artefact into art.

A work of art *is* a part of the world, but it is an element which *appears* and *in* appearing fulfils its 'function'. *It announces the fact of its appearance.* We have already seen that the ready-to-hand appears to us precisely *without* announcing itself, without our usually being aware of it: indeed, it might be said that it precisely does *not* appear to us. The work of art is thus for Heidegger an exemplary phenomenon. One which both shows itself *and* does so explicitly and always, without needing to *fail* in its functioning.

The importance of the art work to phenomenology is that, here, *appearance happens,* and it openly announces itself as happening. And precisely what comes to the fore is that aspect of the world which is usually hidden from us, the earthy, unintelligible aspect of things, which is precisely concealed from us when we work with the ready-to-hand. What appears here is the *being* of things, which is no longer to be identified with the world as the usually inapparent context that allows things to signify, but with the world *plus* the always *in*significant earth. Thus we see that Heidegger has now fully overcome the idea that the source of phenomenal significance is a world which could in theory be illuminated: there is an element involved in the process of manifestation that can never be made intelligible.

Naturally, the earth appears, and precisely in the work of art, but in a way that remains outside of any worldly horizon that would make it *intelligible* in human terms. Artworks precisely cannot remain what they are *and* be made to serve human ends in the practical context of a 'world'. They withdraw from this world. This is to say that they *appear,* but in a *non-*worldly fashion. They shelter their own mystery within themselves, but this very mysteriousness appears.

Thus it becomes clear that the earth is Heidegger's rethinking of *nature* in a way that *does not* understand it solely as a resource for man's productive activity. This is apparent from his beautiful description of the earth as the unchanging cycle of the seasons, summer in its gift of fertility and winter in its barren refusal of growth (*OWA*, 34/19). It is a nature that we have to work *with,* and not force. It comprises those characteristics of nature which we cannot change without 'de-naturing' it altogether. It is not the 'wind in the sails' or the river viewed as a source of 'hydroelectric power' (*BT*, 100/70). It is nature understood as it is 'in itself' *outside* of this instrumental, ready-to-hand context.

Thus the relation between the cultural world of production and the natural world is brought to light in the art work, and so the two absences which we identified in Heidegger's early work, art and nature, are remedied here in one fell swoop.

The work of art relates the world and the earth. It establishes a relation between a historical world and the particular elements of nature which offer themselves to that world.

Traditionally, nature has been understood to lack a history. Culture is the place of history. The work of art would thus seem to act as a link between history and the ahistorical. In fact, this relation is for Heidegger precisely the precondition *of* history itself.

Heidegger describes works of art – '*great* works' (*OWA*, 40/26, my italics) – as remnants of past worlds that have decayed; the work of art has survived, but the world has died. The art work has outlived the world of which it was once a part. It is as if the work of art can retain some value even after the world which gave it significance has vanished. We know that a piece of ready-to-hand equipment can *not* do this. What it is is defined only by its references to all the other elements in the 'work world'.

How does the art work retain its value? Is it to do with the fact that it has never denied the fact that it was made of natural materials? Natural materials are not historical, they are not something that need die with the passing away of a culture. The stone of the ancient Greek statue *endures*, and precisely this endurance allows it to stand as a *historical* monument or 'memorial'.

In a way, the entire world is encapsulated in this one entity. Heidegger would later identify *other* kinds of entities besides the artwork which could do this. He called them 'things' (*Dingen*). They are precisely those entities which are phenomena *par excellence*, where appearance *itself* appears, and in particular, appearance in its *historical* character; and this occurs by means of the appearance of a world that stands in contrast to the world in which the art work actually exists, a strange world, or a world of the past.

(c) History as condition of possibility of experience

Heidegger realized that he too had been blinded by certain features of his own age and that his understanding of the world in his early work, which was presented as if it were ahistorical, in truth reflected the way things appeared at that particular point in history. He had postulated his notion of worldhood as an ahistorical structure and his ontology as a permanently valid categorization of things. Following the so-called 'turning' (*Kehre*) in his thought, he came to see that this was insufficient: history needed to be given an even deeper role in phenomenology. There is not just one 'world', there are many, and history happens when the world changes,[9] and precisely what changes is that world's relation to the *earth*.

This would lead us to something like a 'transcendental history', which is to say precisely *not* an *empirical* history, and this means that history is not just a contingent succession of facts with no fundamental effect on the way we experience things. This history must be governed by some sort of necessary principle, *and* it becomes a necessary part of the conditions of possibility for experience. The limits of what we can experience contract and expand according to our position in history. Hence, today, in the technological era, as is frequently said, our experience is particularly impoverished, even brutalized.

We cannot examine this here, with the all the rich detail and nuance that Heidegger's texts give it, but we must say that the principle which Heidegger recognizes in history is that of a more or less progressive *forgetting of being*, and that means, in practical terms, a destruction of singularity and our experience of it. He understands the history of the West to be co-extensive with the history of metaphysics, which he describes as 'onto-theo-logy', a totality of metaphysical 'positions' whose possibilities he believes to have been exhausted. But this completion of metaphysics is in fact the ongoing *installation* of metaphysics in another form, in the guise of its very 'over-coming': science and technology.

Onto-theo-logy: Heidegger's understanding of metaphysics or 'first philosophy' as it has been practised since Aristotle. Aristotle in his *Metaphysics* described it as the science of beings as such and as a whole. Metaphysics is the most basic form of philo-sophical thought and attempts to understand the being of all things, that which is common to all things, 'common being' (*ens communis*), and also that particular entity (usually God) which is the effective cause of everything that exists, of the *fact* that they exist and of *what* they are. The first aspect of *prima philosophia* is often referred to in modern and mediaeval thought as 'general metaphysics' (*metaphysica generalis*), while the latter is referred to as 'special metaphysics' (*metaphysica specialis*), for it deals with specific entities rather than that which is common to all beings: it comes to deal not just with God but with the soul and the universe as a whole. In general, the former is called 'ontology' or the science of being (*to on, ousia*) and the latter 'theology' or the science of the divine or god (*to theion, ho theios*). Hence, 'onto-theo-logy', combining three Greek words (including '*logos*') which Heidegger uses to indicate that the entirety of philosophy has unfolded an understanding of things which is basically Greek. Heidegger needs to draw attention to these implicit inheritances in order to consider the possibility that today we might move beyond metaphysics, to another way of thinking, and a way of relating to the world that goes beyond the ruinous technological exploitation of contemporary mass production and consumption.

Further reading

Heidegger, Martin (1971), 'The Thing' [1950] in *Poetry, Language, Thought*, pp. 163–86.

—(1973), 'Art and Space' [1969]. Trans. Charles H. Seibert in *Man and World* 6/1.

Taminiaux, Jacques (1991), *Heidegger and the Project of Fundamental Ontology* [1989]. Trans. and ed. Michael Gendre. New York: State University of New York Press, chapter 2.

8 Technology

Chapter Outline

Main primary literature

'The Question Concerning Technology'.
'Building Dwelling Thinking'.
'The Thing'.

(a) Technology as realized metaphysics

Heidegger proposed that in the twentieth century the forgetting of being was not just – if it ever was – confined to the texts of philosophy. Metaphysics had come to dominate the globe. The theories of metaphysicians had been *practically* realized, and indeed are perhaps being *developed,* which is to say originated *in* the world. This is precisely what is taking place in the theory that is science and the practice that is technology, as well as a kind of science that goes beyond simple empirical observation and requires techno-logical instruments in order to carry out its observations, forming a peculiar co-dependence of science and technology: 'techno-science'.

In this practical realization of metaphysics, metaphysics achieves its ultimate domination, and precisely because this passage to the practical realm covers over the metaphysics that it realizes. Metaphysics could dominate the globe only by making everyone forget that it exists. Metaphysics, a theory concerning being, which understands it as 'substance' or 'presence', assumes the guise of its opposite, an *absence* of metaphysics, or an '*overcoming* of metaphysics', which is proclaimed by Anglo-American analytic philosophy (e.g. Rudolph Carnap) and science itself – for which being is quite simply 'nothing' (*WM,* 84/3–4).

This denial of being is a crucial step, because if being is nothing, then there is nothing to stop us from *treating* beings in any way that we want. Why? Because being is the singular manner in which each thing appears, the possi-bilities that are *naturally appropriate* to a certain thing. If things *have* no such singularity today, if everything is just a resource for production and con-sumption, or mass-reproduced trash, why *shouldn't* we treat beings as means to our ends, distorting them into whatever form we require?

The history of metaphysics as the forgetting of being culminates in techno-logy's attitude to the earth, which lacks any idea of a timeless, unmodifiable essence, and any conception of the purely 'natural'. Technology itself is under-stood to have no essence, merely a practical function.

By contrast, Heidegger proposes to demonstrate that such an essence exists, that technology has certain conditions of possibility, which require that beings as a whole are revealed in a certain way, and, correlatively, that man has been prevailed upon to experience beings *in* this way. This is to say that technology's essence is *being,* in the current, historical mode of its manifestation.

Heidegger describes the essence of technology as a call (*ein Ruf*).[10] Man is not merely passive when it comes to technology: the way things are uncon-cealed makes *demands* on him, man is *called* to respond in a certain way. This is simply because revelation cannot happen unless there is someone *to whom* it is revealed. Presence, appearance, always has *two* poles for Heidegger: the appearance, and the one it appears *to.* If beings are unconcealed in a way that allows them to be exploited, man is the one *called* upon to reveal nature as an energy resource, man is the one who is *capable* of exploiting it. Things must already be 'unconcealed' in a certain way for man to set upon them with his technological implements.

The name for this call, for this way of being unconcealed, and hence the name for 'being' today is '*Ge-stell*'. In German, '*ge-*' implies both the past tense and a 'gathering together', while '*-stell*' derives from '*stellen*' meaning 'to place or set', to posit, stand, and stabilize.

'*Ge-stell*' is generally translated as 'enframing', and literally means a frame, rack, chassis, or skeleton; some formal framework into which things are forced and with which they must comply, an immutable *mould* according to which things are cast. Heidegger is here reworking the Platonic idea of essence, and thus drawing attention to the wholly metaphysical approach that underlies technological production: first one has a template (essence) and then one uses a machine to produce an actual instance of it (existence). Fordist mass-production at the very end of the history of being.

Gestell, then, is the current name for *being*, a word that can be used to understand the essence of everything that is. It describes the predominant way in which beings as a whole are currently manifested to us: as a *resource* or 'standing reserve' (*Bestand*).

> **Gestell**: The essence of technology. It literally means 'frame' or 'chassis' and refers to a number of other terms in Heidegger's German, but most importantly it refers to the notion of a template, a fixed mould from which a potentially infinite number of identical copies can be produced, as happens in modern machine technology. It has been translated in a Heideggerian context as 'En-framing' and even as 'System', taken in its literal sense of 'standing together (*syn-stema*)' to emphasize the way in which beings as a *whole* are gathered together and homogenized by this process. Heidegger uses it to show how the practical effects of technology may be seen to be a consequence of the ways in which 'being' has been understood in history. Technology consummates the 'productivist' understanding of being, which is present in Greek thought, and is most pronounced in Plato. According to this understanding, there exists in advance an archetypal idea or transcendent essence, purely intelligible, that is then instantiated in material reality, to form the particular 'existents' (beings or entities) that surround us in the sensible world.

So, in the terminology which Heidegger introduces in 1949, *being* is *Gestell*, and beings are *Bestand*. *Gestell* refers to the way in which man is gathered up into the process of setting upon beings to exploit their resources. Technology, in the hands of man, is to reveal beings as *Bestand*, constant resource, under the sway of the general mode of unconcealment or being, called '*Gestell*'. *Gestell* is the gathering of man into the process of revealing entities as resources, energy, standing reserve. It is the gathering of man into a process which he did not initiate, a process of '*stellen*', which man is called upon to carry out: setting up or setting upon beings in order to make them deliver up their riches (*Bestand*).

Being, understood in a metaphysical way as constant presence, is consummated here in this technological understanding of entities as permanently on hand. *Bestand* was an early Heideggerian word for the present-at-hand: that which merely subsists (*bestehen*). In the later Heidegger, it is reworked to become the paradigm for the way in which all beings appear in the technological epoch: as fully present, which is to say, maximized in their actuality or potential actuality. Nothing is to remain purely virtual, incapable of being actualized. Hence the dreadful threat that hovers over the 'earth'.

(b) On causality

In 'The Question Concerning Technology', Heidegger attempts to show that the standard 'instrumental' understanding of technology as an artificial means to a human end, does not touch on the 'truth' about technology, and 'truth' for Heidegger is understood not as 'correspondence' or 'adequation' (to use the mediaeval term for the same idea) but as 'unveiling' or 'revealing' (*Entbergen*). In other words, the truth of technology is what it can be shown to *reveal*.

Heidegger investigates the notion of instrumentality and finds it to rest on a certain interpretation of *causality*. The way in which a product is understood to be produced by technological instruments is roughly equivalent to the relation between cause and effect, but *only* if 'cause' is understood in its modern sense, which Heidegger goes on to show is only a very restricted understanding of the full essence of 'causality': it takes all causality to be '*efficient* causality'.

For Heidegger, the Greeks knew almost nothing of this kind of cause, and this 'cause', which we understand in such a mechanical way, is more fundamentally a manner of *revealing*. When Aristotle speaks of a 'cause' (*aitia*) he is referring to whatever allows an entity to *appear*, to come towards us in the way that it does. An entity's 'cause' is *responsible* for the way in which that entity appears.

We have already identified the four forms of Aristotelian causality in *Being and Time*, efficient, formal, material and final. Here, Heidegger rethinks this in the context of the *technological* world.

Heidegger investigates the nature of causality in order to show that *technē*, the origin of technology, is a form of *poiēsis*, which we call 'production' but which for the Greeks is a manner of *revealing*. *Poiēsis*, 'production', is a way of *revealing*. It is a way of bringing things to appearance, bringing them forth (*Hervorbringen*).

The potter at his wheel coaxes shapes from the raw clay, gently moulding the material into the shape of a jug that he will then use for dispensing water. The difference between this simple craft and modern machine-powered technology is that there is nothing gentle about the latter's attitude to its material. It does not just lend assistance to an emergence that might not have come forth by itself (as one does when moulding clay), nor does it foster a natural process that was already in motion (as one does in cultivating a vine): both of these gestures characterized *technē* as Aristotle understood it, as either a perfecting or a *mimēsis* or 'mimicking' of natural processes (*physis*). Technology *demands* that things reveal themselves, and it demands that they reveal themselves in a particular way: as a source of energy and ultimately, today, as electricity, which will then be used 'in order to' power machines, or stored and put on standby in the form of batteries, capacitors, circuits and grids.

Technology sets upon *nature* and forces it to yield up energy in a way that can leave it quite exhausted: 'That revealing concerns *nature, above all*, as the chief storehouse of the standing energy reserve' (*QCT*, 21/22, my italics). Technology is *concerned* about nature only insofar as it will not be able to use it any more if it is irretrievably depleted. The worker, so to speak, is to be exploited just as long as he does not die of exhaustion.

(c) The modern world and the peasant world: enforced constancy

This is the shift that interests Heidegger, an epochal transformation in the way that nature appears to man, the way in which a *technē* that works *with* nature becomes a *technology* that more or less works *against* it. A hydroelectric dam can destroy a river in the way that a water-wheel cannot. This is where Heidegger clearly refers back to an idea from 'The Origin of the Work of Art' with regard to the *artist* and his materials. We find this reference most explicitly when Heidegger differentiates the use of power machinery in agriculture from the farming practices of the *peasant*:

> The field that the peasant formerly cultivated and set in order appears differently than it did when to set in order still meant to take care of and to maintain. The work of the peasant does not challenge the soil of the field. In the sowing of the grain it places the seed in the keeping of the forces of growth and watches over its increase. But meanwhile even the cultivation of the field has come under the grip of another kind of setting-in-order [*bestellen*], which *sets* upon nature [*stellt*]. It sets upon it in the sense of challenging it. Agriculture is now the mechanized food industry.[11] (*QCT*, 14–15/15–16)

The distinctive features of modern technology are its interest in *storage* and its insistence on the value of *constancy*. Nature must yield energy *constantly*, and to ensure this we need to produce a surplus, which we can then store so as to provide a *permanent* supply of energy: 'Regulating and securing even become the chief characteristics of the challenging revealing [that technology carries out]' (*QCT*, 16/17). This leads us to make absolutely unbending demands on the earth, quite irrespective of whether this approach is – to use a contemporary term – 'sustainable'.

The peasant derived energy from the land, – the wind powered the sails of the windmill, the water turned its wheel – but never in a way that *demanded* that the earth yield up its potential *come what may*. If the earth proved infertile for a season there was nothing to be done, indeed part of what it meant to farm well was to work in harmony with the earth and its 'cycles'. Today one has to have backups, reserves, an 'uninterruptable power supply', which is to say that one has to have something standing by in case nature, for its own reasons, refuses to yield and remains barren, while demand peaks.

We are now enmeshed in and generally dependent on a *grid* which covers not just a single nation but the entire globe, particularly in the form of the supply of fossil fuels such as gas and, most prominently, oil. There is a highly structured system that 'en-frames' nature, a network upon which we are becoming ever more dependent, and which is becoming ever more violently protected as its precariousness increases.

So much of modern technology is premised upon the *unending* nature of its energy supply. Even planes have emergency batteries: if these fail, the plane drops from the sky. The aeroplane, even more than the automobile, is a perfect symptom of the essence of technology.

What is clear is that the world-system absolutely *depends* upon technology. For Heidegger, this is the difference between the traditional world and the modern world, and it is this dependence that Heidegger wants us to relinquish: 'we should like to prepare a *free* relationship towards [technology]' (*QCT*, 3/7, my italics). This is what Heidegger means by the notion of '*Gelassenheit*' or 'releasement' (*DT*, 54/24–5).

It is curious that in *Being and Time*, the technical device revealed its *essence* when it *broke down*, for where else is our dependence upon power-generation so clear as during a power cut, and why else is the very notion of the destruction of an oil pipeline from the East one of the most terrifying prospects for Western European governments? Everything is done in order to ensure that things do not break down, that, in particular, fuel as potential energy never runs out.

Thus the crucial features of the energy supply demanded from nature are: constant presence, permanence, and stability, and these are *precisely* the features that have always characterized *being*. Being as presence, a timeless permanence, a constant support: '*Bestand*'. Technology is oblivious to its own essence, which is the culmination of the history of metaphysics, which in turn is the history of being. Constancy, presence, stability: being has become *energy*. This is the way in which, today, beings as a whole are for the most part revealed: potential energy. This is the nature of the *phenomenon*.

What governs this lust for maximization, which requires that the energy reserve remain permanently on call? Is it our economic system? For Heidegger – and this is why ultimately he is not a Marxist – more basically than that, it is the absence of *limits*. Nature does not appear to technology in a way that presents any *limit* to technical activity. It is as if the earth appears to it to be completely *consumable*. Even when the countryside is *not* being mined or used to supply power, it is being used to generate wealth as part of the tourist trade (*QCT*, 16/17).

(d) Man as called to reveal

Naturally, this is how *man* sees things. Man sees nature as an energy source. But Heidegger does not attribute sole responsibility to man, he does not consider him to be entirely in control of his actions in this regard: man does not decide how beings as a whole are revealed. Man's excessive nature – his infinite, insatiable desire, his *hubris* – is not called upon to *explain* why nature should have been revealed as an exploitable resource. Rather, since man in no way stands outside of history, he cannot simply *choose* to view nature in this way or in another.

Instead of attributing the appearance of nature to man's free understanding, Heidegger says that *there is* (*es gibt*) a certain 'unconcealment'. There is an event, an event takes place, opening up a space in which things can appear, and in that space, within its circumscribed limits, beings are *given* to us. Man's role is limited to finding the proper *response* to this – historical – event. A space of possibilities is opened up, something like a new 'world': Heidegger's name for this open place in which things are revealed is a *clearing* (*Lichtung*), a cleared space in a forest thick with trees. Within this space, things can move, unfold, become what they are, or indeed be exploited and destroyed. The event of the clearing of this space is just what Heidegger means by 'being' (*Sein*) in his later work, a sudden and then enduring *revelation* or 'unconcealment' (*Unverborgenheit*), a historical event (*Ereignis*) that opens up a new world.

Appearance happens, phenomena show themselves to us, and we are thus called to respond to them.

Thus it is clear that Heidegger is decisively shifting phenomenology away from the notion of a transcendental subject, which would control how things appear to it, and eliminating the residue of this way of thinking that still haunted *Being and Time*. This is why he stops using the word 'Dasein' in his later work and returns to 'man' or the 'mortal'.

(e) Truth

Ge-stell is the *essence of technology*, it is the *truth* of technology, the way in which technology *reveals*, for truth is a way of revealing. Heidegger here appeals to, and discusses at great length, the Greek word for truth, '*alētheia*', '*a-*' being a privative prefix and '*lanthanein*' meaning 'to conceal', whence our word for the oblivion that comes from drinking the water of the river that runs through the field of *Lēthē*, which Plato describes in the *Republic*: 'lethal'. Thus, when Heidegger speaks of the instrumental and anthropological interpretation of technology, he describes it as '*correct*' but not *true*. It does not say in what way technology is itself a form of truth or 'un-concealing'.

Truth is *being*, the event of unconcealment that determines the limits within which the possibilities of things can extend. So the essence or the truth of technology is the *way* in which technology reveals. The essence of technology is *Ge-stell*: the call issued to man by the event of being, which demands that he participate in the manifestation of things as *Bestand*, standing reserve.

Heidegger describes *Ge-stell* as 'the supreme danger' (QCT, 26/27), 'the extreme danger' (QCT, 28/29), precisely because it conceals the fact that it *is* a form of 'truth' or revealing:

> Enframing conceals that revealing which, in the sense of *poiēsis*, lets what presences come forth into appearance. [. . .] Where enframing holds sway, regulating and securing of the standing-reserve mark all revealing. *They no longer even let their own fundamental characteristic appear, namely, this revealing as such.* [/] Thus the challenging Enframing not only conceals a former way of revealing, bringing-forth, but it *conceals revealing* itself and with it that wherein uncon-cealment, i.e. truth, comes to pass. (QCT, 27/28, my italics)

This is due to the absolute constancy which prevails in the technological world. It lets us believe that ultimately there need be no absence or death, no fundamental limits, and hence no *being*, because being *needs* limits: limits ensure that, when it comes to manifestation, there can only ever be a certain *perspective*, from which one can see only as far as the horizon, *rather than* a vision of the universe from no point of view, without situation in space or time, as metaphysics and science have almost always wished for.

Thus for Heidegger, the principal problem of technology is that it encour-ages us to believe that there is only *one* way for beings to be, rather than a whole historical sequence which may not be over: 'Enframing, which threat-ens to sweep man away into ordering as the supposed *single way of revealing*' (QCT, 32/33, my italics). This is Heidegger's description of what is today called 'globalization'. This assertion of a single, universal way of revealing threatens the existence of revelation *as such*, for what is covered up hereby is the very fact that an event of revelation has taken place: 'The coming to presence of technology *threatens revealing*, threatens it with the possibility that all revealing will be consumed in ordering and that everything will present itself *only* in the unconcealedness of standing-reserve' (QCT, 33/34, my italics). With the urge to achieve constant presence, a maximization of the actual, technology's ideal is the closing out of mystery and of any open spaces, any gaps in beings as a whole, such as those interstices which we encountered in *Being and Time* and which formed the structure of the world. These little nothingnesses, the significations and possibilities of things, are what Heidegger means by a 'clearing', and they are the very precondition of any appearance taking place at all.

Technology in its globalized, planetary form, is the final stage of the forgetting of being, of the unquestioned acceptance that being is constant presence, and the realization of this ideal in *actual* reality. The gap between being and beings is closed.

The question is whether there will ever come a time when beings will *not* be revealed to us as exploitable, and, as we have seen, technology itself militates against this by concealing revelation itself and its historical mutability.

The ultimate ethical question of Heidegger's phenomenology is: what might bring this about? Or, failing that, what can we do today to resist the predominant way in which beings are revealed, to escape our dependence upon technology and energy? How can man relate to this epoch of being in a 'free' way, and avoid becoming a mere docile slave of the contemporary system?

At the very end of the essay, 'The Question Concerning Technology', Heidegger suggests that the *artwork*, that other form of *technē*, has a role to play here, and we may presume that it is precisely because here an event of revelation takes place, an event of *truth*, which does *not* conceal the fact that it is such a revelation, and precisely because the work of art does not display the indifference to the earth that technology does (cf. *QCT*, 34–5/35–6).

Here revelation happens explicitly, as if to remind us that, despite its general obliviation, *being* nevertheless endures. The artwork would be one of the memorial stones that creative men raise to the memory of being, in the hope of a resurrection. But there are others: Heidegger calls them 'things' (*Dingen*).

(f) The thing

The 'thing' is Heidegger's word for an entity which is manifestly unique. A thing can be something written, like a poem – Heidegger examines several of these in great detail – or a simple entity that one comes across in the world. It is an entity which manages to escape from the prevailing form of revelation, today, the technological. It is an entity which cannot be made fully present in a functionalized, energetic form. It refuses to be contained within the horizon of the contemporary world. The thing presents a contrast with the entities that *are* a part of this world, and thus it constitutes something like an absence *in* that world, precisely a 'clearing' of the kind Heidegger recognizes as necessary to an event of manifestation.

The technological world refuses to reveal itself, or to reflect on what it is; and at the same time it refuses to believe in an ongoing historical process. By contrast, the thing offers both. In general, the thing is a survivor from an historical world which has now decayed. It thus testifies to a *different* mode of revelation, and since today revelation as such is being closed out, it testifies to the event of revelation as such, and thus brings to light the eclipse of being in the contemporary world. Things *refer* to an entire world that is absent or in some way beyond our grasp. By enduring in the midst of a *new* world, things are a sign of history, or simply of *difference*. They indicate that there have been other worlds, other ways of revealing, and thus by implication, that there could be others. Since Heidegger understands history as a change in world, this means that the sign is a reminder of the continued possibility of history, of new historical events. By acting as a reminder of the fragility of entities within the world, the thing reveals to us that this world is not eternal. It criticizes this semblance of permanence and thus allows us to hope for another world, a new turning in the course of history. Heidegger sometimes speaks of a turn (*Kehre*) within being itself, whereby it would unveil a new aspect of itself, and being *is* history. This is not a change that we can bring about, but by believing it to be possible, we can prepare for it.

Thus, like the work of art, the thing makes manifest an entire world. The thing also seems to embody a certain relation between world and earth. If the globalization of technology amounts precisely to the ubiquity of the human *world* and the exclusion of the *earth*, then the thing will be something in which one can still discern *earth*. It will precisely reignite the strife between world and earth which has today been eradicated by the *victory* of the world.

Thus, today, when singularity has been more or less eradicated by homogenizing technology, *being* can show itself *only* in singular instances. In this way, the 'thing' is the culmination of Heidegger's attempt to refute the metaphysical understanding of being as an empty universal. When Heidegger speaks of the forgetting of being, he means that this singularity is being closed out: this takes the form of the *scarcity* of the thing, and of our ability to appreciate it (*Th*, 182/184).

Technology demands that, in the interests of constant presence, all individual entities should be immediately replaceable, and this is possible only if that entity is essentially nothing more than the instance of a certain type, and that we have a sufficiently rigorous production process to ensure that there is no difference between repeated instances of the same thing. This is achieved by the use of a 'template' (*Gestell*). In contrast to this stands the singularity of the thing, an entity which – for whatever reason – cannot be replaced.

In the early Heidegger, man was this irreplaceable thing, and the reason for this was that man could die. If Heidegger now thinks that singularity can be bestowed upon the inhuman thing, then it is perhaps because death is not the only thing that renders an entity unique. Certainly, Heidegger continues to insist that man has some privilege over other entities, and that privilege is often spoken of as the fact that man alone is capable of dying, but this simply means that his relation to death allows him – and him alone – to appreciate the singularity of *other* things. Death gives us an experience of a genuinely irreversible process: our own life. This lets us experience an entity as something that has undergone, or is undergoing an irreversible disappearance.[12] Man, far from being immersed in his world, is the only entity that is capable of taking a distance from whatever world he occupies and thus of instituting a certain *distance* between things and their context, and in this way restoring to them their singularity. This is why the thing is often an entity that once had a place in a functioning world, but a world that has now decayed, leaving only the 'thing' as a monument to that world, a thing which, being removed from its context, no longer functions. Greek temples, ancient monuments, an old bridge that crosses a river: *incongruous* things.

(g) Phenomenology as an ethical task

Just as metaphysics translates itself practically into the global domination of nature, today, phenomenology should take the form of *ethics*. Phenomenology is one way to describe the attempt to cultivate an experience that would do justice to the singularity of the thing. Phenomenology would amount to an attention to the many layers and finesses that go to make up the singularity of an entity, its being or its *phenomenon*.

Being itself calls upon us, Heidegger often says: the call is thus 'ontological', but to respond to it is 'ethical'. Ethics would thus be a way of 'dwelling' (*ethos*, in Greek) or simply 'living' (*wohnen*) on the earth.

If phenomenality itself has been endangered by technology, the question arises as to just where phenomenology is to *look* for traces of a phenomenon. One answer is *texts*, written works from the past. Again, in the case of discourse, as in the case of the artwork and the thing, something is clearly being revealed. Revelation is not suppressed here, provided that discourse is not reduced to the level of abbreviation, shorthand, or telegraphic message, as Heidegger had anticipated.

Thus, to conclude, for Heidegger, phenomenology becomes the ethical task of revealing the truth or essence of a phenomenon, an experience that attains to the singularity of a thing, which is precisely *absent* from the way in which we normally encounter it. It thus becomes an attempt to return us to the thing in its simplicity, and to return simplicity to the thing, despite the technological enframing of the world which militates against this.

Further reading

Derrida, Jacques, (1989 [1987]), *Of Spirit: Heidegger and the Question*. Trans. G. Bennington and R. Bowlby. Chicago: University of Chicago Press.

Janicaud, Dominique, (1996 [1990]), *The Shadow of That Thought: Heidegger and the Question of Politics*. Trans. M. Gendre. Evanston, IL: Northwestern University Press.

Lacoue-Labarthe, Philippe, (1990 [1987]), *Heidegger, Art and Politics*. Trans. C. Turner. Oxford: Basil Blackwell. (This and the previous two works investigate Heidegger's thinking of technology in relation to his political engagement with Nazism.)

Stiegler, Bernard, (1998 [1994]), *Technics and Time, 1: The Fault of Epimetheus*. Trans. R. Beardsworth and G. Collins. Stanford, CA: Stanford University Press. (A fascinating study of the relation between Heideggerian thought and anthropological studies of the connection between the origin of man and the use of tools.)

Part III
Jean-Paul Sartre (Paris, France, 1905–Paris, France, 1980)

Jean-Paul-Baptiste-Eymard Sartre wrote about more than just phenomenology, although all of his work was informed by phenomenology. Since we must confine ourselves to his contribution to phenomenology, we shall have to neglect many of his works which are still of the greatest interest. This also means that we must confine ourselves almost entirely to Sartre's early works, written prior to *Being and Nothingness* in 1943, since it is perhaps here that he makes his most innovative contributions to the method of phenomenology. We shall even have to neglect his later *philosophical* works, including the colossal, *Critique of Dialectical Reason* (1960 & *posth.*), which are only now beginning to be appreciated as the remarkably prescient works that they are, and should prove an exceptionally rich resource for philosophical and political thinking in the future. His fictional work includes four excellent novels, a collection of exceptional short stories, numerous plays, which are certainly his most accessible works and a fine introduction to the most basic thrust of his philosophy in terms of contingency, freedom and our relations with others. Beyond fiction, he wrote many occasional pieces, often of a political or aesthetic character, many of which are collected in the numerous volumes comprising his *Situations*. He wrote entire books on Charles Baudelaire, the French writer, Jean Genet, and Gustav Flaubert, essays in 'existential psycho-analysis', which attempt to isolate the singular *project* that can be said to define an individual life.

While the specific contents of these works need not be addressed here, the *fact* that Sartre found it necessary to write in such a variety of forms is a consequence of his understanding of 'human reality', human existence, and the particular phenomenological method that must be used to study human life, a method which requires us to invoke other means in order to describe the nature of this reality. In particular, an attention to the contingent features of a situation and a certain entity, which lend it its unique character, a character which cannot be predicated without actually experiencing that thing from the 'inside', as it were: all of this is crucial for Sartre, hence his use of *fictions* to help us get 'inside' certain situations that we may not at that moment be experiencing ourselves.

These individual situations and contingencies are both beyond the ken of traditional philosophy and essential to philosophy as Sartre understands it. This is connected to the central tenet of what later came to be known, without Sartre's help, as 'existentialism' (a title apparently coined by the 'Christian existentialist', Gabriel Marcel). This is the thesis that the essence of human beings is to be in each case unique, and that the peculiar character of this uniqueness is freely decided upon by each one of us as we live through our particular life: no absolute values beyond those which we choose to adopt and no actual facts about ourselves and our situation can entirely extinguish this freedom. Nevertheless, a crucial part of existentialism is its insistence on man's 'situatedness', the thesis that what we *are* depends on certain contingent facts about our situation in history, geography, and society. Hence our decisions have to take these into account when making the fundamental choices that come to determine what we are.

Sartre would spend his entire life attempting to understand the balance between the free human subject and the inert, material and symbolic structures and institutions in which he finds himself involved from the very moment he becomes conscious. The confluence of these two currents creates the individuality of the human being. It might be said, with some exaggeration, that Sartre, after *Being and Nothingness* (1943) – which had been interpreted as focusing almost exclusively on the individual at the expense of the community – later came to address these 'political' questions more explicitly, particularly in the *Critique of Dialectical Reason* (1960). A concern for the institutions and other elements of the environment which we as a community share, naturally involved attending to the notion of history and historical revolutions, which destroy and reconfigure the institutions and laws of a society. This in turn led him to an ever more explicit *philosophical* engagement with Marxism – for in terms of his political activity, like so many of his generation in France, he felt compelled to define his relation to the French Communist Party (PCF, *Partie Communiste Française*). At the same time, he will always have persisted with the idea that freedom is free with respect to even the most parlous and restrictive of external conditions – which does not however imply that anything is possible.

This opposition between the free human subject and the external world was described by the early Sartre as the opposition between 'being-for-itself' and 'being-in-itself'. These twin elements of freedom and contingency dictate the ever changing but always original shape of Sartre's own understanding of man and the method of phenomenology with which he strove to achieve it.

Phenomenology and the Empirical Sciences: Sartre's Early Work

9

5

Chapter Outline

Main primary literature

Sketch for a Theory of the Emotions, Introduction, chapter III and Conclusion.
Imagination, chapters 1, 9 and 10.
The Imaginary, part I, chapter I, and Conclusion.

(a) Phenomenology and the empirical sciences: the actuality of consciousness

Sartre may be distinguished from many earlier phenomenologists not only by his interest in literature, theatre, and political and cultural phenomena, but by his intimate concern for the findings of empirical science. In this chapter, we shall attempt to show that one of the most original aspects of his work in phenomenology is his attempt to relate phenomenology and contemporary empirical psychology, which would enjoy a brief influence in phenomenology, in the middle of the twentieth century, largely thanks to Sartre and his colleague, Maurice Merleau-Ponty. This brief and extraordinary attention to the natural sciences may now be thought, after this brilliant excrescence, to have subsided in the most advanced and interesting forms of contemporary phenomenology, but perhaps this will in time be viewed with regret.

Most philosophers address the natural sciences, but for the most part this is only to define philosophy's relation to them in a very general way. This is especially so in the transcendental phenomenological tradition, where, for essential reasons, philosophers do not find it necessary to take account of actual empirical-scientific *results*, the facts that natural science identifies. Sartre, on the other hand, found it absolutely necessary to do so. This has its philosophical foundation in Sartre's insistence that the nature of consciousness is to exist not as a general, non-specific possibility, but only in *particular, contingent, factual* forms. Consciousness itself is defined by the fact that it has no generic characteristics and exists *only* in a multiplicity of particular forms. The only one of these forms to which we have access is *human* consciousness in the form that it takes today, here and now. If one wishes to compose a true account of the human being, it is therefore essential to pay a certain empirical attention to the way man has actually turned out.

While Sartre criticizes Husserl's and Heidegger's understanding of phenomenology, for him it is precisely phenomenology which allows us to see the necessity of this recourse to the sciences: it demonstrates the way in which consciousness is not trapped within its own representations of things, but is *actually related* to *real* things in the world, and since it is always outside of itself in this remarkable way, it is always 'infected' with the contingency of this empirical universe. This is the upshot of Sartre's inheritance of Husserl's concept of 'intentionality', the characteristic that defines consciousness as a reference to an object beyond itself.

It is not only contingency – that with regard to which we are *unfree* – that necessitates the recourse to the sciences and to fiction, it is also man's freedom itself: what a man is cannot be decided in advance of that man's actual existence, because he is free and at liberty to form his life as he chooses.

In his early work, then, Sartre criticizes traditional philosophy and the way this still finds expression in certain aspects of Husserl's phenomenology, for its rigid distinction between transcendental philosophy and empirical science, the concern with essences and the concern with facts. For Sartre, phenomenology in its Husserlian guise was concerned only with the structures of *any possible consciousness*, the *essence* of the transcendental ego. Sartre's contribution to phenomenology is to show that this is insufficient to the very particular nature of consciousness, and what we need to show in addition is how this *possible* consciousness is *actualized* in the case of human beings, and indeed how this *always particular* actualization is part of the most basic nature of consciousness 'as such'.

This is a critique that he later extends to Heidegger, and it explains why he refuses Heidegger's word '*Dasein*' and in a deliberately anti-Heideggerian move – which Heidegger mistook for a simple misunderstanding – returns to the phrase 'human being' or 'human reality' (*la réalité humaine*). This is Sartre's 'humanism'. Heidegger makes many advances on Husserl, and in particular with his assertion that Dasein is always ontologically entwined with a contingent world that is not of its choosing. But for Sartre, Heidegger does not attend to the particular nature *of* this facticity in his descriptions, focusing solely on the *essence* of 'facticity' as such. For Sartre, this is a paradoxical way to approach the factual, since the latter has no essence. All we can do here is to *describe*, and for this we need to have recourse to the empirical sciences, which investigate purely contingent facts which in the end can only be described, not logically deduced, and a recourse to 'fiction'.

Human reality: Henri Corbin's translation of Heidegger's '*Dasein*' in his partial French translation of *Sein und Zeit* from 1937 in an anthology entitled, *Qu'est-ce que la Métaphysique?* with which we must assume Sartre was acquainted, despite his ability to read German reasonably well. Perhaps this would be indicated by the fact that he often places 'human reality' in quotation marks. The phrase indicates in two ways Sartre's stress on the actual, contingent way in which consciousness is instantiated in each case: he is concerned with consciousness as it has come to exist in the *human*, and in his individual *reality* rather than his – or consciousness's – general *possibility*. Thus the term embodies a critique of the transcendental subject, which Sartre discerns even in Heidegger, who hoped he had done away with it.

This means that *a priori* logical reasoning will *not* be able to determine what consciousness is *in the particular case of man*. Husserl had already seen this, which is why for him, unlike Kant, phenomenology is not a study of what *by rights* or *in principle* (*de jure*) belongs to any consciousness whatever, but 'a *de facto* science' with *de facto* problems, and this is why it is ultimately a *descriptive* science (*TE*, 2/15–16). At the point where transcendental consciousness is specified – but strictly speaking it is inseparable from its empirical instantiation – description is the only way to speak of consciousness. We must, 'draw up an inventory of its content in a non-positional way' (*TE*, 7/30).

The profusion of examples which proliferate in Sartre's works suggests that we cannot draw conclusions about the human essence if we do not examine the way in which he actually 'exists'. We shall see when we come to the explicit definition of 'existentialism' that this idea will be incorporated into Sartre's rethinking of the traditional philosophical division between essence and existence.

Sartre describes the idea beautifully at the very end of one of his earliest and most accessible works, *Sketch for a Theory of the Emotions* (1939): 'if phenomenology can prove that emotion is a realisation of the essence of the human-reality in so far as the latter is *affectivity* [affection], it will be impossible for it to show that the human-reality must necessarily manifest itself in *such* emotions as it does [de telles *émotions*]' (*STE*, 64/66). He then continues: 'that these are such and such emotions and not others – this is, beyond all doubt, evidence of the *factitious* character [*la* facticité] of human existence. It is this factitiousness that necessitates a regular recourse to the empirical' (*STE*, 64/66–7). Sartre's very first book had already reached this conclusion: 'It might be that on the way we would have to leave the realm of eidetic psychology and resort to experimentation and inductive procedures' (*Imagination,* 143/159). Empirical sciences study the world as it actually is, they bring to light positive, contingent facts, which a traditional 'transcendental deduction' of the nature of consciousness would – according to Sartre – leave out.

Since Sartre was concerned above all with consciousness, the science which Sartre found most relevant to his study of the human being was one in which he had been well-versed: psychology.

(b) The project of a phenomenological psychology

Sartre's idea was certainly not to *abandon* philosophy in favour of the empirical sciences. One reason for this is that contemporary science, for all its claims to focus purely on the facts as they present themselves in experimentation, shared exactly the same metaphysical presuppositions as a whole philosophical tradition, but in a form that was all the more insidious for being disavowed. Sartre demonstrates this with particular brilliance in his first book, *Imagination* (1936).

Sartre's two earliest works of philosophy – initially intended to be one volume – were concerned with the image. More precisely, they were concerned to indicate the historical prejudices that had perverted the theory of the imagination and the image, and to correct them. The first, *Imagination*, reveals the presuppositions inherited from a long philosophical tradition which had become entrenched and hidden beneath the supposedly non-philosophical pronouncements of contemporary psychology, while the second, *The Imaginary* (*L'Imaginaire*) (1940), presents at great length Sartre's own theory of the image.[1]

In its most basic form, Sartre's theory sets out to refute atomism, along with any materialist understanding of the way the human mind, and in particular the imagination, works. This is an understanding which he finds in Descartes, Leibniz and Hume, and which is then tacitly and perhaps unknowingly inherited by contemporary psychology. Rather than borrowing this atomistic model used by the physical sciences and applying it to consciousness, Sartre uses the peculiar qualities of the imagination to demonstrate that human con-sciousness *cannot* be understood in this 'naturalistic' way: the imagination is governed by its own *sui generis* laws. This for Sartre is crucial if we are to understand human beings, and – for him – the peculiarly human capacity to imagine, which liberates us from the material world and which indeed Sartre might well be said to think of as the origin of our freedom, our capacity to project possibilities beyond the actual and thus 'nihilate' it.

Sartre is one of the first in a long line of twentieth-century philosophers to oppose a 'naturalist' tendency in philosophy, by asserting that there is something specific to the human being which cannot be understood by natural science. He is however among the most interesting since he does not then leave natural science behind.

Sartre believes that this insight into the uniquely different '*being*' of con-sciousness may be gleaned from an attention to Husserl's phenomenology. Phenomenology and empirical psychology are then the two disciplines which must be encouraged to learn from one another, if we are properly to under-stand the human being. This would be to construct a 'phenomenological psychology' (cf. *STE*, 14/19). If psychology deals with empirical facts about human consciousness, what is it that *phenomenology* will bring? For Sartre, it will demonstrate what is *ontologically* or *essentially* different about conscious-ness. The 'being' of consciousness is distinguished from that of the physical world by two characteristics: *intentionality* and *significance*. Both of these are concerned with the way in which purely positive facts, which simply *are* what they *are* and express nothing beyond themselves, in the case of consciousness *refer* to something beyond themselves. Consciousness is a form of *relation*, it refers to things in the world, and it is thanks to this capacity to extend itself that it can understand 'significance' and indeed attribute it to a meaningless, inert, physical world for the very first time. It is only by joining facts together to form a 'totality' or system that the individual parts of that totality acquire a fixed and definite signification. Sartre calls this totality 'the world'.

This is what an attention to the imagination and the imaginary will have allowed Sartre to understand: consciousness would be unable to imagine if it were not intentional. For, as Sartre goes on to show, imagination is itself a form of consciousness in the sense of a relation to an actual world in which there is significance and into which we are plunged by our consciousness.

(c) Phenomenology: intentionality and significance

Sartre wishes to demonstrate that a positivist understanding of man, one which confines individual facts and phenomena purely to themselves, in their positive existence, considering them as they are in themselves – 'being-*in*-itself', Sartre will say – will never understand the ability of consciousness to experience things as *signifying* or 'standing for' something other than themselves. This is precisely what the Husserlian notion of conscious 'intentionality' allows us to understand. It supplements a purely empirical approach to human psychology with a notion of consciousness that depicts the way in which it extends beyond itself, into the world. Consciousness has the capacity to *be* something that it is *not*, and hence its very nature eludes those reductive disciplines which think only in terms of the 'in-itself', of things which are and remain only what they are, which never leave themselves and never return, and hence never relate to anything, even themselves.

This is intentionality; what of significance?

Sartre distinguishes phenomenology from empirical science by stating that the empirical sciences concentrate on *facts*; but these facts suffer from two deficits: they are not linked together in some form of system, and they comprise a potentially infinite series. For Sartre, in order to be *meaningful*, facts need to form a totality, and this totality needs to be finite (*STE*, 2–4/8–9). Thus phenomenology needs to find some centre around which it can organize the facts that empirical science provides, and so to select from a potentially infinite number of such facts and reduce them to a finite totality. This can be achieved by examining the facts themselves *phenomenologically*, which is to say insofar as they *signify*. It can then determine what it is that they refer to, and this 'referent' will act as their organizing centre. Sartre will show that what these psychological facts refer to is the totality of 'human reality' itself. This notion will allow us to select from among a potential infinity of facts those which are relevant to a determination of what the essence of the human psyche actually is.

Indeed, Sartre demonstrates that the scientist is not actually entitled to his avowed lack of interest in such metaphysical questions of essence because his very activity presupposes that such an essence is already known. For instance, if he is describing and classifying various emotions he must have some idea of what emotion *as such* is; *he* must have a principle that allows him to sift the limitless number of facts. Therefore, in order to clarify what the scientist is doing – and for the scientist himself to become clear – the philosopher is entitled to ask questions of essence: not just what the essence of emotion is, but what *essence as such* is, and with such questions he moves definitively beyond the scope of science (*STE*, 6/12). Sartre suggests that science not only presupposes the essence of various different kinds of psychic phenomena, but also involves an implicit idea of the essence of man itself, and it is ultimately this idea that gives to all of the various facets of the human being studied by science their synthetic totality and hence a unified meaning.

In other words, phenomenology takes facts to express something of the *essence*, without which they would refuse to make sense. So already Sartre is troubling the purely transcendental nature of philosophy and the isolation from the empirical which accompanies its fascination with the absolute. Philosophy needs psychology and its facts, but it examines these facts with a view to the essence: 'To the phenomenologist [. . .] every human fact is of its essence significant' (*STE*, 11/16). And the phenomenological goal is to 'find precisely the thing signified [*le signifié*]' (*STE*, 11/16). Thus, 'the phenomenologist will interrogate emotion *about consciousness* or *about man*' (*STE*, 10/15). But we must remember that the opposite is also the case, since Sartre does not propose a one way relation of essence and existent, essence and fact: 'And conversely, he will interrogate consciousness, the human reality, about *emotion*' (*STE*, 11/15, my italics). Thus once again, neither fact nor essence is to be left behind. To acknowledge that science has its own realm and autonomy with respect to philosophy, Sartre insists here that psychology does *not* have to wait for this phenomenology in order to proceed with its experimental work, but – ultimately – it should not simply collect facts, as if psychological phenomena were just 'meaningless' physical events. It should determine their signification, for what characterizes consciousness is that it is capable of spontaneously attributing meaning to facts.[2]

(d) Appearance announces essence

The notion of essence is precisely the province of philosophy, and more particularly, of phenomenological philosophy. Sartre clearly states that phenomenology began with Husserl's distinction of essences and facts, along with the realization that it would be impossible to reach the essence if one began from mere facts, by induction from particulars to generalities (*STE*, 7/12).

What phenomenology alters in the distinction between essence and fact is the quasi-Platonic notion that appearance is the appearance of something beyond appearance, of an essence that does not itself appear in its every aspect, but remains hidden, 'absolute' in the sense of utterly distinct from the *relative* way in which it touches our senses. The phenomenon is itself an 'absolute' for phenomenology. The appearance is the appearing *of* the essence. This is why almost all phenomenologists speak in terms of 'announcement': the phenomenon 'announces' the entity that appears through it. Sartre later on frequently uses the word 'expression'. In *Being and Nothingness*, Sartre states that the phenomenon with which phenomenology deals is not the appearance of anything *else* (*BN*, xlv–vi/11–12); the phenomenon is rather the *announcement* of an entity, and so it is the entity *itself* that appears. In phenomenal appearance the existent does not simply appear, it *announces* the fact that it appears (*STE*, 10/15).

The non-mental object can never present itself all at once in its totality. It is comprised of an infinite series of possible profiles which it can present to consciousness, an infinite number of possible meanings that we are able to attribute to it (*BN*, xlvi-iii/12–16). There will always be some facet of the object that we cannot see. But precisely what distinguishes consciousness is that *here* there is nowhere to hide, because the conscious sphere is fully transparent to itself and hence thoroughly illuminated, and thus all conscious experiences as such display themselves fully to consciousness. This Sartre often insists upon, particularly in his arguments against the psychoanalytic unconscious.

Thus when we reflect on our own emotions, for instance, nothing is hidden from us, and nor is that which these emotions *signify*, which Sartre tells us is man itself, and its intimate relation with the world: emotion 'is that human reality itself, realizing itself in the form of "emotion"' (*STE*, 12/17), and it signifies 'the totality of the relations of the human-reality to the world' (*STE*, 63/66).

Sartre believes that the phenomenology which can illuminate the foundations of psychology would deal with certain fundamental notions which he himself will later elucidate in *Being and Nothingness*: 'man, world, being-in-the-world, and situation'. That text would only appear in 1943, so in 1939, Sartre can say that, 'phenomenology is hardly born as yet' (*STE*, 13/17).

What sets a phenomenological (or 'eidetic'[3]) psychology apart from *phenomenology as such* is that the former focuses on a single determinate region and examines the particular *way* in which it signifies the totality of human reality, while the latter focuses on human reality as such – 'the totality of man' (*STE*, 13/17), on *what* is signified by these conscious facts, not from any one particular point of view, such as emotion, but for itself. This is what Sartre will carry out most thoroughly in the 'phenomenological *ontology*' that is *Being and Nothingness*. So we might say that, in terms of the back and forth exchange between philosophy and science, we are here on the side of science, psychology in this case, – the faculties of the imagination and the emotions – which must be illuminated by philosophy in order to become an *eidetic* science, studying the significance of facts – *still focusing on facts*, but *in* their signifying capacity (*STE*, 14/18). Phenomenology will focus on *what* these facts signify, and thus approaches the confluence between facts and essence from the point of view of essence.

Further reading

Sartre, Jean-Paul (1967), *Imagination: A Psychological Critique*. Trans. with an introduction by Forrest Williams. Ann Arbor: University of Michigan Press, chapters IX & X.

—(2002), *Sketch for a Theory of the Emotions*. Trans. Philip Mairet. Preface by Mary Warnock. Routledge Classics. London and New York: Routledge. (First published by London: Methuen and Co., 1962, Routledge: 1994.)

—(2004), *The Imaginary: A Phenomenological Psychology of the Imagination*. Revised with a historical introduction by Arlette Elkaïm-Sartre. Trans. with a philosophical introduction by Jonathan Webber. London and New York: Routledge, pp. 179–87.

Cumming, Robert (1992), 'Role-playing: Sartre's transformation of Husserl's Phenomenology' in *The Cambridge Companion to Sartre*. Ed. Christina Howells. Cambridge: Cambridge University Press.

10 Self-consciousness and Intentionality

Main primary literature

'Intentionality'.
Transcendence of the Ego, part I.
Being and Nothingness, part II, chapter 1.

(a) Intentional consciousness and its immediate self-relation

What Sartre next comes to investigate, and what forms a bridge between his earliest works and the work of his middle period in *Being and Nothingness*, is a certain feature of intentionality which we have not yet brought to light, and this is the way in which all intentional consciousness is minimally *self-related*. This comes clearly to the fore in Sartre's earliest essay, 'The Transcendence of the Ego' (1936–7). Here he begins his attempt to eradicate what he describes as a misunderstanding of the relation that consciousness has to itself, by demonstrating that the ego itself, which we might have thought to be identical with the self-conscious subject, is in fact a *product* that only arises through the process of reflection: before consciousness is reflected upon, there is in it strictly speaking no 'ego', no 'I'. In that case, something other than the ego must be carrying out this reflection, and it is this 'something' that Sartre proposes to investigate. In the first place, when we are experiencing the world, for the most part – this is particularly apparent in the case of infants – there is no reflection, and hence no ego. Nevertheless, in order for such reflection to be possible, consciousness must already have a reflexive relation to itself, which Sartre will call 'the pre-reflective *cogito*'.

The 'world' for Sartre is a totality of interrelated entities all of which are endowed with significance. A mere collection of isolated entities cannot be said to warrant the title 'world'. The world is that which is experienced by intentional consciousness. Now we need to understand how consciousness nevertheless experiences *itself in* its experience of the world, and it is not by simply folding back on itself in explicit reflection, by an effort of will.

In *Transcendence of the Ego*, Sartre contrasts his approach to Kant's statement in the *Critique of Pure Reason* that in order for experience to *be* experience it must be unified by an 'I', an '*ego*': it can be said to constitute a single unified experience only *because* each component part of it, each aspect, can be said to belong to *me* (*TE*, 1/13–14). For Kant, the question of how a unified field of consciousness is synthesized is a *de jure* question, a question of right or principle: Kant asks how any consciousness at all must be constituted in order to enjoy an *objective* experience. But Sartre wishes to ask a *de facto* question, a question of fact. How *in fact* is this generic consciousness *actually* instantiated in human beings? 'Kant never bothered about the way in which empirical consciousness is *de facto* constituted' (*TE*, 2/15). While it may need to be possible for the 'I' to accompany each of our 'representations', Sartre asks whether in *fact* in most cases it actually *does*.

Sartre applies the same critique to Husserl, but in a different way. The transcendental reduction was supposed to eradicate all empirical worldliness and contingency from the consciousness that is examining itself through self-reflection, but for Sartre, 'the phenomenological reduction is never perfect' (*TE*, 42/73). This is a consequence of Sartre's 'realist' understanding of intentionality as consciousness's projecting itself *beyond* itself and into the world of contingency and factual existence (*Intentionality*, 382–3/32–4). Sartre sees in Husserl's notion the proof that consciousness opens directly onto an outside, and indeed that it *is* this opening, for it has no interior space of representations which would be akin to a 'cabinet' where consciousness would store the trace of the impressions that the outside has made upon its surface. Sartre then takes Husserl's notion to what he believes to be its logical conclusion, while Husserl himself, in 1913, developed it in an 'idealist' way. So, for Sartre, the concept of intentionality shows that we cannot simply describe consciousness in its reflective isolation from the world, because consciousness is always consciousness *of* factical, contingent things, and hence this facticity infects the essence of consciousness itself, and it will always already have done so.

(b) The impersonal field of consciousness

Sartre agrees with Husserl that the empirical 'me' – the 'psychological ego' – is not a subject but an *object*, something that exists in the world, and which forms the topic of empirical psychology. This means that it is something which must be explicitly *posited* by consciousness in order to exist at all. 'Positing', the setting before oneself of an object, is precisely what a scientific, theoretical or reflective kind of consciousness does: 'the *me* appears only with the reflective act, as the noematic correlative of a reflective intention' (*TE*, 20/43).

While Husserl and Kant believed that the only way the field of consciousness could be unified was through the constituting activity of a transcendental subject which would transcend that field, Sartre shows that in fact the empirical field of consciousness is sufficiently unified *without* such transcendent intervention. Therefore we can understand this unification *without appealing to anything beyond this immanent field itself* (*TE*, 5/23). Consciousness would then be something like a self-organizing field, eschewing any reference to a transcendent principle that would organize it.[4] '*[A]ll transcendence* must fall under the scope of the *epochē*' (*TE*, 8/34), and that includes the transcendental ego or – in Kant's terms – the transcendental unity of apperception itself. Ultimately, Sartre wishes to explain this unity of consciousness in terms of time, and perhaps one can conjecture that it is the temporal endurance of a single selfsame object which allows one single finite field of consciousness to persist as the same: 'It is consciousness that unifies *itself*, concretely, by the interplay of "transversal" consciousnesses that are real, concrete retentions of past consciousnesses' (*TE*, 4/22).

Sartre wishes to say that there is no need for this recourse in order to unify a field of experience. Ultimately, the reason why we can, upon reflection, eventually apply the pronoun 'I' to our experiences is *because* they are *already* unified, and unified by an object that is really out there, beyond the field of consciousness itself, 'trans-phenomenal' as Sartre will say a few years later. But this does not mean that we are speaking of some cosmic or divine consciousness that would be undifferentiated and without location or individuality. Each particular field *is* distinct from any other consciousness, and so 'mine' is a different consciousness to 'yours', 'an *individuated* and *impersonal* spontaneity' (*TE*, 46/78, my italics). But what explains this unity is intentionality, consciousness's directedness to a real unified *object*, the object is what gives to experience its unity: 'it becomes conscious of itself *insofar as it is consciousness of a transcendent object*' (*TE*, 4/22). We may therefore say that it is Sartre's original 'realism' about the world outside of consciousness that allows him to understand consciousness as unified without the help of any transcendental agency, such as the 'ego'.

We now need to examine the intentional nature of consciousness in order to understand in what sense it may be said to be 'self-conscious'.

(c) Consciousness as non-thetically self-conscious

The philosophical and scientific tradition has, for Sartre, understood consciousness's relation to itself as primarily epistemic, a reflective self-knowing, analogous to a subject's relation to an *object*. To refute this primacy, Sartre indicates certain strange and extreme situations where this notion of consciousness *demonstrably* does not apply, as for instance in the case of emotions and the imaginative relation to the world. For Sartre, emotions, like the image, are themselves a form of consciousness, and consciousness is intentional, it stretches beyond itself to refer to the world. Sartre criticizes psychologists for believing that the primary form of consciousness is a 'thetic' or 'positional' consciousness, 'thesis' being the Greek word for a 'positing'. Here again they show themselves to labour under a properly philosophical prejudice, in this case, the *epistemological* prejudice, the idea that our primary access to the world is one of *knowing*. What a phenomenological description of emotion shows is that emotions *are* a basic form of consciousness but *can not* be understood in this way, and cannot adequately be described as reflective, since they are merely forms of openness or 'dis-closure'. And yet, for Sartre, they show that while it is not explicitly self-conscious, consciousness by its very nature has a certain relation to itself, one which *makes possible* the explicit self-contemplation of reflection. There are forms of consciousness (imagination, emotion) that can not be understood as first of all thetic or epistemic, and yet they must have some form of self-relation. Sartre calls this a *non-reflective* or non-positional self-consciousness: 'every positional consciousness of an object is at the same time a non-positional consciousness of itself' (*BN*, liii/19).

Once one ceases to think of consciousness as primarily theoretical, which is to say as consciousness of an object, one can begin to understand consciousness's self-relation in a more appropriate way, according to which the consciousness reflected-on is *not* reduced to a separate object, with a theoretical consciousness reflecting *upon* it (cf. *TE*, 10/35–6). Sartre wants to guard against the splitting of consciousness into two consciousnesses: this is the way of knowledge, which splits everything into subject and object, a 'first order' consciousness and a 'second order' consciousness reflecting on the first. We suffer, Sartre tells us from 'the illusion of the primacy of knowledge [*connaissance*]' (*BN*, liii/18), which makes us think that 'consciousness of consciousness' is a 'knowledge of knowledge [*une connaissance de connaissance*]' (*BN*, liii/18).

Sartre tries to describe the experience of consciousness in which it is entirely absorbed in what it is doing, without returning to the reflective plane or being explicitly conscious that its action is one that *I* am producing. 'The self does not appear at all in this' (*STE*, 38/41).

If a field of consciousness relates to itself, but not in the way of self-*knowledge*, then it becomes inaccurate to describe this particular experience with statements of the form, 'I think . . .' or 'I experience . . . (this or that)': 'there is no I on the unreflected level' (*TE*, 17/32). This is why Sartre describes consciousness as in the first place 'impersonal'. It is impersonal in the sense that the person pronoun 'I' cannot truly be applied to every experience, in fact, even if *by rights*, as Kant states, 'I think' should be able to accompany all my experiences.

This non-thetic nature of self-consciousness means that our conscious experience of objects will be falsified if it is expressed in philosophical '*theses*' of the propositional kind, '*S is p*'. Hence more experimental styles of writing are required, even of *philosophical* writing, hence the intrusion of dramatized examples *in* the philosophical text itself.

Everything that one can say, if indeed any such explicit, positive statements are appropriate at all, will take the form of a *passive* construction: '*There is* this conscious experience taking place at this moment' (cf. *TE*, 16–17/32). But, slightly more naturally, one experiences and expresses this passivity in terms of the properties of *objects*. This is the meaning of Sartre's frequent statements to the effect that we do not encounter the world and at the same time experience the reflective proposition 'I hate this', for example; we encounter the world *as* hateful (*Intentionality*: 383/34).

Consciousness does not, either at the time or later, in some temporary respite from practical action, become theoretical and turn back upon itself. It *is* conscious of itself, but not in a way that remains distinct from the action, withdrawn from the world: rather it is conscious of itself *out there in the world*. In other words, consciousness finds itself *in* the intentional relation itself. '[U]nreflective conduct is not unconscious conduct. It is non-thetically conscious of self'. Its way of being conscious of itself is 'to transcend and apprehend itself out in the world as a quality of things' (*STE*, 38/42). 'This self-consciousness we ought to consider not as a new consciousness, but as the *only mode of existence which is possible for a consciousness of something*' (*BN*, liv/20).

(d) Consciousness's consciousness

Consciousness is conscious, as Sartre never tires of repeating. What does this only apparent tautology mean? It means that the conscious awareness of an object would not *be* conscious if it were not *aware* that it was aware. In *Transcendence of the Ego*, Sartre seems to say that this is simply part of the very definition of consciousness: it is an awareness, and if it is not aware of itself as awareness then it is not aware at all. This suggestion is present in *Being and Nothingness* as well, but here he is quite explicit that this is simply a matter of logic: 'all knowing consciousness can be knowledge only of its object' (*BN*, lii/18). But it is a necessary and sufficient conditions of this 'that it [consciousness] be consciousness of itself as being that knowledge' (ibid.). Sartre immediately goes on to describe the idea of a consciousness that does not know itself to be conscious as simply 'absurd' (ibid.), an *unconscious* consciousness simply does not make conceptual sense: taking as his example once again a non-epistemic form of consciousness, Sartre states that, '[p]leasure can not be distinguished – even logically – from consciousness of pleasure' (*BN*, liv/21).

Perhaps, then, we can only describe this relation, and have no need to prove its existence, if it is simply a part of the very definition of consciousness.

In fact, as we shall see in the next chapter, Sartre later went beyond this and demonstrated the necessity – or at least the nature – of this self-relation in the form of its underlying *ontology*. Thus he will come to describe precisely what it means to be self-conscious in this way, with his notion of 'being-for-itself'. 'The law of being of the *for-itself*, as the ontological foundation of consciousness, is to be itself in the form of presence to itself' (*BN*, 77/115).

Sartre speaks then of a *pre*-reflective 'I think' or '*cogito*', a word which in Latin needs no explicit pronoun (*ego*), since its very grammatical form tells us that it is meant in the first person singular. It is a self-consciousness without 'ego'. Sartre attempts to show how this non-explicit self-consciousness is the condition of possibility for reflection and the reflective self-relation of the theoretical kind which he identifies with *Descartes*' '*cogito*'. This is why he refuses to say even that consciousness *relates* to itself or *refers* to itself, since this would imply a prior separation.

Only by positing such an unreflective self-consciousness can one halt the infinite regress of consciousnesses (the consciousness that is conscious of the first consciousness itself needs its own superordinate self-consciousness, and so on to infinity):

> In fact, all reflecting consciousness is in itself unreflected, and a new, third-order act is needed to posit it. Moreover, there is no infinite regress here, since a consciousness has no need of a reflecting consciousness in order to be conscious of itself. It merely does not posit itself to itself as its own object. (*TE*, 6/29)

In this way, Sartre accepts the thrust of the Heideggerian critique of a self-enclosed sphere of reflective, transcendental subjectivity, and yet retains a certain conception of self-'consciousness' or self-relation, which Heidegger will perhaps have left behind (cf. *BN*, 73/111, 85/123–4). Contrary to the latter's notion of ecstatic being-in-the-world, for Sartre the subject is *not* 'all outside', which would be to take intentionality to its extreme limit as a directedness or projection into a world *without remainder*, while in fact, consciousness is of necessity *still* self-related. But this self-relation has to be understood in a particular way, and indeed it is in this that Sartre sets himself apart from later post-Heideggerian thinkers such as Jacques Derrida who precisely attempt to criticize traditional understandings of consciousness for assuming that one can simply posit such a self-proximity without demonstrating how it comes about. Sartre on the other hand speaks quite openly of 'the absolute proximity of consciousness to itself' (*STE*, 8/13).[5] What protects

Sartre from the Derridean critique, which is at the same time very close to Heidegger's, is that for Sartre this self-relation need not be understood along the lines of the signifying relation of reference, as it is for Derrida. Indeed, it is prior to this and constitutes its very precondition.

Further reading

Bernasconi, Robert (2006), *How to Read Sartre*. London: Granta.

Howells, Christina (ed.) (1992), *Cambridge Companion to Sartre*. Cambridge: Cambridge University Press. 'Conclusion: Sartre and the deconstruction of the subject'.

Existentialism

Chapter Outline

Main primary literature

Heidegger, *Being and Time*, pp. 68–71.
Sartre, 'Existentialism is a Humanism'.

Without too much exaggeration, we might say that of the two poles between which Sartre's thought unfolds, the early work focuses on the contingent significance of the inert material environment into which man is thrown; the middle period, which we shall address here under the heading of 'existentialism', without leaving contingency behind, concentrates on freedom. (Although we shall not ultimately deal with it here, the later work might be said to 'sublate' the two and finally attain something like a balance.) At the same time, the relation between philosophy and science seems to be synthesized into a totality in which philosophy and *fiction* merge into one.

(a) Essence and existence: technical objects and humans

There are too many stereotypes and misunderstandings surrounding existentialism for us to have time to work through them patiently, so let us proceed directly to its definition. We shall go no further in Sartre's thought, simply because the doctrine that is existentialism is a consequence of Sartre's ontology, which he describes in the subtitle to *Being and Nothingness* as 'phenomenological', and it is directly related to our theme in that it provides the ontological foundations for the innovations in phenomenological method that we have analysed above.

Sartre describes existentialism as 'of all teachings the least scandalous and the most austere: it is intended strictly for technicians and philosophers' (*EH*, 289/16). It is to be understood in contrast with '*essential*ism', the doctrine that asserts the existence of timeless, generic essences for certain types of entity.

Thus in terms of the traditional, metaphysical differentiation of essence and existence, this is to focus on the world of existence, and indeed to posit that it is in some ways prior to the world of essence. Indeed, one of the great tenets of 'existentialism' is that the way existence actually turns out in fact *shapes* the world of essence. Human life does not need to unfold according to some pre-conceived notion of what man is, – his essence – it simply unfolds according to the contingency of the facts of its world and the free choices man makes in light of those facts.

Sartre describes existentialism as the belief that, in the case of the human being, 'its essence [. . .] precedes its existence' (*EH*, 289/17). This in turn is more or less a quotation from the opening pages of Heidegger's *Being and Time* (*BT*, 67/42), Heidegger being one of the 'atheist existentialists' whom Sartre identifies along with himself and – implicitly – Albert Camus, at least, in contrast to 'the Christian Existentialists', Gabriel Marcel and Karl Jaspers.

He then produces a superb explanation of what existentialism means by comparing and contrasting the human being with an object produced by human art (*technē*), the manufactured thing. In order to be produced, the 'artefact' requires two things to exist in advance: a *concept* of the final product, and an understanding of the *technique* needed to produce it – in other words, the *theoretical* knowledge and the *practical* know-how. Sartre also appears to identify the concept of a thing with its purpose: to know what something *is* is to know what it can be used *for,* or what it can *do.* The concept and the technique, the end (but also the end of the end, the ultimate purpose) and the means, constitute the 'essence' of the thing: 'the sum of the formulae and the qualities which made its production and its definition possible' (*EH,* 289–90/18).

Now, this seems to be an adequate understanding of a technical object, but if we understand *man* in that way, it can only be because we are – if only implicitly – presuming a creator *god* who made man along the same lines as the artisan makes the artefact. God has the idea and the technical know-how, and he makes man. Even when atheism predominates in philosophy, this conception still holds: man has a pre-existing essence, only it is not an idea in the mind of god but a certain universal 'human nature'. In either case, theist or atheist, 'each man is a particular example of a universal conception' *(EH, 290/20)*, and he has a single ultimate goal or purpose, fixed in advance, merely waiting to be discovered and achieved.

If we truly believe that this kind of God does not exist (the so called 'God of the philosophers' (Pascal), which is to say God as it is understood by metaphysicians, as the efficient cause of man), we must infer that 'there is at least one being whose existence comes before its essence, a being which exists before it can be defined by any conception of it' *(EH, 290/21)*. And this is man. Sartre's text is not quite unambiguous with regard to the question of whether we should extend this notion to other entities, particularly natural entities, which were formerly thought to be just as much a part of god's creation as man.

Each individual instance of man exists unconstrained by a pre-established essence that dictates what he will be, what man's ultimate purpose as a species truly is: 'man is still to be determined' *(EH, 310/92)*. Man is precisely an entity which has the potentiality and thus the freedom to become whatever he chooses: 'to begin with he is nothing [...] he will be what he makes of himself' *(EH, 290/22)*. But unlike god, who has infinite possibilities, Sartre makes it clear that in the case of man, due to his finitude, his situatedness in an environment which he is unable to choose for it will always have preceded his immersion in it, the choice of what to make of oneself is nothing like the magical fulfilment of a desire, as if anything we wish for might come true.

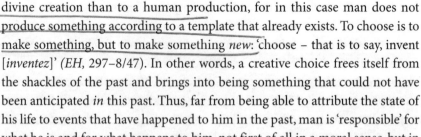

However, there is a crucial way in which man's act is more akin to a divine creation than to a human production, for in this case man does not produce something according to a template that already exists. To choose is to make something, but to make something *new*: 'choose – that is to say, invent [*inventez*]' *(EH, 297–8/47)*. In other words, a creative choice frees itself from the shackles of the past and brings into being something that could not have been anticipated *in* this past. Thus, far from being able to attribute the state of his life to events that have happened to him in the past, man is 'responsible' for what he is and for what happens to him, not first of all in a moral sense, but in the sense that he is the origin of what he is, as god the artisan is responsible for his creation. Sartre is quite explicit in connecting the human being's act of self-creation not with artisanship but with another kind of *technē*, 'art': 'the moral choice is comparable to a work of art' *(EH, 305/75)*. 'There is this in common between art and morality, that in both we have to do with creation and invention' (*EH*, 306/77). And what is created is ultimately a *value*, something that man *ought* to be (cf. *BN*, 84ff./127ff.).

So a decision is an *act*: 'there is no reality except in action' (*EH*, 300/55) and since man makes himself through these decisive acts, 'he is therefore nothing else but the sum of his actions' (ibid.). This explains why choice is nothing like a wish: a free choice is an act, not necessarily a physical act in the world, but an act of *projection*, the free projection of a value and a future in which our acts will be guided by the attempt to realize this value.

So this choice to be a certain kind of being is for Sartre an evaluative choice. It attributes a certain value to that which we choose to be. If it is a valuable thing to be, it becomes more than just a simple subjective 'preference' or desire, it must be something that we believe *others* ought to be. So from the very start, far from being *simply* 'individualist', existentialism involves a collective project (cf. *EH*, 292/26–7). Sartre will stress this much more clearly in his later work, for there is a sense in which Sartre's work at the time of *Being and Nothingness* is an ontology which demonstrates the *essential individuality* of man. In *essence* man is an individual, and not a type.

The choice of our individuality is without a ground, in the sense that it would not be a free choice if it were *caused* by some preceding entity or event. And this groundlessness of decision, which is precisely the necessary condition for anything that may properly be called a 'decision', is what makes man capable of anxiety (*angoisse* or 'anguish') (cf. *EH* 292–4/27–36). Precisely by putting its past out of play in making its free decision about the future, consciousness deprives itself of any *basis* for its decision, and as Kierkegaard and Heidegger have attempted to show, the experience of groundlessness is the experience of anxiety, in which for Sartre we actually and undeniably experience our freedom (*BN*, 28/63–4).

Sartre speaks of consciousness's *bracketing* the past, in the manner of a phenomenological *epochē*, and thus being allowed to initiate an action which is unconstrained by it (*BN*, 27/63). This 'denial' of the world is a necessary condition of freedom: in order to be free, consciousness must first extricate itself from the clutches of the past, for only then will it be free to 'surge' forward into its projected future, 'as being both this past and this future and as not being them' (*BN*, 29/64). Sartre indeed often uses this word to describe consciousness's 'arising' into the world: an *upsurge* (*surgissement*), a wave that engulfs and washes over the rocks. But at the same time this remains dependent on freedom's captor, which it uses precisely as a launching pad for its projectile.

This idea of a transcendent value, a 'good' that has inherent value, beyond and before any choice is made to pursue and value it, vanishes with the death of god. Sartre quotes Dostoyevsky: "'If God did not exist, everything would be permitted'; and that, for existentialism, is the starting point' (*EH*, 294–5/36). 'Existentialism is nothing else but an attempt to draw the full conclusions from a consistently atheistic position' (*EH*, 310/94).

Sartre thus suggests that 'existence' also has the more Heideggerian sense of being projected into the future. This is where man is free after all, not in what has happened to him in the past, which is over and done with, but in what is to come, and at the same time how this past is *viewed*, and this changes depending on the particular future that he wishes to have: it can be an obstacle or a challenge. Certainly man is constrained by his situation, but there is no circumstance in which he will not be free to make a choice, which then affects the *light* in which this circumstance appears, its very *meaning* is altered, and as we know, for a phenomenologist, appearance and meaning, however insubstantial, are not nothing.

For Sartre, as long as one is alive, one will always at least be able to choose to die rather than put up with the events one is living through. Indeed, he describes this as the highest form of freedom, the very most basic kind (*Situations III*, 3, cf. *BN*, 525/607–8). Thus, circumstances, while absolutely relevant to our choice, can never utterly stifle freedom, indeed the harsher and more constraining they become, the more extreme are the choices that face us: 'every human purpose presents itself as an attempt either to surpass these limitations, or to widen them, or else to deny or to accommodate oneself to them' (*EH*, 304/69).

Existentialism: the doctrine that there is no generic essence of man. The nature of man's existence is freely decided by the individual entity as he or she develops. Hence 'existence precedes essence'. Sartre contrasts man with the products of the artisan, a model which is frequently but tacitly applied to man when we understand God to be his creator, moulding man out of raw clay, along the same lines as the artisan, who has both a theoretical knowledge of the ideal model or template and a practical knowledge of the technique that will actualize this potential in some appropriate matter. If anything, this role of creator and artisan is to be taken on by the individual himself, in the absence of god and the consequent lack of any ideal archetypes for human existence.

Further reading

Birchall, Ian (2004), *Sartre against Stalinism*. New York, Oxford: Berghahn Books.

Flynn, Thomas (1984), *Sartre's Marxist Existentialism*. Chicago: University of Chicago Press.

McBride, William (1991), *Sartre's Political Theory*. Indianapolis: Indiana University Press.

Sartre, Jean-Paul (1957), *Being and Nothingness: An Essay on Phenomenological Ontology*. Trans. Hazel Barnes. New York: Methuen, part IV, chapter 1, especially section 'I'.

12 The Ontology of Existentialism

Main primary literature

Being and Nothingness, Introduction.

(a) Being-in-itself and being-for-itself

What is the justification for Sartre's assertions concerning the existential nature of man in 'Existentialism is a Humanism'? We find the answer in his 'essay in phenomenological ontology', *Being and Nothingness* from 1943.

Here it becomes clear that for Sartre consciousness is the defining feature of the human being whom he spoke of in his – chronologically later – piece, 'Existentialism is a Humanism'. After quoting Heidegger, Sartre states that

> consciousness is not produced as a particular instance of an abstract possibility but that in rising to the centre of being, it creates and supports its essence – that is, the synthetic order of its possibilities [. . .] Since consciousness is not *possible* before being, but since its being is the source and condition of all possibility, its existence implies its essence. (*BN*, lv/21)

The primary ontological distinction, which splits the notion of 'being in general' in two, lies between being-in-itself (*être-pour-soi*), and being-for-itself (*être-en-soi*). This distinction appears on the first page of Sartre's very first book, *Imagination,* from 1936, and so was clearly of foundational importance to him. It might roughly be equated with the distinction that we have suggested to be crucial to Sartre's thought, between the contingent material world and the free self-consciousness of man (cf. *EH*, 303/65–6).

> ***Being-for-itself and being-in-itself****:* consciousness and the non-conscious. Being-in-itself is non-relational and has none of the oppositional qualities that language and man's consciousness apply to things: it is neither possible nor necessary, neither active nor passive, it simply *is* what it *is*, but without even the self-relation of an entity that would be 'self-identical', which is to say governed by the principle of identity, 'A=A'. This implies that an entity would already have left itself, in order then to return to itself, to become equal or co-extensive with itself. Only the for-itself does this and thus enjoys a minimal self-relation, which Sartre calls 'the pre-reflective cogito'. It is clear that Sartre thought that this opposition was posited by the for-itself rather than being one which simply applied to reality in itself, splitting it in two after the fashion of Descartes, and indeed he is concerned precisely with finding those extraordinary moments when the two come into contact, relate and mix.

Sartre states that his reason for writing a book that entwines 'Being and Nothingness' (which we may identify with being-in-itself and being-for-itself, respectively) is to answer the following questions: 'For what reasons do they both belong to *being* in general? What is the meaning of that being which includes within itself these two radically separate regions of being? [. . .] these regions which *in theory* are without communication' (*BN*, lxvii/34, cf. *BN*, lxiii/31). Thus Sartre immediately problematizes his only apparently Cartesian division and spends the rest of *Being and Nothingness* trying to heal it. Sartre suggests that while the two are in theory, by rights, without communication, *in fact* they find themselves related in various crucial phenomena, and it is precisely these factual situations that will be described in the book. It seems that, given the factual nature of this connection, they must be the subject of description *alone*, perhaps not even (inductive or deductive) argument, but mere *description*.

At the same time, the way in which the two relate will tell us everything about *man*'s basic nature, which involves an essential relation to others, and to things outside of him: 'the relations of the for-itself with the in-itself [...] are constitutive of the very being of the for-itself' (*BN*, 172/220). Sartre's book is largely comprised of examples of precisely such intertwinings: his famous examples of 'bad faith' (*la mauvaise foi*), in which we attempt to substantialize what we are and effectively deny our freedom by rendering it substantial or 'in-itself', and our finding ourselves petrified by the gaze of the other, in which our freedom and our situation are objectified, indicate the way in which the human being is precisely the *juncture* of being and nothingness, being-in-itself and being-for-itself, and hence the very focus of Sartre's book.

To express their relationship Sartre invokes the rhetorical trope known as the 'chiasm', based on the graphical form of the Greek letter *khi*, χ, in which one reverses the order of corresponding words as one repeats them, thus being-in-itself is 'the *being* of the phenomenon', while being-for-itself is the '*phenomenon* of being'. The former is the unknowable materiality of things and the latter is 'the pre-reflective cogito' to which any significant appearance must manifest itself (cf. *BN,* xlviii–l/14–16).

But this presentation risks suggesting that we are speaking here of the opposition between subject and object, and precisely what Sartre thinks phenomenology has overcome is this Kantian dualism of a transcendental ego and a thing-in-itself that never appears as such. Rather, phenomenology shows that consciousness *is* a direct relation to the thing itself, which announces or expresses itself to consciousness through one of its aspects. What distinguishes phenomenological consciousness from the intellectual intuition which Kant allowed only to God, is that nevertheless this experience is limited. It is limited to a certain point of view and a certain period in time. The objects of consciousness are thus both directly accessible to consciousness in the aspects that appear to consciousness, but also escape it in the sense that the series of aspects which they display is *infinite*, and finite consciousness is quite unable to intuit an infinity. It is precisely this totality of possible appearances that can be said to be what the object itself *is*. It is the *being* of the phenomenon, what that phenomenal object really *is*; and yet this being, while always displaying itself through the phenomenal aspects of the object, *never* appears in its totality. This is why Sartre states that the being of the phenomenon is not a noumenal entity but 'transphenomenal', taking the word '*trans-*' to mean both 'beyond' and 'across' or 'throughout' (*BN*, l/16). The being of an object is never fully captured by any one phenomenon, but, at the same time, in itself it is nothing that is *not* phenomenal. Every single aspect of the object *can* appear, but it can *not* appear *all at once*.

Nevertheless, Sartre distinguishes the transphenomenality of objects from another transphenomenality, the transphenomenality of consciousness. His intention here is to avoid idealism with respect to consciousness, by showing that consciousness does not even found itself, let alone the beings that lie outside of it.

For Sartre, the 'being' of an entity is its 'transcendental' condition, it is what makes it possible, what *allows* it to be such as it is (*BN*, xlix/15–16). Sartre opposes idealism by insisting that something must *be* before it can be *known*. So there is no sense in which consciousness decides *what* a thing is; rather, it is precisely limited in the number and range of appearances which it can apprehend: the object will always be *more* than consciousness conceives it to be. Sartre encapsulates the idealism he is here countering with Berkeley's phrase *esse est percipi*, to be is to be perceived and to be *as* it is perceived, an idealistic deviation which Husserl himself had authorized for phenomenology, and which Sartre found it necessary to resist. The invocation of this phrase 'in itself' then describes the (non-metaphysical)[6] *realism* of Sartre's phenomenology: 'The *esse* of the phenomenon can not be its *percipi*. The transphenomenal being of consciousness can not provide a basis for the transphenomenal being of the phenomenon' (*BN*, lx/27). 'The transphenomenal being of what exists *for consciousness* is itself *in itself* (*BN*, lxii/29).

(b) Being-in-itself is, being-for-itself is what it is not

Being-in-itself may properly be called *being*, it can rightly be said to *be*, since it simply is what it is (*BN*, lxvi/33). While being-for-itself *cannot* be said to be, for as Sartre curiously describes it, it *is* what it is *not*. This is a consequence first of all of the intentional nature of consciousness, in that it has the capacity to refer beyond itself to a non-conscious reality. If Sartre calls this the 'phenomenon of being', it must be because he sees this extension beyond oneself as the very condition of possibility for phenomenality. This would mean that the intentional directedness of consciousness and hence a relation between two entities, one of which exceeds itself and so opens itself up to this other thing, would be needed in order for anything at all to appear.

If being-for-itself, the being of consciousness, is pure relationality, being-in-itself is nothing of the kind, it is not defined by being differentiated from any other thing, by being related to what it is *not*: 'it can encompass no negation. It is full positivity. It knows no otherness; it never posits itself as other-than-another-being [*autre qu'un autre être*]' (*BN*, lxvi/33–4).[7] There is no reference or relationality of any kind in the in-itself, not even to the minimal extent of a pre-reflexive *self*-relation:

> [W]e should not call it 'immanence', for immanence in spite of all connection with self is still that very slight withdrawal which can be realised – away from the self. But being is not a connection with itself [*rapport à soi*]. It is *itself*. [. . .] if being is in itself, this means that it does not refer to itself as self-consciousness does. [. . .] That is why being is at bottom beyond the *self*, and the first formula ['being-in-itself'] can be only an approximation due to the requirements of language. (*BN*, lxv/32–3)

Due to this lack of relation, the in-itself is *contingent*, for there is no way to *derive* its existence from anything beyond itself (*BN*, lxvi/34). If it has no relation to anything, nothing can even make it *possible*, let alone necessary: 'the possible is a structure of the *for-itself*' (*BN*, lxvi/34). It is not even linked to itself and so it is not self-causing or even immanent to itself. This is the meaning of Antoine Roquentin's sickness in *Nausea*, Sartre's most accessible novel, in which he has the feeling that his consciousness is being invaded by the contingency of being-in-itself.

The in-itself is superfluous (*de trop*), and absurd (cf. *BN*, 479/558), since it is without reason. This is what is unbearable about it.

(c) Being-for-itself and self-relation: the nihilation of the actual in favour of the possible

We have said that being-for-itself is the ecstatic relation that consciousness has to the things of the world. But this would not yet explain why it is described in its very being as 'for *itself*'. The for-itself that is 'pre-reflexive self-conscious-ness' is a certain kind of self-relation, and in this self-relation the 'for-itself' relates to itself in the form of what it *might be* but *is not*. Sartre names this reflexive motion the 'circuit of selfness [*ipséité*]' (*BN*, 102/147). In fact, this reflex returns to an endpoint that is *different* from its point of departure. What it returns to is not its *actual* self, for only the *in-*itself might be said to be actual. When consciousness relates to itself, it cannot therefore be in the way that a being-in-itself relates to another entity of the same kind, for what it relates to are its *possibilities*; man is 'a being which is for itself in its own possibility' (*BN*, 98/143). And since possibilities are currently *not* actual, what it relates to is something it 'is *not*'; it relates to the future (cf. *BN*, 104ff./149ff.). Being-in-itself is what it is, it cannot have potentiality, for that would be to relate to something else, that it might have been or might become in the *future*: 'The in-itself is actuality' (*BN*, 98/143).

Human existence in its self-relation is thus a relation to the future, projecting into the future a value and a project that tends towards this value (cf. *BN*, 96/135). Thus human existence is a free projection of possibilities, and the self-relation of the self, the way in which it is *for* itself, is constituted by its turning towards its own futural possibilities. Thus there is no contradiction between consciousness's relating to itself and yet *not* being itself, for it relates to itself in its non-actual futural possibilities: 'to be its own possibility [. . .] is precisely to be defined by that part of itself which it is not' (*BN*, 100/144).

And yet, the human subject's folding back on itself is not a return to a purely transcendental subject that has separated itself from the world. The return first leaves itself and returns to itself *via* the world in which it finds itself. So one's understanding of what one is, by means of a fundamental futural project and value, is never independent of the world in which one is contingently placed. The possibilities that one conceives oneself to *be* are drawn *from* the world. Thus the possibilities appropriated by the for-itself are circumscribed by the world in which it finds itself:

> the For-itself is separated from the Presence-to-itself which it lacks and which is its own possibility, in one sense separated by *Nothing* [Rien] and in another sense by the totality of the existent in the world, inasmuch as the For-itself, lacking or possible, is For-itself as a *presence to* a certain state of the world. In this sense the being beyond which the For-itself projects the coincidence with itself is the world. (*BN*, 102/146)

(d) Nothingness, nihilation

If being-in-itself is the *positive* being of the phenomenon, the for-itself is a *nothingness* (*une néant*) by comparison. It is precisely what introduces nothingness into a world that can only be said to enjoy a positive fullness of being. Thus the two elements of Sartre's title, *Being and Nothingness*, may be mapped onto being-in-itself and being-for-itself, respectively, the being of the phenomenon and the phenomenon of being.

This nihilation (*néantisation*) is consciousness's ability to transcend the mere actuality of the in-itself and to project possibilities, meanings, and values, to go beyond the actual and to see in it more than is actually there, by relating it to something else, in the future. 'The possible is a new aspect of the nihilation of the In-itself in For-itself' (*BN*, 99/144). It is only thanks to consciousness and its ability to synthesize and relate, that the entities of the world come to form totalities, whose individual elements can then be individuated by being related to and thus differentiated from one another.

(e) Imagination, fiction and nihilation

Sartre's concept of nihilation will become clearer if we examine his early work on the *imagination*.

The image, produced by imagination, is for Sartre a form of consciousness in which the latter finds itself able to escape from its strict ties to the actual matter that lies before it, and take off into endless, and endlessly elaborated, variations. Imagination *irrealizes* things, it nihilates them.

By means of imagination, the real object in which consciousness is directly immersed, is reduced to a 'noema', in the sense that it becomes something 'irreal' and can then be imaginatively varied (*Imagination*, 138–40/152–4).

Sartre suggests indeed that nihilation is the basic ground of what Husserl describes as imaginative fantasizing, the imaginative variation of the particular qualities of real individual things, which is necessary in order to attain an idea of the universal form of that thing. Perhaps this is what occurs in Sartre's infinitely varied examples, which fan out into entire novels that are created in parallel with the philosophical works (cf. *Imagination*, 141–3/155–9). One way of viewing Sartre's work is as an imaginary varying of reality that aims to reach a universal truth about human beings, and perhaps to show that no matter what situation human beings are put in, contingently (or by the whim of the author), they nevertheless share in certain universal structures that characterize human reality.

In any case, the imagination, with its freedom and nihilation, which will have produced such variegated fictions, scattered among Sartre's monumental works of philosophy, stands as a fitting figure with which to describe Sartre's lifelong philosophical attempt to understand the intertwining of consciousness and its world, and indeed the very method of phenomenology itself, which also veers between these two extremes.

> **Nihilation (*néantisation*)**: the distinctive ability of consciousness to reduce the in-itself to a certain nothingness (*néant*). It is the ability to see beyond the actuality of an entity and to see its *possibilities* or its *meaning*. Hence it is to be distinguished from annihilation, of which it is nevertheless the condition, which would mean to destroy the actual thing altogether. Nihilation rather refers to man's capacity to free himself from his actual past, from his very 'being' and the inert being of things around him. Nihilation is thus what allows him to be free, since it allows him to project beyond the actual certain possibilities which are *not* currently actual, and certain ideals that change the way in which the actual appears.

We have seen that in order to be an object for finite consciousness, certain of the object's aspects must be absent from the phenomenon. Indeed the very *being* of the phenomenon is the sum total of all these aspects, present *and* absent. Sartre does suggest that nothingness is necessary in order for there to be such a thing as an 'object', an enduring presence that does not rely on its being perceived in order to exist. The always outstanding unfulfilled intentions which go to make up the infinite series are crucial to there being an object at all, rather than just a series of subjective impressions. Sartre suggests that if all the profiles of an object ever *could* be made present, the object would be reduced to a pure hallucination (*BN*, xlvii–iii/13–14).

At certain times, Sartre explains this crucial co-existence of presence and absence with the help of the *Gestalt* theory of perception, another of his innovative additions to the discourse of phenomenology, greatly expanded upon by his friend Merleau-Ponty. The only way in which a field of experience can exist is if one element or group of elements raises itself to prominence against a background of undifferentiated insignificance: 'in perception there is always the construction of a figure on a ground [*d'une forme sur un fond*]' (*BN*, 9/44). In other words, a difference between figure and ground must be established, and for Sartre, this can only happen by way of consciousness's power of nihilation. One aspect of the object or one element of the world must be brought to full presence, while the rest is relegated to a background of which we are only marginally aware.

Once again, we find Sartre laying the ontological ground for the empirical sciences: it is only because consciousness is capable of nihilation that perception *must* be organized into a structure containing figure and ground. 'No one object, no group of objects is especially designed to be organized as specifically either ground or figure; all depends on the direction of my attention' (*BN*, 9/44). Sartre describes this organization as 'an original nihilation' (ibid.). 'Negation is the cement which realises this unity [of the Gestalt]' (*BN*, 21/57). Thus the nihilation of consciousness amounts to the reduction of a certain field of perceptual experience to the level of a background, against which a genuine phenomenon raises itself. So 'the original nihilation of all the figures which appear and are swallowed up in the total neutrality of a ground is the necessary condition for the appearance of the principle figure' (*BN*, 10/45).

The ground is a nothingness in the sense that it is attended to marginally, but more essentially because it is 'undifferentiated' (*BN*, 10/45). Thus nothingness is the indetermination of an undifferentiated field: there is 'no *thing*' there, because no thing has yet been individually picked out from the background by consciousness: 'non-being supposes an irreducible mental act. Whatever may be the original undifferentiation of being, non-being is that same undifferentiation *denied*' (*BN*, 14/50). Nothingness then is precisely the differentiating force which allows entities to individuate themselves, by means of relation and differentiation, the ability to affirm that, 'I am not this, nor anything else', and thus to achieve individuality at the level of the for-itself from out of the pure undifferentiated existence of being-in-itself. To express this, Sartre reverses Spinoza's dictum, *omnis determinatio ist negatio*, by stating that 'every negation is a determination' (*BN*, 16/51–2).

> **Gestalt**: A theory of perception which states that the relation between a figure and a ground is indissoluble and essential to any genuine perception. This theory of perception was created in opposition to the atomists who affirmed that perception was ultimately compromised of distinct atoms which are combined only later by conscious synthesis. Gestalt theory states that it is a law of perception that a certain element is either a figure or a ground and cannot be both at the same time, as in the famous picture of the Eskimo and the rabbit and the two faces that are also a vase. But at the same time, neither could be what they are *without* the other one, hence the indissolubility of the two. Most basically, this means that perception involves a primordial *difference* rather than an absolutely homogeneous mass that is only subsequently synthesized to form collectives that are then differentiated from one another. For Sartre, human consciousness 'nihilates' in the strict sense that when a certain element of a perceptual field comes to the fore as a 'figure', the rest of the scene is reduced to nothingness in becoming the 'ground' of that figure, the background against which it stands out.

Ultimately, in order to retain an objective status, the thing we are experiencing must have certain aspects that remain absent. In fact, extra-mental objects always will retain elements of absence because consciousness has only a limited capacity. It is finite, and this of itself makes it necessary that in the field of its attention, certain elements, indeed the majority, must be relegated to the background, as empty, unfulfilled intentions, that are nevertheless crucial in making our perception the perception of an *object*.

Consciousness always sees the world with some particular *end* in mind, and as a result all but one part of this world must then be relegated to the background of our attention while the part *most relevant* to our current projected intention comes to the fore.

This nihilation in the perception of the world is crucial since we have seen that when consciousness relates to its own possibilities, it only does so *by way of* the world. Hence the world of things must be there prior to consciousness in order for the latter to have something to nihilate, and thus produce possibilities for itself. In this way, it becomes apparent that freedom remains deeply indebted to the contingency of the in-itself, for it is precisely this factual world that freedom *nihilates*. 'Nothingness can be nothingness only by nihilating itself expressly as nothingness of the world' (*BN*, 18/53).

(f) From 'world' to 'situation'

First of all, the possession of concepts, or at least the ability to individuate entities from one another allows consciousness to create individual, meaningful things from the undifferentiated mass of being-in-itself. But since things can be individuated only if we differentiate them from whatever *else* occupies the field of perception, consciousness must create an entire world. Projecting possibilities that give a unified sense to a collection of entities turns an unconnected multiplicity of things into a *world*: 'it is these possibilities as such which give the world its unity and its meaning as the world' (*BN*, 104/144). But there is yet a further transformation in our perception of the in-itself, that will transform this 'world' into my particular 'situation'. And this will be the value and the ultimate goal of my existence.

So far, we have only a generic world, which could be anybody's; it is not yet my individual 'situation'. The peculiar way in which a generic world appears to me depends on what I am aiming to achieve in this world. The precise way in which things appear depends upon the projects that I have, upon what I intend to *do* with them, and these projects in turn depend upon the *values* that I hold, which ultimately guide my action.

Sartre defines 'situation' as the 'contingency of freedom in the *plenum* of being of the world inasmuch as this *datum* [. . .] is revealed to this freedom only as *already illuminated* by the end which freedom chooses' (*BN*, 487/544). 'The inapprehensible *fact* of my condition [. . .] causes the for-itself, while choosing the *meaning* of its situation and while constituting itself as the foundation of itself in situation, *not to choose* its position' (*BN*, 83/121).

For Sartre, there are two limits to my freedom, both of them stemming not from the being-in-itself but from *another* being-*for*-itself. These limits become active when I myself am objectified (reduced to the level of the in-itself) by entering the field of another person's awareness. This Sartre describes largely in terms of 'the look' or 'gaze' (*le regard*) (*BN*, 252–302/310–64). But not only can *I* be objectified, so can my *situation* (*BN*, 525/582–3). As a result, the supposedly free choice of a project that turns the world of possibilities into a particular situation is revealed to be *un*free since it is to some extent constrained by the contingency of being-in-itself. But Sartre adds an extra twist to this: this objectification of my choice does not simply render us unfree, indeed he describes at great length the way in which a *struggle* is instituted when I experience the gazing, objectifying other in turn and hence objectify *him*: this putative objectification of myself and my situation depends upon *my* recognizing the other *as* an other, as a fellow human-being, and in truth it is always possible for me to view them as mere objects, rather than as subjects, thus neutralizing their power (cf. *BN*, 526/584–5).

(g) Beyond being and nothingness?

It is precisely this intimacy and interdependence between the freedom of the for-itself and the contingency of the in-itself that Sartre's most famous work goes to such great lengths to describe.

Sartre goes on to give his famous descriptions of the attempts that human beings make to deny their freedom, terrifyingly revealed to them in the experience of anxiety, and he describes the basic form of all these attempts as 'bad faith' (*BN*, 43ff./83ff.). Sartre indeed comes very close to identifying the two trajectories of human life, freedom and bad faith, with Heidegger's notions of projection and thrownness respectively. In the case of bad faith, as so often, we find Sartre providing his reader with an elaborate *example* whose very existence demonstrates a universal feature of human consciousness, which is, broadly speaking, that it can combine being and nothingness: 'If bad faith is to be possible, we should be able within the same consciousness to meet with the unity of being and non-being [*de l'être et du n'être-pas*]' (*BN*, 45/83).

The remainder of the examples that seem to make up the greater part of Sartre's book express more or less exactly the same thing: for instance, desire, the for-itself's attempt to return to the in-itself, as would be impossible, and the various relations with the other which never resolve the conflicts in which one or other of us is reduced to the level of the in-itself, a mere object, albeit never entirely or once and for all.

This all testifies to what Sartre describes – provisionally – as the ultimate aim of human activity, which is 'the in-itself-for-itself', in other words, a for-itself which has achieved the status of an in-itself, and thus the ideal coincidence marked in the book's title, *nothingness* and *being*, the being *of* nothingness, which Sartre ultimately identifies with God, an entity which is both free and yet depends on nothing else for its existence (*BN*, 90/129 *et al.*). The human being would then be defined by the effort to achieve a substantial existence but without dying, without simply becoming another part of the in-itself. However, in the closing pages of *Being and Nothingness*, Sartre begins to wonder if this striving to become god *is* in fact the inescapable fate of man, or whether he might be able to exist in some other way, which would precisely allow him to embrace his freedom absolutely and *not* attempt to render it substantial, in the form of an in-itself (*BN*, 628/722). Sartre asks whether man can live without such transcendent ideals as 'god' and escape the bad faith that seems always to push him towards the sanctuary of the actual. In which case, the task of the entire book will have been to reveal this ideal to us, in order to free us from its hold.

Further reading

Sartre, Jean-Paul (1957), *Being and Nothingness*. Trans. Hazel Barnes. New York: Methuen, part I, chapter 2 (on bad faith); part III, chapter 1, section iv & chapter 3 (on the look and concrete relations with others).

(Time should also be made for part IV, chapter 1 and the conclusion of the whole book which contain some of Sartre's most fascinating insights. Some answers to the questions with which Sartre ends *Being and Nothingness*, and which he entrusts to a 'future work', are to be found in his *Notebooks for an Ethics*.)

Part IV
Maurice Merleau-Ponty (Rochefort-sur-Mer, France, 1908–Paris, France, 1961)

Maurice Merleau-Ponty was born in Rochefort-sur-Mer on 14 March 1908. He studied at the École Normale Supérieure in Paris where he met Sartre and Simone de Beauvoir. In 1942, he published *The Structure of Behaviour* which explores the affinities between Gestalt psychology and phenomenology. In 1945, the *Phenomenology of Perception* appeared. Merleau-Ponty held positions as Professor of Philosophy first in Lyon, then in Paris (at the Sorbonne and the Collège de France).

Merleau-Ponty and Sartre participated in a number of joint endeavours, such as a resistance group during the Second World War and the journal *Les Temps Modernes* which they co-edited from 1945. In the 1950s, Merleau-Ponty took a critical (and self-critical) distance from Marxism (*Adventures of the Dialectics*, 1955) which led to a split with Sartre and de Beauvoir. When Merleau-Ponty died in 1961, he left behind the uncompleted manuscript of *The Visible and the Invisible* (published posthumously in 1964).

The Lived Body 13

Main primary literature:

Phenomenology of Perception, Preface (pp. vii–xxiv/i–xvi), 'The Body as Object and Mechanistic Physiology', 'The Experience of the Body and Classical Psychology', 'The Spatiality of One's Own Body and Motility' (pp. 84–170/87–172), 'The Body in its Sexual Being' (pp. 178–201/180–202).

In his early work manuscripts, Merleau-Ponty described the general goal of his philosophy as the 'search for a third dimension' – a dimension where subject and object, activity and passivity, autonomy and dependency would no longer contradict one another.[1] The entity which best fits this description is the 'lived body'.

The **lived body** designates my body as I ordinarily 'know' it, with special emphasis on the way in which that body is 'lived' or experienced. My body is never a mere physical body (in opposition to a pure mind) but an inhabited body. For Merleau-Ponty, I am my body, and I also 'have it' pre-reflectively available to be used to further my various projects. Human existence is necessarily an incarnate existence.

My body shares many features with a merely physical, spatio-temporal body: for example, it has mass, collides with objects and can be looked at from the outside; yet it is at the same time 'lived' and 'experienced' from within. The strange intermediate character of the lived body creates obstacles for a faithful description of it because it is tempting to disambiguate this character and focus either on the physical or on the spiritual side of the body in isolation. The first approach is designated by Merleau-Ponty as 'empiricism', the second as 'intellectualism'; we shall see how these two approaches play out in the case of several examples. The alternative account which avoids the pitfalls of the two extreme positions is that of phenomenology. Phenomenology takes a third way and explicates rather than resolves the complex character of bodily phenomena. Before turning to some specific bodily experiences, let us first shed light on Merleau-Ponty's idea of phenomenology and the phenomenological method.

(a) Phenomenology

In the 'Preface' to his *Phenomenology of Perception*, Merleau-Ponty formulates his position with regard to Husserl's idea of phenomenology. He writes explicitly about the Husserlian phenomenological *epochē* and the reduction, the suspension of judgements regarding a being-in-itself of the world[2]: 'The most important lesson which the reduction teaches us is the impossibility of a complete reduction' (*PP*, xv/viii). What does this statement mean? Merleau-Ponty's 'Preface' presents the state of Husserlian phenomenology as one that is inherently determined by tensions and even contradictions. Phenomenology wants to describe our actual experience of the world, but it also wants to be a science – these dilemmas are familiar from Husserl's own reflections. From Merleau-Ponty's perspective, Husserl does not sufficiently acknowledge the problems involved in founding phenomenology as a rigorous science. Merleau-Ponty follows the inspiration of Husserl's phenomenological project but deems it most important to reflect on the limits of that project. In Merleau-Ponty's view, phenomenology can be practised as a way of thinking even though it has not yet been able to achieve a complete understanding of its own methodology (*PP*, viii/ii). Phenomenology consists in constantly reassessing and transforming its own method. Whenever a certain formulation of the phenomenological method is produced, the praxis of phenomenology can in turn put this particular formulation in question and a transformation of phenomenology then becomes necessary. The strength of phenomenology is to allow for such transformations – it is a procedure of perpetually beginning anew.

According to Merleau-Ponty, phenomenology needs to be honest about the fact that it will never be able to account fully for the fact that there is a world, and that a complete reduction of this world is impossible. It is crucial for an understanding of Merleau-Ponty's statement about the impossibility of a complete reduction that we consider the immediately preceding sentence: 'All the misunderstandings with his [Husserl's] interpreters, with the existentialist "dissidents" and finally with himself, have arisen from the fact that in order to see the world and grasp it as paradoxical, we must break with our familiar acceptance of it and, also, from the fact that from this break we can learn nothing but the unmotivated upsurge of the world' (PP, xv/viii). This sentence contains several claims. First, it states that many of the problems which occur when we try to interpret Husserl's phenomenology are the result of misunderstandings (including misunderstandings on the side of Husserl himself). Secondly, it announces that there is something paradoxical about the very nature of the world itself. The paradox of the world consists in the fact that even though we continuously make sense of and give meaning to the world, the world can never fully be brought to conscious immanence and transparency. There is always an excess, a remainder of the unintelligible fact that 'there is [*il y a*] (world)' which we cannot account for.[3] The 'unmotivated upsurge of the world' describes the same excess, but with an additional implication: the break with our familiar acceptance of the world must ultimately also be unmotivated; it cannot be fully accounted for. Merleau-Ponty refers us to Eugen Fink whose talk of '"wonder" in the face of the world' would be the 'best formulation of the reduction' (PP, xv/viii).[4]

When correctly understood, the reduction is not a series of steps prior to phenomenology, but already a part of the phenomenological inquiry itself. This means that the question as to how the reduction should be performed is itself a matter of phenomenological inquiry open for discussion and improvement. As a result, Merleau-Ponty does not outline his phenomenological method beforehand (in abstraction from the phenomena), but examines specific phenomena to reveal the need for a phenomenological examination. The main achievement of phenomenology, in comparison with alternative approaches, stems from its emphasis on the world.

> **World**, for Merleau-Ponty, is 'what we perceive' (*PP*, xviii/xi). This does not mean that he abandons the phenomenological concept of world as a context of references and takes it to mean a totality of perceivable objects. Rather, the meaningful references between objects are part of what we perceive (in a wider sense of 'perception'). Furthermore, it does not mean that the world is fully transparent and available to us; rather, it harbours opacity, resistance and 'shadows'. Merleau-Ponty describes our existence as a transcendence towards the world, or as a being destined to the world.

Our existence becomes disclosed as 'being-toward-the-world', and our involvement in the world as a context of meaning needs to be investigated if we are to make sense of all the significant phenomena of human existence, be they temporal or spatial, cultural or natural, normal or abnormal.

(b) A third way

In his *Phenomenology of Perception*, Merleau-Ponty investigates a variety of bodily phenomena to show how both intellectualism and empiricism encounter severe problem in giving an account of our bodily experience. Two of the central themes of the book will be discussed in the present and subsequent chapters: sexuality and speech. At this point, let us first introduce the example of the 'phantom limb' to exemplify the shortcomings of intellectualism and empiricism. It is unnecessary for Merleau-Ponty's analyses to name specific proponents of the empiricist and intellectualist approaches because both designate general 'types' of investigation.

> **Empiricism** focuses on physical reality and takes experience to be a collection of stimuli and qualities that can ultimately be explained in causal, natural scientific terms. **Intellectualism** focuses on the spiritual or mental realm, stressing the productive, conceptualizing role of consciousness.

The problem of the phantom limb describes the experience of a limb which has been amputated. The empiricist account of this phenomenon is unsuccessful in a variety of ways: it cannot account for the wide spectrum of experiences which patients with similar amputations report, and it cannot explain why anaesthesia fails to eliminate the experience. But the intellectualist explanation does not succeed either; the limb is more present than a memory or a phantasy. We do not take the subjects of our memories or imaginings to be present at the moment we experience them, but the patient takes the limb to be present and relies on it to a certain extent. The limb is not taken to be present in an intellectual way, but in practice. Furthermore, the intellectualist account is undermined by the fact that the severance of the nerves connecting the former limb to the brain abolishes the phantom limb (*PP*, 99/101).

What is the response to this dilemma? Merleau-Ponty concludes that psychic factors (memories, emotions) and physiological conditions 'gear into each other', to the extent that there is nothing purely physical or purely psychological in experience (*PP*, 89/92). The existence of the nerves makes a difference because 'they keep an area which the subject's history fills' (*PP*, 99/101); they are a condition for the psychic factors to take root and become manifest. In the end, it turns out that the phantom limb emerges out of a meaningful situation, from a way of projecting myself towards the world. The way in which a person relates to the world (their history, profession, preferences, and so on) is reflected in their experience of an anomaly or pathology such as the phantom limb.

For Merleau-Ponty, anomalies have a disclosive role because they show how we *normally* relate to the world. We usually expect to be able to move in the world without accidents and interruptions. Everyday activities like walking, climbing stairs or eating food are habitualized in such a way that we do not need to reflect on them, and we do not need to be aware of our environment in terms of specifically measured distances or qualities. Only if I have sustained an injury to my leg or if the stairs are broken will I need to start reflecting on my activity of climbing the stairs. Otherwise, these movements are habitual, where 'habit expresses our power of dilating our being-in-the-world' (*PP*, 166/168). An expansion of my bodily existence can include certain instruments, such as the automobile which I drive or the blind person's cane. Merleau-Ponty introduces such examples to show that the automobile and the cane are no longer external objects for their possessors, but extensions of their bodies that have been incorporated into their bodily space. In driving or in walking with the cane, the wings of the car and the end of the cane have come to mark the boundaries between the embodied self and its world.

The emergence of a 'habit body' can again serve to show how intellectualism and empiricism fall short of a satisfying explanation. The empiricist account fails because the acquisition of a new activity which then becomes habitual has a systematic character. A habit cannot be built up from a collection of individual stimuli, but responds to a situation of a general type, such that it can cope with a different situation of the same type (for instance, in the habitual ability to cycle, the need to ride a different bike, or take a more treacherous road). What situations of such a type share is not a set of similar elements but rather a similar meaning that the habit body 'comprehends' in its practical coping. For its part, the intellectualist explanation would describe the acquisition of a habit as the comprehension of a meaning; yet it fails to see that this meaning is not merely an intellectual one, but also a motile one, a 'motor meaning'. The body grasps this meaning on a pre-reflective level; the person performing the movement may well be unable to give account of the relevant factors which would need to inform the movement according to the intellectualist. It turns out that 'habit is neither a form of knowledge nor an involuntary action' but rather, a 'knowledge in the hands' or in the body (*PP*, 166/168). My hands know how to type or to play the piano even though I may not (intellectually) know the place of the keys.

In general, the intellectualist approach toward the lived body neglects the materiality of the lived body that becomes most obvious when we encounter obstacles or suffer injuries. The empiricist approach, by contrast, does not sufficiently attend to the spiritual dimension, but takes the lived body to be an object, exposed to stimulations from other objects. The distinct character of the lived body will now be described from the phenomenological perspective.

(c) Characteristics of the lived body

Merleau-Ponty states that '[t]he body is the vehicle of being in the world, and having a body is, for a living creature, to be intervolved in a definite environment' (*PP*, 94/97). This statement might at first glance appear Cartesian in spirit, as if there were a clear split between mind and body, with the body serving as an instrument that allows the mind to connect to the world. This is certainly not Merleau-Ponty's intention. A few interrelated thoughts are expressed here. First, we only have access to the world by way of the lived body. Merleau-Ponty insists that our only mode of existence is to have a body or to be essentially incarnate, fleshly; this fact cannot be altered or circumvented. There is no purely spiritual existence for living creatures. For Merleau-Ponty the lived body is the expression of our existence – and existence, in turn, is continuous incarnation. Secondly, there is an essential connection between body and world; not only do we gain access to the world by being embodied, but as embodied we are always in a world, and more specifically, involved in a world that surrounds us: an 'environment'. This holds for all living creatures, as Merleau-Ponty points out, and it is possible to explicate the way in which the world-relation of humans differs from that of the other animals.

The peculiar character of the lived body becomes particularly obvious when compared with mere physical bodies that it resembles in many ways; yet there are a number of significant differences that make the body unique among objects. The lived body appears more accessible than a physical object because I experience it from within; yet it is in several ways less accessible, or at least given in a different way:

(i) The lived body is a 'constant here', always proximate and always with me. I can throw a ball, but I cannot throw away a part of my body. Because I cannot take a distance from my body, it is not accessible to me like other objects that I can see and touch from all sides (though never all at once). Although it might be argued that a mirror gives me such complete access to my body, there is no question that the mirror is an artificial means and does not alter the basic inaccessibility of my rear side. On the basis of the permanence of my lived body, I can perceive other objects that are not always perceptible. It turns out that 'the presentation of objects in perspective cannot be understood except through the resistance of my body to all variation of perspective' (*PP*, 106/109). I can never see an object from all sides because I am always in a specific location by virtue of my body, from which I approach objects and deal with them.

(ii) My lived body allows for 'double sensations': my right hand that is touching my left hand can itself be touched, that is, can feel itself being touched. When we describe a touch, it seems that the one hand is never really experienced as touching and touched at the same time. Touching and being touched never quite coincide, but the touching hand exhibits the possibility of being touched, or being experienced as touched, in the next moment. This example helps to show that when I am immersed in the world in my everyday coping and investigating, my acting body is not thematically present. When my body comes into the foreground of my attention, by contrast, the presence of the world outside me recedes into the background.

(iii) The lived body is given as 'affective'. A physical object can be the cause of a pain, whereas if my foot hurts, it is not causing pain but is itself hurting. My foot becomes the place where the pain manifests itself, but it is not the cause of the pain like the chair that I have just crashed into. The lived body is an 'affective background' which allows things to appear as helpful or as harmful (*PP*, 107/109).

(iv) My lived body is determined by 'kinaesthesis': movement (Greek: *kinesis*) and perception (Greek: *aisthesis*) go together. Movement is not something secondary or external to my body; I move directly in and with my body. When I reach for a physical object, I do not conceive of myself as another object which has to move and traverse the distance between me and the object. Normally, as I think about looking in a book, I am already stretching out my arm to pick it up. To put it another way, there is no gap between the intention and the action, and the very way that I extend my hand and arm at the outset of the action demonstrates the anticipation of its purpose and its result. The beginning already contains the end; therefore, Merleau-Ponty can claim that 'the relationships between my decision and my body are, in movement, magic ones' (*PP*, 108/110).

Our lived body thus turns out to be similar to and yet different from mere physical bodies in at least four respects. These differences are not entirely Merleau-Ponty's discoveries: Husserl had already described them more briefly in the second volume of his *Ideas* to which Merleau-Ponty refers in footnotes. But Merleau-Ponty systematizes these discoveries and presents them in a more accessible fashion. There are two ways in which Merleau-Ponty moves beyond Husserl.[5] First, he develops a more comprehensive account of motility. Although Husserl introduces the phenomenological notion of *kinaesthesis*, he is mostly concerned with our perception of an object, and with the possibility and necessity of moving around it, perceiving its other aspects in acts of seeing and touching. Merleau-Ponty examines various kinds of movements in which we actually deal with things, and he also includes those that do not aim at an object. Going even further, he accounts for how we acquire new abilities (such as dancing or riding a bicycle). Secondly, based on this expanded notion of motility, Merleau-Ponty explores the unity of the body, one which is not merely accomplished by thought, but is a lived, experienced and habitualized unity, one for which he introduces the term 'body schema'.

> The '**body schema**' describes our body as an organic unity or a system of inter-connected senses. Perception relies on this 'prelogical unity of the bodily schema' (*PP*, 270/268).

The body schema (*schéma corporel*) has often been mistakenly translated as 'body image', even though such a mistranslation does in fact pick out one of the ways in which Merleau-Ponty uses this phrase. In this first signification, the body schema denotes my overall postural awareness, mediated by the ways in which I have employed my body and seen it 'from inside' (the end of my nose, forearms and hands more usually fall within my visual field). Here my body schema is my body image.

In its second signification, the body schema refers to my habitual body as the set of acquired skills that I bring to bear on certain things in certain situations. Through this set of skills (which most obviously evolves and broadens in childhood and early adulthood), I am able to perceive things in certain ways. Here the body schema is my integrated system of skilled motor capacities as it practically comprehends the world. From what has already been stated above it can be guessed that my current body image is heavily conditioned by this system of skills.[6]

Merleau-Ponty alerts us to several dimensions which operate on a level prior to fully fledged perception and which yet contribute to it. The 'prelogical' unity of the body schema is one such dimension, where the body is synthesized and experienced as a unity without relying on any explicit logical operations in order to establish this body as 'one'. Furthermore, perception has elements which are intrinsically pre-objective: this becomes apparent when we are not given fully-fledged objects with properties but things that are more vague and primordial than that.[7] For example, if I jump because a shadow is approaching me, this is not because I am avoiding a known, typified object; I am responding to something pre-objective which might turn into an identified and hence conceptualized object on closer inspection.

In Merleau-Ponty's account, the lived body functions pre-personally and pre-reflectively. There is an anonymous element to perception, expressed in statements such as 'It's cold!' In perception, I take over a legacy that is always already given to me before I have emerged as an ego. The concept of the 'habit body' captures the fact that a large proportion of my actions happen habitually or passively. When I subsequently reflect on them, I may not even be able to capture all of the essential elements, and yet the action took place successfully.

If an impression has arisen from the characterizations given so far that Merleau-Ponty considers our existence to be determined by various kinds of bodily facts and necessities, it is essential to remember that existence is always both necessity and freedom. The characteristics of our lived body certainly determine our perception of the world, but at the same time, it is our task – which we are fully able to undertake – to freely appropriate these necessities and respond to them. The skills that I must possess in order to negotiate the world when I leave infancy also provide me with my freedom. Precisely because they are taken for granted or are unthinkingly available, they do not swamp my present awareness. The irreducible tension between necessity and freedom becomes particularly obvious in the realm of sexuality, to which we will now turn.

(d) The body in its sexual being

When he introduces his account of the body in its sexual being, Merleau-Ponty argues that our affectivity or ability to feel is an area which has existence only for us (humans), and we will gain a better insight into existence in general if we see 'how a thing or a being begins to exist for us through desire or love' (*PP*, 178/180). It is important to note that Merleau-Ponty's interest in this chapter lies with the affects or emotions since one might otherwise receive the impression (from the discussion of a specific pathological case) that the focus of the chapter lay merely with a functioning sexuality. Yet it turns out that a full understanding of sexuality requires us to take affectivity into account, and at the same time, shows that the sexual and the erotic are intertwined.

The pathological case in question is that of a certain Schneider, to whom Merleau-Ponty turns several times throughout the *Phenomenology of Perception*, always relying on the case history and hypotheses originally provided by the neuropsychologists Adhemar Gelb and Kurt Goldstein. Schneider suffered a brain injury in the war, and as a result, experiences a number of abnormal motor functions which empiricist and intellectualist approaches cannot account for. Schneider can still perform concrete movements more or less normally (for instance, lighting his lamp), but he can perform abstract movements (like tracing a figure in the air) only if he is able to watch his limbs and position them as if they were external objects (for example, he first has to watch his arm and lift it parallel to the floor before commencing the figure). He has lost the ability to carry out movements without representing the body parts in question and having to consciously move them into the relevant starting positions.

Schneider's difficulties in the sexual realm serve to show that neither empiricism nor intellectualism can capture the full nature of sexuality. According to an intellectualist account, 'any sexual incapacity ought to amount [. . .] to the loss of certain representations', whereas according to an empiricist account, such an incapacity would result from 'a weakening of the capacity for satisfaction' (*PP*, 179/181). Yet Schneider's problems are neither of the first nor of the second kind. To describe his symptoms briefly: he does not seek sexual intercourse of his own accord, and if the intercourse initiated by another is somehow interrupted, he has no urge to continue. Though he is capable of orgasms, they are always brief and perfunctory. He does not have erotic dreams, and his nocturnal emissions are very rare. What Merleau-Ponty designates quite appropriately as 'sexual inertia' (*PP*, 179/181) is thus not the result of any genital dysfunction because bare physical satisfaction is in principle possible for Schneider, and is unaffected by his injury.

Yet the intellectualist account is also unsuccessful, because a loss of representations does not explain the difficulties encountered during actual intercourse, and the absence of dreams seems 'an effect rather than a cause' (ibid.). Overall, erotic perception does not aim at a consciousness; rather, it comes about because a living body aims at another living body. But as his own descriptions show, Schneider fails to find a woman's body attractive as a body and considers mainly her personality. In this sense, Schneider's perception of others and of the world shows itself quite similar to the intellectualist picture of our worldly interactions. Yet such an over-intellectualized approach (which also determines Schneider's motility) is not normal, but pathological; and intellectualism cannot count this approach as a pathology. In short, there is no physical or intellectual aspect of sexuality in isolation that is missing in Schneider, yet the entire character of sexual experience has changed.

What would be the alternative account of sexuality provided by a phenomenology of the lived body? According to Merleau-Ponty, '[w]hat has disappeared from the patient is his power of projecting before him a sexual world' (*PP*, 181/182) which would allow him to endow a situation with sexual meaning, recognize such meaning in a situation, or respond to and follow up on this sexual meaning. He has ceased to ask 'this mute and permanent question which constitutes normal sexuality' (*PP*, 181/183). The erotic question is not permanently asked, but it is continuously present in a dormant form and can be awakened. Schneider has lost the erotic structure of perception, in which we not only project ourselves into situations, but get so caught up in them as to be temporarily lost within them.

Sexuality does not constitute a specific, clearly delimited area of existence. It is impossible to determine the boundaries of sexuality (*PP*, 194/196). The erotic can make itself present quite suddenly because it is 'at all times present there like an atmosphere' (*PP*, 195/196). It goes to the merit of psychoanalysis to have alerted us to this. In the case of Schneider, his sexual difficulties go hand in hand with difficulties in maintaining friendships, where he also shows a certain kind of inertia. However, it would be misleading to equate existence with sexuality. If psychoanalytic theories sometimes convey the impression that existence and sexuality are co-extensive, they go too far. For example, someone can be very active and successful in his professional life, and passive to the point of inaction in his sexual life, or the other way round (as in the case with Casanova; *PP*, 184/186).

From a phenomenological perspective, the task becomes to rethink sexuality, rather than to ask how much of life rests on sexuality. Sexuality is part of a general openness to the world, as is speech. My body can shut itself off and open itself up, and in this way, psycho-symptomatic pathologies like aphasia (loss of speech) or certain sexual dysfunctions come about. The result is that sexuality cannot be clearly delimited but permeates existence but at the same time is not co-extensive with the latter. This shows that sexuality is one of the more striking parts of the ambiguity that determines our overall lived existence.[8]

Further reading

Casey, E. S. (1984), 'Habitual body and memory in Merleau-Ponty'. *Man and World* 17, 1984, pp. 278–97.

Smith, A. D. (2007), 'The flesh of perception: Merleau-Ponty and Husserl.' In Baldwin, T., *Reading Merleau-Ponty. On* Phenomenology of Perception. London: Routledge, pp. 1–22.

Waldenfels, B. (2008), 'The central role of the body in Merleau-Ponty's Phenomenology', *Journal of the British Society for Phenomenology*, vol. 39, no. 1, pp. 76–88.

Language and Painting

Chapter Outline

Main primary literature

'The Body as Expression, and Speech' (in *Phenomenology of Perception*, pp. 202–32/
202–32); 'Cézanne's Doubt', 'Indirect Voices and the Language of Silence', 'Eye and
Mind' (all in *The Merleau-Ponty Aesthetics Reader*).

Merleau-Ponty's analysis of corporeality finds an exemplary application in
his treatment of language and speech. Here, the benefits of his approach
can be seen with respect to the central topic of language (arguably the most
important philosophical theme of the twentieth century). It turns out that
one-sided approaches fail to capture our experience of language. According to
Merleau-Ponty, our misunderstandings regarding language stem from the fact
that we focus on ready-made formulations rather than the creative use of
words. His considerations of expressive, creative language take him to the
realm of art where these creative possibilities become most obvious, and at

the same time, the difficulties of describing the phenomenon of expression come to the fore.

Merleau-Ponty has engaged with art in various phases of his writing, from the early essay on 'Cézanne's Doubt' (1945) to 'Indirect Voices and the Language of Silence' (1952) and finally, 'Eye and Mind' (1961). In the second part of the current chapter, these three essays will briefly be examined with respect to three themes which are developed there, but extend throughout Merleau-Ponty's work as a whole: the affinity between painting and phenomenology; the relation between language and painting; and, finally, the fundamentally different approaches which art and science exhibit towards the world.

(a) The paradox of expression

Merleau-Ponty shows that language is not a totality of signs. A sign would be an arbitrary placeholder, devoid of meaning, and could be replaced without any loss of meaning by a different such placeholder in another language. Learning a language means learning to orient oneself in a new world rather than learning to replace an ever greater number of familiar signs with new signs.

The realization that language is akin to a world rather than an accumulation of signs is accomplished in the already familiar way, through a discussion of the flaws in the intellectualist and empiricist accounts of speech. Merleau-Ponty begins with the question: how do speech and thought relate to each other? We tend to presume that thought precedes speech, but Merleau-Ponty shows that speech accomplishes thought. Despite their opposition, intellectualism and empiricism share the same basic assumptions about speech, including its separation from thought. For both of them, words do not really have a meaning or a true significance. Throughout the chapter, Merleau-Ponty explains how empiricism and intellectualism come out on different sides while employing the same basic assumptions. For neither of them does the word has a meaning; and yet, '[i]n the first case [i.e. the empiricist case], we are on this side of the word as meaningful, in the second we are beyond it' (*PP*, 205/205). The empiricist explains the usage of a word as a response to a certain stimulus, thus making it part of an objective causality (for example, an experience of pain resulting in the exclamation 'Ouch!'). This account does not even need to introduce meaning to account for our employment of words. The intellectualist, in turn, makes thought and meaning primary, but the word then appears almost superfluous, a mere container which does not bear any essential connection to the meaning it transports because the thought has been completed prior to the utterance.

To phrase the same problem in terms of the relation between the speaking subject and language: 'In the first [case], there is nobody to speak; in the second, there is certainly a subject, but a thinking one, not a speaking one' (*PP*, 205/205). The empiricist account eclipses the subject since the word is summoned up by stimuli; it is subject to neurological or associative laws. The precise formulation of the empiricist account and the extent to which it takes a straightforward or a more refined scientific approach does not alter the basic fact that there is no place here for a speaking subject since the account simply does not require it. As a result, the approach can explain neither our normal, subjective experiences of speech, nor certain pathologies such as an inhibition or loss of speech. The intellectualist account, by contrast, includes a subject, but it is merely a thinking subject, and speech would be secondary, arriving on the scene only after thought has already established a meaning.

To provide an alternative account, Merleau-Ponty makes a rather daring announcement: 'Thus we refute both intellectualism and empiricism by simply saying that *the word has a meaning*' (*PP*, 206/206). What is Merleau-Ponty's evidence for this statement? The first argument he provides concerns the way in which 'thought tends towards expression as towards its completion' (ibid.). Naming, saying, or writing down the thought gives it a reality; otherwise, it has only a fleeting, uncertain, incomplete existence. The relation between thought and speech then turns out to be a relation in which thought and speech are not identical; but rather, speech 'accomplishes' or completes thought (*PP*, 207/207).

The meaning of a word is not to be conflated with the way in which we usually presume a concept to function. Merleau-Ponty explains that when I identify an object in dim light as, say, a brush, this does not usually mean, and does not have to mean, that I use 'brush' as an explicit concept, acquired by repeated usage, under which I subsume the object that I reach for. If somebody asks me what I am holding in my hand, the linguistic concept 'brush' might not even immediately come to mind. Yet the word 'brush' bears the appropriate meaning, and by reaching for this object, I confirm this meaning. The success in identifying the object as a brush shows that the word has this meaning, and that the meaning leads me to the object.

There are, however, two phenomena of speech which challenge this understanding and contribute to misconceptions along intellectualist or empiricist lines: first, the difference between speaking language and spoken language, and second, the paradox of expression.

> By **spoken language** (*langage parlé*), Merleau-Ponty designates language that we have at our disposal: familiar words and phrases. **Speaking language** (*langage parlant*), in contrast, designates creative language which brings about new meanings.

Speaking language expresses our experiences in a new fashion, without falling back on set phrases and clichés. The examples which Merleau-Ponty gives include a child uttering its first word, lovers revealing their feelings, and the attempts of writers and philosophers to express experiences which have not found expression before (*PP*, 208n./209n.). These are rare occurrences, but they reveal the essence of speech in the emphatic sense, as creative; they show how thought indeed calls for speech as its very completion. However, in everyday usage, we exchange set phrases and use language as a mere container to convey messages. In this way, the impression arises that speech would be secondary to thought (as the intellectualist account has it) or that we use a word mechanically (as the empiricist account implies).

Speech is neither the pure clothing of thought, nor is expression its translation. 'Speech is therefore that paradoxical operation through which, by using words of a given sense, and already available meanings, we try to follow up an intention which necessarily outstrips, modifies, and itself, in the last analysis, stabilizes the meanings of the words which translate it' (*PP*, 452/445). This statement brings out several features of speech that relate to its paradoxical character and leads us on to a discussion of the so-called paradox of expression.

> The **paradox of expression** describes the paradoxical relation between that which is yet to be expressed, and the accomplished expression. Before the expression, there is no complete thought, but just a 'vague fever' (*CD*, 69) or an 'uneasiness' (*Signs* 19/27). Only the expression shows that there was something rather than nothing there, and in that sense the expression is a necessary condition for knowing what was there to be expressed. At the same time, this 'fever' has a certain determinacy which becomes obvious, for example, when we realize that we have not yet found the appropriate expression.

The difficulty of this paradox consists in describing what is there prior to the expression, and how the term 'expression' is justified despite the fact that there is only an intention or a fever, and no already complete idea to be expressed. Expression is creative, and yet it is neither a creation from nowhere, nor a mere externalization or reproduction of an internal content. The intention to be expressed, so Merleau-Ponty states, 'outstrips' and 'stabilizes' the meaning of the expression. Expression is excessive, in both directions: it is never possible to express the entirety of our 'uneasiness' and, at the same time, there is a surplus in the expression compared to what preceded it. When Merleau-Ponty, in the sentence cited above, designates expression as a kind of translation, this requires us to rethink translation in a new way, as itself creative in the same ways that expression is. It is important to note that Merleau-Ponty employs 'expression' in a rather wide sense, including bodily expressions such as gestures, which will be examined in the following section.

(b) Body and speech

In order to develop the alternative, phenomenological account of speech further, an exploration of the link between body and speech may prove helpful. Merleau-Ponty announces this connection already in the title of his chapter, 'The Body as Expression, and Speech'. There are several ways in which body and speech condition one another, and also certain parallels which can help elucidate both. Merleau-Ponty states that our body is the 'condition for the possibility of all expressive operations' (*PP*, 451/455). At first, this announcement is not particularly surprising given that Merleau-Ponty points out that our existence is necessarily embodied and expression is one aspect of this embodied existence. And yet the connection is stronger; our corporeality conditions expression in a stronger sense than other aspects of existence. There is a certain reality to expression which requires our bodily involvement. This reality can be that of a word or a sentence, but also a gesture, or the more obvious reality (and materiality) of a sculpture. Through our body, the expression acquires a place in the world. Before the expression, what was yet to be expressed did not have this reality; it was confined to one mind, and even within this mind, it was not available as such. However, the expression, especially when manifest in an artwork, has the ability to unite 'separate lives' and 'dwell undivided in several minds', including a claim on future minds to which the artwork will speak (*CD*, 70).

While it is important to note that Merleau-Ponty's concept of expression includes artworks and bodily gestures, the more striking connections between body and speech will become obvious if we return once again to expression through words. The following two instances confirm the close connection between speech and the body, and at the same time show once again how intellectualism and empiricism fail to capture the essence of speech. The first example describes what happens when we are searching for a word, the second considers the way we learn a foreign language.

When we search for a word, the distinction between thought and speech becomes tangible, and our frustration at not finding the right word reaffirms Merleau-Ponty's insistence that thought tends towards expression as towards its completion. Yet even when we find the word fairly easily, the experience discloses something about the nature of speech. 'I reach back for the word as my hand reaches toward the part of my body that is being pricked'; yet this is precisely not an instance of empiricism: 'the word has a place in my linguistic world' (*PP*, 210/210). The crucial concept which connects reaching for a word with reaching for a part of the body or for a certain instrument, is the concept of 'world'. Rather than being signs and thus empty containers for thought, words form part of a linguistic world.

Merleau-Ponty builds on Husserl's and Heidegger's phenomenological notions of world as a context of references. Like Heidegger, he emphasizes that hiddenness or concealment is crucial to the world and that our existence is essentially being-in-the-world, or more precisely, being directed towards the world. A linguistic world is thus a context of interconnected meanings, and our home language or mother tongue is the linguistic world we are most familiar with, allowing us to move with most ease.

The example of learning a foreign language confirms the significance of the concept of world for understanding speech. If a language were a system of signs which stand in for specific objects, we could learn a foreign language mechanically, by studying a dictionary. Yet such an approach would never really allow us to *speak* the foreign language (where speaking is taken here not in contrast with writing, but as the employment of a language in the full sense, being able to understand and communicate, and thus make our way in the foreign linguistic world). Merleau-Ponty tells us that 'in a foreign country, I begin to understand the meaning of words through their place in a context of action, and by taking part in a communal life' (*PP*, 208/208). Learning a foreign language means familiarizing oneself with a foreign world, thus being able to follow references and detect regions of meaning. A translation program on a computer which necessarily looks at a sentence word by word will never fully be able to do this. Merleau-Ponty says that we 'deduce' the conceptual meaning of a word from its 'gestural' meaning (*PP*, 208/208). Words gesture or point, and we understand them by recognizing them within their context of references.

The connection between body and speech culminates in Merleau-Ponty's theory of style. Important examples of style are an artist's style (which allows us, for example, to recognize a certain painting as 'a Picasso') and a person's style of bodily comportment, such as their mimicry, gestures and mannerisms. Imitating somebody means imitating their style. A style remains implicit while it is enacted, and can only be recognized indirectly or at a distance.[9]

> **Style** designates a recognizable structure of expression or comportment which cannot, however, be reduced to a list of features. In accordance with our everyday usage of the term, there are artistic styles, personal styles, and so on.

Merleau-Ponty draws several connections between art and other areas of life which may at first appear puzzling, but which he works out convincingly with the help of such concepts as style, world and body. 'The body is to be compared, not to a physical object but to a work of art' (*PP*, 202/203). In turn, the phenomenology of the lived body allows for a new exploration of the artwork in which the traditional aesthetic scheme of matter and form is replaced by an intertwinement of spiritual and material dimensions. The artwork is able to stand within itself and express itself, like a lived body. This new approach to art places the painter in close proximity with the phenomenologist.

(c) The painter and the phenomenologist

In his early essay 'Cézanne's Doubt', Merleau-Ponty tackles several important themes and questions. A few of those themes will be mentioned here before we turn to our main topic, the connection between painting and phenomenology. As the title indicates, Merleau-Ponty focuses on the artist, in this case Paul Cézanne (and the final part of the essay deals in some detail with Leonardo da Vinci). With this focus, Merleau-Ponty distinguishes himself from Heidegger (although this difference is not thematized): Heidegger had criticized the discipline of aesthetics for its subjectivist tendencies which manifest themselves in a concentration on the artist and the spectator. Against this typically modern focus, Heidegger begins his detailed investigations in 'The Origin of the Work of Art' from the artwork and emphasizes that it is part of the artwork's nature – and, in fact, its strength – that it can stand by itself or rest in itself without necessarily pointing to the artist. There are artworks, for example, where the artist is unknown to us, and this does not detract from their character as artworks.[10]

Merleau-Ponty would not object to this Heideggerian insight as such; as we have seen, he sometimes draws a parallel between the artwork and the lived body, thus emphasizing that the artwork has a material bearer, but also a spiritual component. The traditional alternative of form and content has failed to account for the unity of an artwork which manifests itself, as in the case of a lived body, through a style and a certain 'life' which the artwork has. Nevertheless, according to Merleau-Ponty, the focus on the artist can be useful, especially if this focus includes a criticism of classic accounts. This criticism is developed from an existentialist perspective and builds on the insight that our life is determined by contingency *and* necessity. In 'Cézanne's Doubt', this intertwinement of necessity and freedom which is constitutive for our existence is examined specifically with respect to the history of a life: 'Two things are certain about freedom: that we are never determined and yet that we never change, since, looking back on what we were, we can always find hints of what we have become' (*CD*, 72).

In retrospect, we can give a coherent story of our life and our decisions (provided that we want to). Yet this does not prove in the least that our life was predetermined to develop in a specific way. In the case of an artist, this possibility of a retrospective account gives us the false impression that the connections between life and work are determined by necessity, and that we can understand an artist's work if we know everything about his or her life. This impression is misleading because we again arrive at our explanations in retrospect, after already knowing the artist's work, which makes it easy to find hints and reasons in the artist's life: 'If Cézanne's life seems to us to carry the seeds of his work within it, it is because we get to know his work first and see the circumstances of his life through it, charging them with a meaning borrowed from that work' (*CD*, 70). This does not mean that it would be useless to examine an artist's life; Merleau-Ponty deems many aspects of Cézanne's life relevant, especially his self-doubts, his decision to part ways with the impressionists, his obsession with depicting the world as it presents itself to us, and his need for recognition from others. But we already know the limits of such accounts and should avoid the assumption that the artist's life explains his work. Rather, 'it is true both that the life of an author can teach us nothing and that – if we know how to interpret it – we can find everything in it, since it opens onto his work' (*CD*, 75); life and work shed light on one another.

The doubts and struggles of the artist confirm the ambiguity of our exist-ence, and Merleau-Ponty thus concludes his essay with the following thought: 'We never get away from our life. We never see ideas or freedom face to face' (*CD*, 75). Yet along the way, several insights are gained which confirm the need for and difficulty of a phenomenological examination. Merleau-Ponty says about painting what he *could* also say about phenomenology: 'Cézanne later conceived painting not as the incarnation of imagined scenes, the pro-jection of dreams outward, but as the exact study of appearances' (*CD*, 61) – it is this exact study of appearances which the painter undertakes by way of looking and painting, and the phenomenologist by way of 'looking' and describing in words. Because the painters' means of expression is the visible, and what they are studying is also the visible, they find themselves in a particularly good position to try and show how vision comes about, or how the visible makes itself seen.

A few brief comments concerning the emphasis on vision (without, how-ever, entering into the critical debates about vision instigated by Emmanuel Levinas and other philosophers): First, the emphasis does not mean that qualities like weight or roughness do not play a role; painting a thick red curtain is certainly very different from painting red blood or a red bird's feather. Secondly, there is good reason, from the phenomenological perspec-tive, for the fascination with vision: through vision, the world is experienced as spread out and thus *as* world, whereas other senses tend to give us more of a part or a detail. Thirdly, the painters' preoccupation with the visible does not mean that the invisible would be entirely neglected. The invisible in the interesting sense is actually tied to the visible as its shadow, reverse, or depth, and painters do attend to it, albeit indirectly (cf. Chapter 16).

The most important methodological procedure of phenomenology, namely, the *epochē* which can never be completed, according to Merleau-Ponty, is also required of the painter: 'Cézanne's painting suspends these habits of thought and reveals the base of inhuman nature upon which man has installed himself' (*CD*, 66). The common patterns of thought need to be bracketed or suspended in order to reveal nature, or the brute being which grounds our dwelling. This is where the challenge and also the frustration of painting reside. Both the phenomenologists and the painters thus need to continue trying, making ever new attempts to suspend the habits of thought and disclose how the world comes to appear. However, the phenomenologist uses the means of language, and there are some crucial differences between linguistic works and painting.

(d) Linguistic artworks and paintings

Merleau-Ponty does not shy away from the difficult task of relating and comparing different forms of art to one another. For the purposes of this subsection, the term 'language' will thus be used in the narrow sense to refer to linguistic artworks, or art that involves words, rather than the wide meaning where painting could also be a form of language.

In his essay, 'Indirect Language and the Voices of Silence', Merleau-Ponty confirms several of his earlier findings about language and expression. He emphasizes again that we are mistaken if we conceive of expression as the process of bringing 'a sort of ideal text' to the outside since there is no such text beforehand (*IL*, 80). He also reiterates that we arrive at this mistaken conception partly because we fail to distinguish between 'empirical language' and 'creative language' (equivalent to the distinction between spoken and speaking language) (*IL*, 82). Yet what is new in this text, and allows for the comparison between language and painting, are the themes of silence and history.

Merleau-Ponty states that 'all language is indirect or allusive – that is, if you wish, silence' (*IL*, 80). This formulation is important because it shows that silence, for Merleau-Ponty, is not opposed to language, for language actually 'is' silence in the sense that it is permeated by and depends on silences, pauses, gaps, allusions, blanks and shifts. The 'unsaid' is often as important, perhaps even more important than the 'said'. Therefore, Merleau-Ponty is not discrediting painting when he summarizes his discussion about language and painting as follows: 'In short, language speaks, and the voices of painting are the voices of silence' (*IL*, 117). Painting exhibits its close relation to silence in a more obvious way than language, but both language and painting depend on silence in order to be expressive. Of course, painting is not so much silent because it is inaudible; it is silent because it is indirect and allusive, ambiguous, and dependent on our engagement and interpretation. In all of his texts on painting, Merleau-Ponty points out that painting is not a process of representation or copying. The continuous discussion of the paradox of expression combats the idea that the painter receives a copy of the landscape in his or her mind and then produces a copy of this copy on the canvass. Painting is expression in a much more creative and exploratory fashion, as we have already seen with Cézanne. If it was a mere representation, there would be no silence to painting.

The differences which painting and language exhibit in relation to silence become more tangible when history is taken into consideration. The extensive discussions of history in 'Indirect Language and the Voices of Silence' create some difficulties for the reading because Merleau-Ponty is referring to a Hegelian concept of history and distances himself somewhat from it, albeit not completely. Yet for our purposes, it should be sufficient to conceive of Merleau-Ponty's concept of history as a phenomenological one, with an emphasis on worlds as continuously developing. Merleau-Ponty states that we more easily gain access to a painting after many centuries than we do to a piece of writing. In the case of writing, a greater knowledge of its times is necessary, especially if there are references to historical events, theories or debates. However, Merleau-Ponty argues that 'painting pays curiously for this immediate access to the enduring that it grants itself, for it is subject much more than writing to the passage of time' (*IL*, 117). Painting and sculptures (which Merleau-Ponty here includes in the discussion) have a different materiality and resemble more closely a spatiotemporal object, whereas the elements of writing are words, and 'nothing equals the ductility of speech' (ibid.). A written text from another century is thus at first less accessible than a painting from the same time, but once we have found access to it and its times, it speaks to us more fully and conveys its meaning more easily than a painting.

One could debate whether these characterizations are indeed sufficient or whether the relation to history would need to be investigated in more depth. In any case, it is clear that Merleau-Ponty does not prioritize painting over language or vice versa, but merely investigates their strengths and weaknesses from different perspectives. It is important to note this because some of his statements could in isolation convey the impression of a hierarchy; yet such isolation would break up the argument which Merleau-Ponty is developing.

A further important difference between painting and language concerns their ability to reflect on themselves, which language can do much more easily since it is relatively difficult to 'paint painting' or to reflect on painting by way of painting (*IL*, 117). This difference in the ability and need to reflect means that the writer can and must take a position, as Merleau-Ponty describes it in his later text, 'Eye and Mind':

> Now art, especially painting, draws upon this fabric of brute meaning [. . .].
> Art and only art does so in full innocence. From the writer and the philosopher,

> in contrast, we want opinions and advice. We will not allow them to hold the
> world suspended. [. . .] Music, at the other extreme, is too far on the hither side
> of the world and the designatable to depict anything but certain schemata of
> Being – its ebb and flow, its growth, its upheavals, its turbulence. (*EM*, 123)

Here again, we find statements which might seem to imply a superiority of one
art form over the other, perhaps of painting over music. But it is crucial to
consider that Merleau-Ponty is looking at these art forms here with respect to
one particular feature: <u>the need and possibility to take a position</u>, which the
writer must, the painter does not need to, and the musician cannot. If the
question was, on the other hand, which art form ~~comes closest~~ to brute Being
and the elements, the answer would presumably be th<u>at music is cl</u>osest, with
painting still closer than writing. Furthest removed and thus in stark contrast
to art is science which floats above the world, as it were.

(e) Art and science

The special nature of art – in all its forms – becomes particularly evident when
contrasted with science. A suitable theme to show this contrast is that of space.
Merleau-Ponty returns to this theme in several of his writings and likes to
discuss it with respect to the Renaissance discovery of central perspective with
which art tried to emulate the exactness of science, but failed: 'By remaining
faithful to the phenomena in his investigations of perspective, Cézanne discovered what recent psychologists have come to formulate: the lived perspective, that which we actually perceive, is not a geometric or photographic one'
(*CD*, 64). In his late essay on art, 'Eye and Mind', Merleau-Ponty explores this
topic in depth, employing a historical or genealogical perspective reminiscent
of Husserl's late phenomenology which examines the ways in which certain
ideas are first instituted (see Chapter 3 above). The spirit behind perspectival
painting turns out to be a version of the spirit that guides modern science, and
Merleau-Ponty asks what is lost as a result.

Rather than condemning Renaissance art, Merleau-Ponty identifies the
merit of Renaissance painters, namely, their attempts to 'experiment freely'
with space and depth, trying different approaches to capture them (*EM*, 135).
Yet Renaissance painting has to neglect certain optical and geometrical laws in
order to persist with its proper technique. The natural perspective, '*perspectiva
naturalis*', is replaced by an artificial perspective, '*perspectiva artificialis*',
which forgets about the spherical nature of the visual field or, in terms of

geometry, forgets about Euclid's eight theorems. 'As Panofsky has shown concerning the men of the Renaissance, this enthusiasm was not without bad faith' (*EM*, 135), a bad faith which becomes manifest in such forgetfulness.

Perspectival painting is based on a certain concept of space which coincides with the idea of space conveyed by the modern sciences: space as homogenous and infinite, extending uniformly and boundlessly in all directions. Our space of experience, in contrast, is structured by borders and boundaries. It is divided into regions and territories, and even apart from all social, political and species-related limits, there are limits to my embodied perception, namely, the limits of my visual field or horizon.

In the middle part of 'Eye and Mind', Merleau-Ponty undertakes a discussion of Descartes' *Dioptrics* as a paradigm example of the specifically modern view concerning vision, which is reflected in modern science as well as in art. What motivates Descartes' account is the quest for a 'crystal clear', 'unequivocal' approach to the visual world (*EM*, 130). In order to achieve this, Descartes has to model vision after touch, thereby reducing the world to certain features of size and shape which can be mathematized. As a result, colour and other secondary qualities become negligible, and the world becomes a scenario devoid of 'ubiquity' (*EM*, 131), devoid of mystery, thickness and depth. Renaissance art follows the same procedure. It is interesting to note, however, that the greatest Renaissance artists were those who, in one way or another, violated the rules of the new techniques.

Merleau-Ponty maintains that it is difficult for us to describe our actual experience of space because we are entirely used to the notion of space proposed by the natural sciences. Scientific thought 'looks on from above', and it tries to be so objective that it cannot even focus on specific objects, but rather, concerns itself with the 'object-in-general' (*EM*, 122). The space of the natural sciences is homogenous and infinite, extending uniformly and boundlessly in all three directions, with depth as its third dimension.

In contrast, Merleau-Ponty shows that depth is the most existential dimension since it gives expression to our bodily situatedness. Depth is not a third perspective derived from the other two; from our embodied perspective, depth is the primary dimension because it describes our distance from objects. Furthermore, depth leads us to the realization of the rivalry between objects since depth is the dimension in which objects cover each other and compete for our attention. Art knows about the special significance of depth, and it also knows that space is not uniform and indifferent towards its content. It can therefore also inspire considerations on the difference between space and place[11]: place describes a filled form of spatiality which envelops my lived body and the objects I perceive. Space, in contrast, is always too large and fails to provide stability or orientation.

Further reading

Kwant, R. C. (1963), *The Phenomenological Philosophy of Merleau-Ponty.* Pittsburgh: Duquesne University Press, chapter 2.

Several interesting essays on Merleau-Ponty's philosophy of art and various questions related to it can be found in the following two collections:

Foti, V. (ed.) (1995), *Difference Materiality Painting.* New York: Prometheus Books.
Johnson, G. A. (ed.) (1993), *The Merleau-Ponty Aesthetics Reader: Philosophy and Painting.* Evanston, IL: Northwestern University Press.

A Philosophy of Ambiguity

Main primary literature

Excerpts from *Phenomenology of Perception* as cited in this chapter; 'An unpublished text by Maurice Merleau-Ponty: A Prospectus of His Work' (In *The Primacy of Perception*, pp. 3–11).

Merleau-Ponty's philosophy has been called a philosophy of ambiguity; two important studies of his philosophy in French even use this expression in their titles.[12] Nevertheless, it is not easy to determine quite what Merleau-Ponty means by ambiguity, and there is little sustained discussion of ambiguity as a concept in the literature on Merleau-Ponty.[13] It turns out that ambiguity serves different functions in Merleau-Ponty's philosophy, which are connected but are by no means identical. In this chapter, we will be concerned with these different functions in order to trace out a phenomenological concept of ambiguity: a kind of ambiguity that 'cannot be a matter of reproach, for it is inherent in things', that is, inherent in the phenomena (*PP*, 199/201). In order to approach phenomenological ambiguity, we will outline different functions of ambiguity in the *Phenomenology of Perception* before turning to

Merleau-Ponty's later philosophy where ambiguity is distinguished from ambivalence. The corresponding distinction between good and bad ambiguity will then be utilized to consider cultural ambiguity and the criticism Merleau-Ponty has encountered with respect to this concept.

(a) Ambiguity in the *Phenomenology of Perception*

In the *Phenomenology of Perception*, Merleau-Ponty refers to ambiguity in various contexts and often at crucial moments. He does not discuss ambiguity separately or introduce it as a concept. Especially in his more negative statements, that is, where he discusses a widespread tendency in philosophy and common sense to avoid ambiguity, it seems to be used in its usual or everyday meaning. Yet the concept plays a more important role in its positive usage since it helps Merleau-Ponty to provide a phenomenological description of the body, spatiality, temporality, and so on, and thus develop a 'third way' as an alternative to intellectualism and empiricism. Ambiguity cannot be defined independently of the phenomena to which it applies – just as the phenomenological method also changes depending on the phenomena. At least five functions of the concept of ambiguity can be traced out in the *Phenomenology of Perception*:

(i) Ambiguity is an *inevitable* feature of our existence. Merleau-Ponty points out that we cannot escape ambiguity and that we can encounter ourselves only in ambiguity: 'I know myself only in ambiguity' (*PP*, 402/397); 'our contact with ourselves is achieved only in the sphere of ambiguity' (*PP*, 444/438). In my encounters with myself and with others, there is no complete transparency but always an element of evasion.[14] By pointing out that such ambiguity cannot be eliminated or circumvented, Merleau-Ponty wards off any attempts to approach our existence merely scientifically, in a way that seeks to achieve a certain kind of unambiguous exactitude. Since we are incarnated as well as spiritual beings, no complete exactitude devoid of ambiguity can be reached in the crucial matters of our existence.

(ii) Ambiguity is an *essential* determination of our existence. This point is somewhat similar to (i), but designates a more positive insight. Not only should we realize that 'ambiguity is of the essence of human existence' (*PP*, 196/197), but there is in fact 'a genius for ambiguity which might serve to define man'[15]

(*PP*, 220/220). The expression 'genius for ambiguity' arises in the course of a discussion regarding speech and describes once again our ambiguous situation as beings for whom everything is both manufactured and natural – and yet we orientate ourselves in this world without getting confused by this duality. In fact, we are usually so unaware of this dual nature, indeed even taking it for granted, that we are easily persuaded by one-sided explanations of our existence. Even though we have a genius for ambiguity, we normally employ this genius without explicitly directing our attention towards ambiguity; it simply serves to orientate us in our ambiguous existence. Phenomenology helps to make us aware of the significance of ambiguity.

(iii) Ambiguity describes the *dual* character of our existence, or the character of 'both . . . and . . .'. We are both freedom and contingency, both incarnated and spiritual beings. Our existence always involves both of these opposed dimensions, we can neither eliminate one of them (not even temporarily), nor can we join them together to form a consistent unity (since they are opposites). In an important passage on spatial ambiguity, Merleau-Ponty writes:

> What needs to be understood is that for the same reason I am present here and now, and present elsewhere and always, and also absent from here and from now, and absent from every place and from every time. This ambiguity is not some imperfection of consciousness or existence, but the definition of them. (*PP*, 387/383)

As human beings, we are both present in this place and absent from every place; we are both situated and supersede every situation. We will return to this passage under the heading of cultural ambiguity.

(iv) Ambiguity describes the *vague boundaries* of certain dimensions of our existence. This concerns especially the realm of sexuality, but also other dimensions; it seems that Merleau-Ponty turns to an examination of the vague boundaries of sexuality because he is engaged in a dialogue with Freudian psychoanalysis. Psychoanalysis has rightly emphasized the fact that sexuality encompasses a great deal more than explicitly sexual acts and organs. As an 'ambiguous atmosphere', sexuality appears to be 'coextensive' with life (*PP*, 196/197). The sexual realm cannot be clearly delimited; as an 'atmosphere', it can make itself present unexpectedly, and often even unbeknownst to us. However, caution is required here. It would be wrong to reduce all of life's activities to the promptings of (sublimated) sexual drives and impulses. Even though the limits of the sexual cannot be determined, it is still just one among many dimensions of our life.

(v) Ambiguity *permeates* various dimensions of the world in a parallel fashion: 'Thus, to sum up, the ambiguity of being-in-the-world is translated by that of the body, and this is understood through that of time' (*PP*, 98/100). The structure of the *Phenomenology of Perception* is determined by the way in which bodily ambiguity, spatial ambiguity, temporal ambiguity, and problems of freedom and contingency gear into one another. Although different kinds of ambiguity can be treated separately, it turns out that they can be translated into one another.

While these different forms and functions of ambiguity might appear to operate on different levels, there is a close affinity between the ambiguity of existence and the ambiguity of the world if we bear in mind that existence is being-towards-the-world and that the world in Merleau-Ponty's sense is the world of existence rather than the merely objective (and thus unambiguous) world posited by science. Overall, Merleau-Ponty's reflections on ambiguity imply that we have a tendency to avoid ambiguity and strive for unequivocal exactness – hence the success of the mathematical sciences. While it is indeed attractive to give clear answers and justify them in a universally intelligible fashion, it is easily forgotten that this ideal imposes substantial limitations on the kinds of questions which can be asked. Furthermore, it becomes tempting to seek exact answers even for those questions which resist quantification. Merleau-Ponty's continuous criticism of intellectualism and empiricism combats this temptation.

In contrast, a phenomenological investigation discloses an essential ambiguity at the core of our existence. Yet it is by no means sufficient to merely discover ambiguity and close the examination at that point. Rather, phenomenology needs to face up to ambiguity, as it were, and explore it more closely. In *The Visible and the Invisible*, Merleau-Ponty differentiates between several attitudes toward ambiguity. Most importantly, he distinguishes a 'relapse into ambivalence' (*VI*, 93/130) from a thought which 'envisages without restriction the plurality of the relationships and what has been called ambiguity' (*VI*, 94/131).

(b) Good and bad ambiguity

The distinction between ambiguity and ambivalence seems to correspond to the distinction between 'good' and 'bad' ambiguity which Merleau-Ponty sometimes proposes (*Prosp.*, 11).[16] Merleau-Ponty's example for 'bad ambiguity' concerns 'an analysis of perception' which 'mixes finitude and universality, interiority and exteriority, etc'. (ibid.). This statement should not be read as disqualifying all analysis of perception and thus the entire *Phenomenology of Perception*. Such a disqualifying statement would appear strange not just in light of the consistency of Merleau-Ponty's philosophy, but also because his example of good ambiguity, namely, expression, plays such a crucial role in the *Phenomenology of Perception*. Merleau-Ponty describes expression as a form of good ambiguity because it involves 'a spontaneity which combines the apparently impossible', ultimately joining 'monads into a nexus of past and present, nature and culture' (ibid.).

The tenor of these difficult statements seems to be that a mere 'mixture' is problematic, whereas a 'combination' still retains the tension between the combined elements. Expression proves a particularly interesting phenomenon because a paradox emerges here; expression does not translate a previous thought, and yet neither does it emerge out of nowhere.[17] Furthermore, the phenomenon of expression raises questions regarding 'how' and 'why', that is, regarding genealogy, and ultimately regarding history and culture. Although Merleau-Ponty does not spell out these thoughts, it seems to follow from them that a phenomenological analysis of ambiguity must be as 'concrete' as possible, asking why and how perceptual phenomena are ambiguous.

Overall, ambiguity is 'bad' if it is used to provide a point of closure where further examination is called for. Merleau-Ponty emphasizes that 'ambiguity is of the essence of human existence' (*PP*, 196/197). The main task concerning ambiguous phenomena (such as the erotic) thus consists in diagnosing the ambiguity as an essential one which lies at the very core of the phenomenon. This diagnosis should not prevent further exploration but rather invite a more thorough study of the various dimensions of the phenomenon. Yet where does this exploration lead? It becomes tempting to go beyond a mere 'neither-nor' (or 'both-and') and attempt a more positive determination. These attempts lead to a second, problematic kind of 'good ambiguity' – an ambiguity which Merleau-Ponty later criticizes as simply another 'bad ambiguity'. This might be described as a conceptual treatment of ambiguity, the endeavour to capture the ambiguity in concepts. This enterprise moves the discussion away from the phenomenon to a higher level of synthesis.

Phenomenal ambiguity may also be described as an ambiguity in perception, in contrast to the conceptual approach to ambiguity. Even though the intention to grasp the phenomenal ambiguity in a conceptual way may itself be admirable, it usually results in the idea of a mixture – a mixture of inner and outer, finite and infinite. Merleau-Ponty's analyses show precisely that the phenomena in question make it impossible to determine the precise measure of each component and thus elude the concept of mixture.

Interpreters of Merleau-Ponty's work have suggested that his late philosophy avoids the pitfalls of moving from a phenomenal ambiguity to a conceptual solution of ambiguity by giving more and more significance to the idea of structure.[18] Already in his essay, 'Indirect Language and the Voices of Silence', Merleau-Ponty returns to Ferdinand de Saussure to explain how meaning arises from the differences between signifiers, and hence from an entire structure of interrelated elements. A satisfying account of language can thus take its departure neither from isolated words nor from a mere accumulation of words. It must focus on language as a structural whole and on the relation between words. In his late philosophy, Merleau-Ponty describes not only language, but experience and perception in terms of structure. Experience arises from a field that becomes increasingly organized and meaningful. Structures are formed by way of differences and relations. The quest for an original reality prior to all expression can only be futile; expression is not an externalization of a primordial or inner reality. As a consequence, ambiguity cannot be explained through a synthetic account of mixture. Ambiguity cannot be resolved, but only analysed. This may appear frustrating, but in fact, any other kind of ambiguity would not truly be an ambiguity, it would rather be an intermediary stage in a process of clarification.

> Merleau-Ponty has thus provided a distinction between three forms of ambiguity: (a) a bad ambiguity where the tension between incompatible elements is resolved by way of a mixture such that philosophical questioning comes to an end; (b) a good ambiguity that is a true phenomenal ambiguity, an ambiguity which is essential to the phenomenon in question; (c) a problematic ambiguity which consists in the ultimately unsatisfying attempt to resolve phenomenal ambiguity by way of conceptual synthesis.

Following Merleau-Ponty's insistence on the concrete dimensions of ambiguity, we will now turn to cultural ambiguity and see whether Merleau-Ponty's considerations here are convincing in terms of his own distinction between good and bad ambiguity, and in terms of the criticism directed at him.[19]

(c) Cultural ambiguity

What does it mean to say that I am present here and now as well as absent here and now? Importantly, it means that we are both here and now *and* beyond all here and now. The implications of this statement will become clearer when we consider the question of cultural ambiguity. Merleau-Ponty's philosophy of culture has sometimes been conceived and criticized as a weak cultural relativism. A rather complex and subtle version of this criticism may be found in the work of Emmanuel Levinas; we shall bring out certain moments of this criticism here and suggest the outlines of a Merleau-Pontian response.[20] In his essay, 'Meaning and Sense', Levinas develops a criticism of philosophies of culture which he directs specifically at Merleau-Ponty. The position of contemporary philosophy of culture, according to Levinas, can be summed up as 'truth would be inseparable from its historical expression' (*MS*, 83); Merleau-Ponty would indeed deem the quest for a truth outside of historical givenness nonsensical.

Levinas does not criticize philosophies of culture for their emphasis on culture as such, but for assuming that culture is an irreducible, original structure. Moreover, Merleau-Ponty describes relations between cultures as lateral, thus situating them on one and the same plane, whereas Levinas emphasizes that the relation is vertical or asymmetrical. At the same time, there is a justification for Merleau-Ponty's description even from Levinas's perspective. As Levinas puts it, 'there does exist the possibility of a Frenchman learning Chinese and passing from one culture into another, without the intermediary of an Esperanto that would falsify both tongues which it mediated' (*MS*, 88). There is not one universal language that all languages need to pass through in order for translation to be possible. In that sense, all languages operate on the same level.

Levinas, by contrast, emphasizes verticality as the original mode of our encounter with the Other. According to him, Merleau-Ponty's analysis forgets about 'orientation' – the original orientation that motivates and inspires the Frenchman to learn Chinese, which obviously precedes the actual learning process (ibid.). This original orientation would be our original direction towards the Other who is not just a member of a specific culture, but first and foremost my interlocutor. When it comes to ethical questions, the cultural background of the Other is on the most basic level irrelevant, Levinas argues; we are not exempt from our responsibility because the Other comes from a different cultural world to our own.

Although it is not quite clear which texts by Merleau-Ponty Levinas is relying on, the text 'Everywhere and Nowhere' from *Signs* seems a likely candidate. 'Everywhere and Nowhere' is a rich and complex text. In it, Merleau-Ponty criticizes Hegel's concept of history, but joins in certain ways Husserl's idea of the historical lifeworld. While Hegel bases his philosophy of history on the problematic notion of absolute knowing such that it stands and falls with the possibility of our having such knowledge, 'Husserl had understood: our philosophical problem is to open up the concept without destroying it' (*EN*, 138). Opening up the concept without destroying it is also necessitated by the essential ambiguity which characterizes not just existence, but as it turns out, history as well. In fact, 'it is through their ambiguity that philosophy and history touch' (*EN*, 132).

Does this emphasis on ambiguity mean that Merleau-Ponty excludes the possibility of meaning outside of cultural expressions and values? Interestingly, Merleau-Ponty here introduces the notion of an 'oblique universality': He does not expand on this concept, but it might be permissible to think of it as an ambiguous universality which would bear some relation to the way in which ambiguity connects humans universally. To understand Merleau-Ponty's ideas about cultural ambiguity and oblique universality better, the passage in which the latter notion is introduced should be read in its entirety:

> We would have to apply to the problem of philosophical universality what travelers tell us of their relationships with foreign civilizations. Photographs of China give us the impression of an impenetrable universe if they stop with the picturesque – stop, that is, with precisely *our* clipping, *our* idea of China. If, on the other hand, a photograph just tries to grasp Chinese people in the act of living together, they begin paradoxically to live for us, and we understand them. If we were able to grasp in their historical and human context the very doctrines which seem to resist conceptual understanding, we would find in them a variant of man's relationship to being which would clarify our understanding of ourselves, and a sort of oblique universality. (*EN*, 139)

In its strange simplicity, this passage about photographs of China is plausible as well as puzzling. In the case of a photograph which portrays our idea of China, the Chinese world remains entirely inaccessible to us; all we receive is a picture of our own idea. As an idea, our conception of China is accessible to us; yet it is already an idea of the strangers as *in*accessible. Moreover, the photograph of China which is based on this idea is still a photograph *of* China, thus bringing into view the real China while at the same time shutting it out again since we receive it only through our own lens.

On the other hand, a photograph which is merely receptive and does not bring in a preconceived idea – if such a photograph were possible – allows us to see the Chinese people 'in the act of living together', thus letting us catch a glimpse of how they see themselves. Despite their alienness, there is a sense in which we understand them; and this understanding is not hybrid or violent. It is a more intuitive understanding of the way in which they exist in the world, even though their world is alien to ours. Although their senses of their bodies and their freedom will be very different from ours, they are also exposed to the ambiguity which stems from the fact that we are incarnated *and* spiritual beings, determined by freedom *and* contingency.

The result of these observations is not simply that some photographs are better than others and that Merleau-Ponty helps us to describe the difference between them. Rather, he requests that we think these two observations together. The Chinese are both accessible and inaccessible to us, and this does not mean that they are 'somewhat' accessible; rather, there is something absolute both in the accessibility and in the inaccessibility. What Husserl says about the Other, namely, that he or she is accessible in the mode of inaccessibility,[21] holds also for the stranger. Yet the level of complexity increases since the stranger is inaccessible by virtue of coming from an alien world or 'impenetrable universe'.

At the same time, the stranger is on a fundamental level also the Other, and Merleau-Ponty would seem to agree with Levinas that there are forms of our encounter with the Other – such as the ethical encounter – where the world of the Other remains insignificant. There is an 'oblique universality' which concerns 'man's relationship to being'. The passage about the photographs from China thus complements the passage cited earlier about spatial ambiguity. We are here and now, and present elsewhere and always (for example, when imagining ourselves elsewhere), and yet also absent from every place (for example, when we are concerned with ideal objects). We are here, and everywhere and nowhere. Human existence means being entirely tied down to this place and at the same time, to transcend all place. It means being entirely in this body and yet beyond this body.

From a Merleau-Pontian perspective, Levinas appears to overstate the second dimension of this ambiguity at the expense of the first. Levinas emphasizes transcendence and infinity, especially in the ways in which the

Other infinitely transcends my idea of him or her. If Levinas were confronted with the objection, uttered from a Merleau-Pontian perspective, that he places too much emphasis on our absence from the here and now, Levinas would likely respond that our everyday situation in the here and now is more accessible to us, and yet the difficulty consists in thinking the enigma of transcendence, absence, and that which is beyond space and time. Regardless of how this imaginary dialogue would be resolved, it has become obvious that Merleau-Ponty can respond to Levinas's criticism regarding the absence of all universality.

However, Levinas's main criticism of contemporary philosophy of culture concerns the impossibility of 'judging' cultural meaning from an ethical perspective. Of course, Levinas does not envision judgements in the usual sense where certain cultures would be condemned for violating human rights; that would be a different issue and requires a different kind of analysis. Rather, he points out that the Other's cultural world of origin becomes insignificant when the Other calls upon me. Would Merleau-Ponty allow for such a possibility? We have already seen that Merleau-Ponty acknowledges our dual nature, which also means that we belong to a specific culture and yet transcend this culture. This would allow for the possibility that ethics might go beyond specific cultures – without, however, leading to the formulation of ethical principles in a universal fashion. It seems that Merleau-Ponty could agree with de Beauvoir's conviction that ethics needs to be based on ambiguity (even though his conception of ambiguity differs somewhat from that of de Beauvoir's).[22]

Merleau-Ponty would not exclude the possibility of an ethical calling that transcends cultural limits, it seems. In this respect as well, Levinas's criticism appears questionable or more applicable to certain theorists and philosophers who might be influenced by Merleau-Ponty than to Merleau-Ponty himself. Merleau-Ponty's phenomenology does not proffer a cultural relativism which would demand absolute tolerance and prohibit an ethical response. We are called to attend to various aspects of ambiguity. Yet is this good or bad ambiguity, in Merleau-Ponty's terms? Merleau-Ponty maintains that 'what enables us to centre our existence is also what prevents us from centring it completely' (*PP*, 98/100).[23] As incarnated beings, we are both culturally and historically located *and* transcend this location. In line with Merleau-Ponty's critique of bad ambiguity, it is important not to create a soft 'mixture' from such statements. We are not a little bit situated and a little bit beyond situatedness, as if we had room for manoeuvre in this respect. Rather, we are completely situated and cannot escape the confines of our actual situation, which becomes especially obvious when we would like to escape from the here and now. At the same time, our existence cannot be reduced to the here and now, but goes beyond it by virtue of the fact that we are spiritual beings, concerned with ideas, memories and phantasies. It holds true once again that 'this ambiguity is not some imperfection of consciousness or existence, but the definition of them' (*PP*, 387/383).

Further reading

Glendinning, S. (2007), 'The genius of man' in Baldwin, T. (ed.), *Reading Merleau-Ponty. On Phenomenology of Perception*. London: Routledge, pp. 104–17.

Halda, B. (1966), *Merleau-Ponty ou la philosophie de l'ambiguïté*. Paris: Archives des Lettres Modernes, no. 72.

Langer, M. (2003), 'Beauvoir and Merleau-Ponty on ambiguity' in Card, C. (ed.), *The Cambridge Companion to Simone de Beauvoir*. Cambridge: Cambridge University Press, pp. 87–106.

Sapontzis, S. F. (1978), 'A note on Merleau-Ponty's Ambiguity' in *Philosophy and Phenomenological Research*, vol. 38, no. 4, pp. 538–43.

Waelhens, A. de (1951), *Une philosophie de l'ambiguïté. L'existentialisme de Merleau-Ponty*. Louvain: Publications universitaires de Louvain.

Flesh, Reversibility, Chiasm

Main primary literature

'The Intertwining, the Chiasm' (in *The Visible and the Invisible*, pp. 130–62/172–204).

The idea of reversibility finds perhaps its most lucid formulations in Merleau-Ponty's phenomenology of art; it emerges particularly vividly in his descriptions of painters (e.g. Paul Klee) who state that the trees and mountains look at them. In his late work *The Visible and the Invisible*, Merleau-Ponty develops his ideas about the reversibility of perception into an ontology, based on phenomenological grounds. Written between 1959 and 1961, *The Visible and the Invisible* was left incomplete, but with fascinating working notes for its unwritten sections.

(a) Self-critique and the late project

There are several passages in the working notes to *The Visible and the Invisible* in which Merleau-Ponty situates his late philosophy by way of a self-criticism.

In retrospect, the project of the *Phenomenology of Perception* relied too much on the notion of consciousness, and the constant discussion of intellectualism and empiricism perhaps made it more difficult to see the positive contribution of the phenomenological approach as a third way. However, it is always difficult to identify and describe a 'turn' in a philosopher's work, and with Merleau-Ponty, such an endeavour becomes even more difficult than it is with Husserl (who explicitly distinguished between static and genetic phenomenology) or Heidegger (who sometimes speaks of such a 'turn'). The shift of emphasis in Merleau-Ponty somewhat resembles Heidegger's 'turn' because the former now approaches experience from the side of the world or of being (which, in contrast to Heidegger, he describes as 'mute' or 'wild' being). There are a number of references in Merleau-Ponty's working notes which build on Heideggerian insights, such as the following: 'Perception has me as has language' (*VI*, 190/244). Both language and perception can only be adequately grasped if we acknowledge that they are not something we have at our disposal, but something to which we belong and, at the same time, to which we are exposed.

Yet it would be misleading to regard Merleau-Ponty's late philosophy as a shift from Husserl to Heidegger. Merleau-Ponty still discusses Husserl extensively in this late work. When Merleau-Ponty proposes to examine experiences before they have been split up into 'subject' and 'object' (*VI*, 130/172), he seems to pursue a very similar project to Husserl's investigations of 'passive synthesis' as a level prior to subjective activity, and prior to the subject's having a fully-fledged object (Chapter 2 above). But the self-criticism directed against the *Phenomenology of Perception* is also a criticism of the Husserlian influence in that work. This mixture of continuity and discontinuity already indicates that the question concerning a turn in Merleau-Ponty's work is a complex one which we will not be able to resolve here; yet we shall return to these questions when examining the notion of flesh which both develops and breaks with the earlier phenomenology of the lived body.

By way of the discussions with Husserl and Heidegger, and in several other ways which the examination of flesh will reveal, Merleau-Ponty still undertakes a phenomenology in his late work, albeit in a transformed shape; but he now places a stronger emphasis on ontology as we shall see in more detail at the end of this chapter. Another influence from his early philosophy which persists into the late work stems from *Gestalt* psychology. The focus on *Gestalten* or structures allows him to revise his earlier philosophy of consciousness. Merleau-Ponty states quite explicitly: 'To be conscious = to have a figure on a ground – one cannot go back any further' (*VI*, 191/245).

Any attempt to go back further would involve metaphysical assumptions about the existence of consciousness which Merleau-Ponty strives to avoid.

Perhaps the most fruitful justification for the need to revise his earlier philosophy can be found in Merleau-Ponty's statement that the visible is 'much more than a correlative of my vision'; rather, it 'imposes my vision on me as a continuation of its own sovereign existence' (*VI*, 131/173). For example, if I want to explain how and why I direct my attention at an object, something like a call or allure issued by the perceptual object needs to be examined. Merleau-Ponty sometimes even speaks of a 'rivalry' between things which are fighting for my gaze.

> **Reversibility** is the term Merleau-Ponty chooses to designate the fact that a uni-directional movement cannot account for perception in general and vision in particular. The visible is not merely a correlative of my vision; the visible also looks at me.

Merleau-Ponty points out that reversibility is always on the verge of happening but is 'never realized in fact' (*VI*, 147/194). Although the roles of perceiving and being perceived can be reversed (most explicitly in the case of my hands touching and being touched), there is no complete coincidence, but rather a delay. Furthermore, the way in which the visible looks at me is not the same as my way of looking at the visible. Nevertheless, the description should not be taken as 'purely metaphorical', but as reflective of the way in which I experience my perceptual interaction with the world.

> **Chiasm** names roughly the same crossing-over as reversibility, bringing it to expression with the help of the Greek letter *chi*: χ. Merleau-Ponty states that '[t]he chiasm is not only a me-other exchange [. . .], it is also an exchange between me and the world, between the phenomenal body and the "objective" body, between the perceiving and the perceived' (*VI*, 215/268).

The phenomena of crossing, folding, intertwining and reversing all depend on the concept of flesh which we shall now examine. Merleau-Ponty discusses flesh in much more detail and more explicitly than reversibility and chiasm, and this allows us to trace out its motivation and main characteristics.

(b) Flesh – an introduction

Merleau-Ponty claims that 'he who sees cannot possess the visible unless he is possessed by it, unless he is of it, unless, by principle, according to what is required by the articulation of the look with the things, he is one of the visible, capable, by a singular reversal, of seeing them – he who is one of them' (*VI*, 134f./177f.). This means that perception would only be possible because we are part of the visible, of the 'same flesh'. To be sure, not everybody (certainly not every philosopher) might accept this necessary condition for perception as Merleau-Ponty proposes it; yet it seems plausible that the possibility of bridging the gap between perceiving and being perceived would be inexplicable if we were not already part of the perceptual landscape, ourselves being perceivable.

When approaching the concept of 'flesh', it is important to bear in mind that Merleau-Ponty aims to describe experience prior to the split between 'subject' and 'object'. 'Flesh' sustains both of these dimensions, and it is thus not surprising that Merleau-Ponty will describe flesh as doubled, like two sides or two leaves, such as those of seeing and seen, touching and touched. Later on, he will need to tackle the difficult question as to how, on the basis of flesh, the nature of our lived body can be characterized, and whether his new concept runs the risk of lapsing into a monism (which, according to Merleau-Ponty, it does not). These problems are mentioned here at the beginning to create a horizon within which to investigate flesh, pointing out some of the dangers and difficulties.

Even before introducing the term, let me cite two important reminders by Merleau-Ponty: 'What we are calling flesh, this interiorly worked-over mass, has no name in any philosophy' (*VI*, 147/193). Merleau-Ponty thus warns us that we will not be successful if we try to find an explanation of flesh in some other philosophy. At the same time, we will see below that he refers us to the old notion 'element' to help us understand flesh better. Furthermore, 'the flesh is not matter, is not spirit, is not substance' (*VI*, 139/184). This reminder is important because flesh will at times appear to resemble matter (remember the enigmatic comment cited above about the 'interiorly worked-over mass'), at other times to resemble spirit; but if such connections are to be plausible, they require us to think matter and spirit in a new way, such that they would not be contradictorily opposed to one another.

The following sentence in which Merleau-Ponty introduces flesh needs to be examined closely since it contains several important elements, aside from marking the first appearance of this central notion: 'Between the alleged colors and visibles, we would find anew the tissue that lines them, sustains them, nourishes them, and which for its part is not a thing, but a possibility, a latency, and a *flesh* of things' (*VI*, 132 f./175). Flesh is thus something which arises 'in between' the visibles (one might be reminded here of the way in which meaning, for de Saussure and Merleau-Ponty, arises from the interrelations between signifiers). It is not a collection of visible elements, but arises in between them, as a kind of 'tissue'. The character of flesh as a tissue with nodes and folds will be explored in more detail below. At this point, we are told merely that the tissue sustains the visible, somewhat like a (back-)ground which does not itself appear but is a necessary condition of what does.

(c) Flesh – some characteristics

In line with his 'indirect ontology' (which will briefly be described in the following section), Merleau-Ponty approaches the concept of flesh in several ways, partly through images and comparisons.

(i) *World*: In later marginal comments on his first text which discusses the notion of flesh, Merleau-Ponty indicates several connections between flesh and world (world taken in the phenomenological sense). For example, he writes: 'the world, the flesh not as fact or sum of facts, but as the locus of an inscription of truth' (*VI*, 131/173 n.), and later on: 'we are the world that thinks itself' (*VI*, 136/179 n.). Just as the phenomenological notion of world does not designate facts or a collection thereof, but rather a context of references, so flesh also extends throughout the visible and in the interstices of its elements, as we have seen. The connection between flesh and world is important because the concept of flesh is meant to describe the way in which we are immersed in the world and share the visibility of the world.

However, flesh can only be conceived as world if the latter is taken in a 'thick' or 'material' way. The Husserlian connotation of world as horizon can still be helpful, but it would require us to think 'the horizon as being,'[24] in all its density. When Merleau-Ponty writes that 'we are the world that thinks itself', this certainly does not mean that flesh would be a kind of pure spirit. There is a reflection peculiar to flesh which is not of the purely intellectual kind, but which is rather a kind of crossing that resembles a folded tissue.

(ii) *Tissue, folds, and nodes*: The image of tissue (*VI*, 132f./175) provides us with a helpful way of approaching flesh: like a tissue, flesh provides a background for the visible, carrying it while nevertheless being the same kind of thing. Furthermore, a tissue is often woven: a net of interwoven threads which cross each other and thus engender stability. However, the image of a tissue might convey the impression that flesh has a material nature, which is not the case – at least, flesh is not *solely* material. If we can conceive a tissue that is sensing as well as sensed, we would avoid the misunderstanding that takes Merleau-Ponty to be a materialist.

Tissue is an apposite image also because it can be folded; it can be structured in such a way as to create nodes and folds, which are also helpful images in understanding the nature of flesh. More precisely, folds and nodes designate the ways in which the flesh thickens up to create a landscape of visibility. For example, a specific shade of red 'is a certain node in the woof of the simultaneous and the successive' (*VI*, 132/174); this citation reminds us that flesh is not merely spatial, but – like the world – is also temporal. Even more mysterious are the folds of flesh, which should not be confused with a mere thickening of material, but designate a 'coiling over' of the visible upon itself (*VI*, 140/185) in such a way that vision comes about: Merleau-Ponty speaks of 'this fold, this central cavity of the visible which is my vision' (*VI*, 146/192). In vision, the seeing and the seen come to touch, like two folded pleats flush against one another. There is no abyss between a seeing subject and a seen object that needs to be bridged, but rather a magical event of vision which calls for a different kind of description to capture its strange character of doubling and crossing.

(iii) *Crossing, touching, doubling*: At the beginning of the chapter 'The Intertwining – The Chiasm', Merleau-Ponty offers some reflections on perception which resemble the analysis of double-sensations from the *Phenomenology of Perception*. It has therefore been claimed that the idea of a reversibility at the heart of flesh is a continuation of the earlier analyses of double-sensations.[25] Such a claim is plausible since the connection between touching and being touched, seeing and being seen is indeed the main topic of the text. Vision and touch are mysterious experiences which take place between 'two leaves', as Merleau-Ponty likes to put it. However, the late account differs from the earlier since vision is no longer described as a form of consciousness, but as arising in the very midst of the visible. The interplay between vision and touch then reveals itself as a relation between two 'maps': the maps of the visible and the tangible are complete, but they do not merge into one (*VI*, 134/177).

(iv) *Elements*: In order to explain how flesh is neither matter nor spirit, Merleau-Ponty refers us to 'the old term "element", in the sense it was used to speak of water, air, earth, and fire' (*VI*, 139/184). An element belongs to a particular location or region without being tied to it: air is usually, but not always, 'above' earth. My body is made up of these elements, thus inhabiting an intermediate position. Furthermore, the element in the ancient sense is not strictly speaking material, but 'midway between spatio-temporal object and idea' (ibid.). This midway-character is difficult to capture; it is a material- ized idea or an 'incarnate principle' which introduces a certain 'style of being' (ibid.) thus reminding us of the significance of style which extends throughout Merleau-Ponty's work. The style of water, for example, is not captured in its chemical formula, but concerns the way in which it can undergo consistent transformations from ice to liquid to steam, preserving nevertheless its watery character.

(v) *Intercorporeality, anonymity, and the labor of desire*: Finally, the con- cept of flesh also allows for a new description of the realm which has traditionally been referred to as 'intersubjectivity' and which has always created problems for the phenomenological analysis. According to Merleau- Ponty, the so-called 'problem of the alter ego' is ill-conceived because 'an anonymous visibility inhabits both of us' (*VI*, 142/187). On the most primordial level, there is no subject which needs to bridge the gap between itself and another subject. Rather, my own body is already a crossing or folding of touching and being touched which Merleau-Ponty describes as an original 'narcissism'. This crossing can be extended to other bodies, other 'narcissi', creating an 'intercorporeity' (*VI*, 141/185). This term has proved inspirational for later phenomenologists[26] and designates a relation from body to body which does not require a detour through consciousness. Traditionally, 'inter- subjectivity' was thought to require a kind of realization that the body over there is a body inhabited by a consciousness like my own body. Yet this does not do justice to our experience of relations with other people, especially in desire: 'And henceforth movement, touch, vision, applying themselves to the other and to themselves, return toward their source and, in the patient and silent labour of desire, begin the paradox of expression' (*VI*, 144/189). Desire connects body to body in such a way that the world becomes irrelevant.

In this kind of intercorporeal crossing-over, the reversibility between inside and outside perhaps acquires its most immediate shape.

(d) An ontology of the invisible?

Merleau-Ponty's account of flesh gives rise to a number of questions and problems which he himself thematizes. We shall discuss two of them here: the relation between the flesh and the lived body, and the relation between flesh and the invisible.

If my body is of the same flesh as the world, how can we still speak of the lived body? Where can we identify the limit between body and world? Merleau-Ponty states that the lived body holds a special position because it is a 'sensible for itself' (VI, 135/178); it is capable of double sensations. Although this response is familiar from his earlier philosophy, Merleau-Ponty is careful not to rely on any assumptions about subjects and objects or consciousness and world. Instead, he arrives at the idea of the lived body as a sensible for itself by way of a short phenomenological analysis of touching which shows that there are three different kinds of touching: feeling qualities such as smooth or rough, touching spatio-temporal things, and touching that which feels the touch from within. In some sense, the entire project of *The Visible and the Invisible* stems from the enigma that there is a seeing and touching which is embedded in the world and, at the same time, sees and touches it, thus folding the world onto itself. Bodily sensation 'is immersed in the world that it senses, and it makes the world appear somehow from the middle of itself'.[27] The landscape of the visible becomes 'inhabited' by a touch and a vision (VI, 135/178).

Merleau-Ponty likes to speak of the lived body and the world as two circles or vortices which are usually concentric, but become decentred when I start to reflect and ask questions (VI, 138/182). By way of thought, centres are created in the visible, and the question as to how thought arises, or how the sentient being can also come to think, turns into an attempt to comprehend 'how there is a centre' (VI, 145/191). On the basis of this description, the question of consciousness can be posed anew. Consciousness turns out to be such a centre; yet the unity of consciousness is based on the 'prereflective and preobjective unity of my body' (VI, 141f./186). This prereflective unity which emerges as the visible is inhabited by a touching and seeing makes up the unity of my lived body and confronts me with the limit between lived body and world which is not so much a clear dividing line as the difference between a node and the tissue that surrounds it. Yet it still holds true that my lived body in its thickness is my only means of connecting with the world (*VI*, 135/178), and that we have a world only because we are such strange creatures with two dimensions or leaves: perceiving and being perceived.

Merleau-Ponty's working notes show that he intended to pursue these ideas further. His considerations would probably have led him to explore the realm of 'intercorporeity' in more depth. The problem of solipsism as it is usually posed is ill-conceived, according to Merleau-Ponty.[28] The question 'Do others exist?' is posed by an ego that already finds itself in the midst of others and abstracts from them for the sake of a thought experiment. If there was such a thing as true solipsism, there would need to be only a 'single self', a *solus ipse*. Instead, we find ourselves in the midst of other bodies. If consciousness turns out to be in the first place not an intellectual reflection but rather a crossing and doubling based on a fundamental narcissism which I share with others, the task for phenomenology might be an examination of different kinds of interrelation and separation, desire and evasion.

The second issue, which Merleau-Ponty describes as 'the most difficult point', concerns 'the bond between the flesh and the idea, between the visible and the interior armature which it manifests and which it conceals' (*VI*, 149/195). We have seen in the discussion of the characteristics of the flesh that, for Merleau-Ponty, there is no abyss between the flesh and the idea; rather, the flesh turns out to be an incarnate principle or idea. The bond which he considers difficult to describe is thus an intimate one which, according to Merleau-Ponty, has best been captured by Proust, who manages to present the idea as the 'depth' of the sensible. The idea as depth of the sensible would indeed be a kind of interior of the flesh which it 'manifests' and 'conceals' at the same time. The idea exists only as manifested in the flesh of its incarnation; it does not come to the fore as such, but only indirectly.

The idea in this sense turns out to be equivalent to the invisible; the idea is the 'invisible *of* this world' (*VI*, 151/198).

> The **invisible** is not the opposite of the visible, but its interior or depth. It is the depth of this world inscribed within the visible – a peculiar absence which is not absolute, or a 'negativity which is not nothing' (*VI*, 151/198).

The engagement with such an essential shadow, with the invisible of the world, makes it necessary for Merleau-Ponty to develop his phenomenology as an *indirect ontology* (*VI*, 179/233), approaching the invisible through the visible by trying to uncover the depth dimension or inherent shadow which lies at the bottom of that which shows itself.

At the end of the chapter, Merleau-Ponty turns to language as a theme that has been important throughout his philosophy and which now helps him to explain the difficult concepts of flesh, chiasm and reversibility. The relation between language and silence is analogous to the relation between the visible and the invisible in the sense that silence is not the opposite of language, but rather, 'silence continues to envelop language' (*VI*, 176/230). There is no language without silence, and hearing is essential to an understanding of speech; here, Merleau-Ponty and Heidegger agree. Language is a fascinating phenomenon because as Merleau-Ponty says, following Valéry, 'language is everything' (*VI*, 155/203): it is the voice of nobody and, at the same time, the voice of everybody and everything, including objects and nature.

The discussion of language might also help with the problem of a monism which is often raised with respect to the concept of flesh: Is a monism not implied in the claim that everything is of the same flesh?[29] Here is Merleau-Ponty's own response: 'We are beyond monism and dualism, because dualism has been pushed so far that the opposites, no longer in competition, are at rest the one against the other, coextensive with one another' (*VI*, 54f./80f.). He situates his philosophy beyond monism and dualism, at least in the traditional sense, because it would not make sense, for example, to describe the relation between speech and silence as a dualism: silence envelops language, and language is everything. These latter two claims, despite initial impressions to the contrary, do not imply a monism. They do not dissolve the essential difference between speech and silence, and it would be impossible to decide whether this would be a monism of speech or of silence; neither can be reduced to the other.

The relations between flesh and the idea, between the visible and the invisible, and between speech and silence all have the same structure, but the relation between speech and silence seems most familiar to us and can therefore help to elucidate the others. Merleau-Ponty tells us that the relations which he describes cannot be joined together in a 'synthesis' because 'they are two aspects of the reversibility which is the ultimate truth' (*VI*, 155/204). What prevents flesh from lapsing into a monism is the character of crossing or folding, that is, the reversibility between perceiving and being perceived which is irreducible and cannot be synthesized, but can only be described again and again, with respect to vision, language and painting. In this respect as well, the phenomenological reduction has to remain incomplete: 'the incompleteness of the reduction [...] is not an obstacle to the reduction, it is the reduction itself, the rediscovery of vertical being' (*VI*, 178/232). It is this vertical, wild, mute being which needs to be made to express its own sense, and this is the task of phenomenology, however paradoxical it may be.

Further reading

Barbaras, R. (2004), *The Being of the Phenomenon: Merleau-Ponty's Ontology*. Evanston, IL: Northwestern University Press.

Dillon, M. C. (1998), *Merleau-Ponty's Ontology*. Evanston, IL: Northwestern University Press.

Evans, F. and Lawlor, L. (eds) (2000), *Chiasms: Merleau-Ponty's Notion of Flesh*. Albany, NY: SUNY Press (esp. the articles by Dastur, Barbaras and Waldenfels).

Lawlor, L. (2003), *Thinking through French Philosophy. The Being of the Question*. Bloomington and Indianapolis, IN: Indiana University Press.

Part V
Post-phenomenology and the Future of Phenomenology

Post-phenomenology

Jacques Derrida (El Biar, Algeria, 1930–Paris, France, 2004)

17

Jacques Derrida was the originator of the doctrine that came to be known as 'deconstruction'. Forty years after Derrida's work first appeared on the scene, it remains one of the least understood and most unjustly maligned of all philosophical doctrines. Many of its obscurities can be clarified by exploring Derrida's early writings on Husserl, which at the same time constitute one of the most important critiques of phenomenology that we have, and as such they deserve an unusually extended treatment here.

Others such as Gilles Deleuze and Michel Foucault have also engaged in profound critiques of phenomenology, but Derrida's has, so far, in the English-speaking world, been perhaps the most influential, and he is at the same time the one who engages most minutely with the actual texts of Husserl and Heidegger, making his reading somewhat easier to assess. Derrida's earliest works almost always take the form of an engagement with Husserl, and it is hardly an exaggeration to say that his project is most fundamentally shaped by this encounter.

Derrida's thought involves at least two distinct criticisms of Husserl. The first demonstrates the falsity of Husserl's notion of consciousness, which is taken rather to mean the subject's absolute proximity with itself, particularly in the way that immediately given data are present to intuition – phenomenology's 'principle of principles' (*Ideas I*: 44/52). This amounts to a critique of the possibility of the reflective detachment from the empirical world that Husserl attempts in the 'transcendental reduction'. For Derrida, this reduction allows consciousness to be alone with itself and to have the precise meaning of its experiences clearly and transparently given to it. Derrida suggests that this reflexivity of consciousness is ultimately the very foundation of Husserlian phenomenology, and it is this that Derrida takes apart, to show that it rests on a *prior* condition that in fact renders such an immediate self-relation impossible.

Derrida's second criticism is structurally quite similar to this 'deconstruction': it asks whether Husserl is justified in separating so strictly the transcendental sphere of consciousness from the empirical world of contingency and the unpredictable events of history. Although we will not have time to do justice to Derrida's extremely lengthy and detailed texts on Husserl's understanding of 'genesis' and history, we shall suggest that he attempts to show that the separation Husserl wants to make between static or structural phenomenology and genetic phenomenology cannot be upheld, and that a certain incompleteness inherent in any finite structure automatically calls for a certain genetic account of those structures, and one which is not necessarily subject to an a priori, 'philosophical' account of history.

(a) First criticism: self-presence

(i) The question of what precedes the transcendental reduction

Deconstruction in general is the attempt to show that an oppositional understanding of the relation between two things invariably gives priority to one half of the opposition, and relegates the other to a secondary position relative to the first. Thus it does not address the second in itself, but only in terms of its relation to the first: its genuine 'otherness' or singularity is not allowed to appear.

The history of philosophy understood as metaphysics has given priority to that half of the opposition which is more self-sufficient, more fully present on its own initiative, more substantial or 'absolute' (which literally means, un-related, isolated). Its opposite is then merely relative, and the being of the second half of the opposition is defined *only* in relation to the first. As we shall see in the case of Husserl's self-present consciousness, a deconstruction demonstrates that the very notion of self-sufficiency or self-proximity – which for Derrida is the way in which *presence* has traditionally been understood – involves a prior *relation*. It is the relation of reference or signifying. That which is proximal to itself or 'self-identical' must *refer* to itself. Thus at the very heart of the present, absolute, 'divine' half of the opposition, a referential relation is to be found. Now, relationality is what supposedly characterized the *lower* half of the opposition. But deconstruction shows that it is necessarily the case that a certain form of what is 'lower' (relationality, separation, difference, absence) is actually the *condition of possibility* for the 'higher' (absolution, sameness, presence). And at the same time, it demonstrates that such absolute (self-) presence is ultimately *impossible* if it is understood in the traditional way and elevated to the position of the origin.

'Deconstruction' is the name for any process that demonstrates this.

One such opposition, in which we find immediate self-presence on one side and difference and detachment on the other, the latter understood to be *derived* from the former, is Husserl's distinction between the transcendental and the empirical. This distinction is first brought about by the transcendental reduction. The transcendental sphere of reflective consciousness is understood by Husserl in a way that is fundamentally the same as the predominant philosophical tradition: absolute self-presence, pure transparency, a unique, self-founding source of meaning. What Derrida wishes to show is that everything that is bracketed in the reduction, all the contingencies, differences and opacities of the *empirical* world, will in fact haunt *transcendental* consciousness as its very precondition, and as the very condition of possibility for *meaning*.

If the transcendental reduction proves to be impossible, the question is: what are we left with? What is there before this reduction? Derrida's answer lies somewhere between *life* and *language*. In fact, Husserl himself seems to suggest that it is life, and what Derrida wishes to show is that it is only *language* that allows the phenomenologist to arrive on the scene and divide this 'life' into transcendental life (pure, self-present, capable of self-transparency) and empirical life (opaque to itself). Husserl never says just what this 'life' that exists prior to the reduction itself *is*. Ultimately, for Derrida, this notion of a pure life before any linguistic oppositions have been imposed on it is a *mirage* created by language itself. But this does not mean that we should lose all hope of saying something, however negative, about what lies beyond language's capacity to refer. Indeed it is just this possibility of reaching and speaking about such a place that Derrida is concerned with. This would be a place outside of all oppositions and outside of language, an exceedingly difficult place to get to, though one always dreamed of by philosophers. Here, perhaps, the genuine singularity or 'otherness' of entities might be expressed and experienced.

(ii) *Speech and Phenomenon*: self-presence

Derrida's most accessible work on Husserl is *Speech and Phenomenon* (*Le Voix et la Phénomène*) (1967). It is here that Derrida demonstrates Husserl's desire for a pure self-consciousness, free of empirical contingencies and most of all the empirical contingency that is *language*; but at the same time, he wishes to show that there are *resources* in Husserl's text which militate against this view and demonstrate the truth about consciousness, which is to say that reference or signification is ultimately essential to it.

Effectively, what Husserl wants transcendental consciousness to be is a place where the meaning (*Sinn*) of consciousness's intentions is absolutely clear to it (in the 'intuitive fulfilment' of intentions). When this consciousness is forced to enter the world in order to communicate with others, this meaning, formerly accessed by a pure, indeed mystical intuition, must be *articulated*, and this means split up into concepts and expressed in words. Now at this point, potential misunderstandings creep in, and a certain lack of transparency enters into the meaning of the words. To use technical terms, – adapted from Frege by Husserl, but enjoying a much longer career prior to that – meaning (*Sinn*) becomes *signification* (*Bedeutung*). Derrida wants to show that in fact this reference to the other with whom we communicate, and hence a detour through the world, is *irreducible* and *essential* to the very existence of meaning (*Sinn*). In other words, it *cannot* be reduced in the way Husserl wants, and this will mean that signification infects meaning, that meaning will always already involve signification.[1]

This is ultimately the same as saying that the supposedly absolute sphere of consciousness, in its self-presence, requires the referral-structure of language in order to exist. It is only thanks to language that we are even able to posit such a thing as a consciousness that is immediately present to itself.

This moment of self-presence in Husserl appears in the figure of the 'voice', which speaks in the inner monologue that consciousness is said to have with itself – although in the end, *every* genuine experience that consciousness can have of itself may be likened to this inner monologue – in which its meaning is immediately apparent to itself *without having to be put into words*. To describe this situation, Derrida invokes the phrase 's'entendre-parler', which means both to *hear* and to *understand* oneself as one speaks: as if hearing were immediately and always understanding when it takes place in the supposedly transparent space of consciousness. Language would then be restricted to the empirical world, which is bracketed in the transcendental reduction, and we would end up with this pure reflection of the transcendental subject on its conscious life, without reference to the contingency, historicality, and language that are then strictly confined to the world.

(iii) The alternative reading in Husserl's own text

Ultimately, this stress on the absolute presence of fully adequate self-conscious experience is contradicted in Husserl's *own* text by the implication, perhaps not always fully drawn by Husserl himself, that experience actually presupposes two things it was earlier supposed to do without: time, and intersubjectivity, the existence of other consciousnesses. This latter in particular becomes clear in Husserl's later work, the *Cartesian Meditations*, which was delivered as a lecture and initially published in French (translated by one 'E. Levinas', along with G. Pfeiffer), and has subsequently had a great influence on the French reception of Husserl. Derrida shows that even Husserl cannot but admit that the living present depends on and is ultimately nothing apart from its relations to the past and the future, which are not present and ultimately can never be present, and hence never the subject of a fully adequate intuitive experience. The same goes for the other human being, whose own subjective point of view on things and the self-relation of his consciousness is absolutely hermetically closed in upon itself, forever shielded from my view. And the same goes for the other, but *vice versa*. Husserl himself shows that the existence of other potential transcendental subjects is a *prerequisite* for an experience of objects. In both of these ways, Husserl himself undercuts the prevalent thrust of his text and shows that self-presence and immediacy, ultimately relies on absence and mediation: 'time and the other' (the title of an early work by Levinas, who has tacitly influenced Derrida's reading here in several ways).

These are all empty intentions, signifying relations that are at the very ground of any experience of an object in its live presence to intuition. Thus, in a sense, signifying relations *are* seen by Husserl to be presupposed by presence, and this is just what Derrida wishes to demonstrate: that if a text wishes to propose a moment of fully present meaningfulness at its foundation, or as its goal, it can be shown – by attending closely to the very same text – that this presence in fact depends on a prior network of relations and differences.

(iv) Language and life before the reduction

Derrida's point is that the only difference there can be between transcendental and empirical consciousness is one of *language*, with all its contingency and chance. It is only language that lets us make this distinction. And that makes language, in a certain sense, *prior* to what happens in phenomenology. And at the very least, this will prevent Husserl from rightfully bracketing language and counterbalance his tendency to propose a pure presence to intuition as the ultimate governing principle of phenomenology, since language is its very precondition.

Derrida is quite clear that language introduces the difference between presence and absence. So it is not even as if one can simply oppose Husserl's statement that presence is at the origin by saying, 'no, absence is at the origin'. The opposition as such is something that exists only when language does. Language might then be said to be that which precedes the transcendental reduction and thus to exceed the distinction between empirical and transcendental, as well as the distinction between genesis and structure.

For Husserl, what precedes the reduction is 'life'.[2] Derrida has precisely been deconstructing a certain notion of life, understood as absolute self-proximity, 'auto-affection', an immediate self-relation. In place of Husserl's life, Derrida posits *language*, and he associates language not with life, but with *death*. Why? Because language, as the precondition of immediate self-reference, institutes mediation, relation, and difference at the *heart* of this supposedly immediate self-relation, absence in the very core of presence. Thus there is something like a splitting of life from itself, and ultimately a self-differentiation, a 'mistake' introduced into the process of self-replication that ultimately ends in our disintegration and death. Thus language, as a signifying detour, is the presence of death in *life*.

If there is life, at the origin of the difference between transcendental and empirical, then life is always a kind of death. Death is always involved in life. For it is not as if life could have been itself *without* the dead structure of reference. This is why Derrida will sometimes suggest that to achieve such a thing as full self-presence is ultimately to die, for it is only the delays introduced by difference that temporarily keeps living beings *alive*.

Derrida often speaks of the notion of a 'trace' and of 'archi-writing'. In this context, these extremely precise and profound concepts may be understood as an attempt to understand life differently, not as an immediate self-relation, but as a process of making inscriptions upon oneself, life as the capacity to receive traces and to make traces, upon itself and upon its environment, its 'other'. This capacity opens the living thing to a world beyond itself, making it vulnerable, and thus laying it open to death, but at the same time, allowing it to adapt to the nature of its environment. In his later years in particular,

Derrida's interest in life and animality would lead him to expand on this point in many fascinating ways.

(b) Second criticism: history and genesis

Derrida's second criticism, one to which he devotes more time, and more pages, is slightly more difficult to understand. We shall focus on his most concise account, in '"Genesis and Structure" and Phenomenology', which was his first major public speech (1959) and indeed his earliest major publication. Once again, Husserl at the very start of Derrida's course.

(i) Husserl's middle course

Derrida tracks Husserl's attempts to plot a course between two equally problematic theories of consciousness, Platonism and empiricism: this is to say between a purely atemporal vision of static essences that does not require a theory of the way in which conscious structures actually evolve in the experience of individuals and the experience of the human race as a whole; and an attention to history which treats any account of development merely as a set of contingent empirical facts.[3] Husserl comes to see that phenomenology must find a way to navigate between a pure transcendental philosophy that would ignore history altogether and a simple empiricism that would amount to nothing more than a historicism, thus relinquishing the certainty and necessity of its statements by ending up in a position of relativism and scepticism, which 'reduces the norm to a historical factuality' (GS, 200/237). What motivates Husserl here is the worry that if one traces the necessary structures of experience back to their genesis, one will *impair* their necessity and render them ultimately dependent upon something contingent. Thus the normativity of logic and the objectivity of experience is ruined – logic ('the science of thought') will be forced to confine itself to the contingent way in which the human psyche actually thinks,[4] and objective experience will be reduced to a merely subjective impression.

Husserl must therefore plough a furrow between 'logicising structuralism and psychologistic genetism' (GS, 198/235).

So, Husserl cannot remain content with simply enumerating the structures of consciousness *or* focussing exclusively on their empirical genesis, but the kind of genesis he eventually attributes to his structures is one that privileges the structural side of the opposition between structure and genesis. In other words, it will not properly plot a course *between* the two extremes *or* do justice to the notion of genesis. This is because Husserl is in fact searching for a *necessary* genesis, the way in which historical and individual development *had to* occur in order to arrive at the *structures* of consciousness that Husserl has found to be necessary by other means. In this way, what Husserl rules out in advance is the possibility of a genuine history, which is to say one that could in the course of events throw up something genuinely new. This is the notion of 'genesis' to which Derrida believes it is necessary to do justice. There will never be one final set of structures that are necessary to all experience: history, or some other process of development, will always be capable of throwing up some structure or some *event* (the opposite of structure, an absolute contingency), that will not be catered for by any structures we have enumerated in advance, and indeed that may contradict this enumeration and find no place within the established structures. History is precisely not teleological, but is the ever present possibility of a genuinely *new* event. It is 'danger' in the sense of a threat to any supposedly complete structure (cf. *OG*, 5/14).

So the idea is that there is a *necessary* strife between structure and genesis and that this opens up the possibility of an 'untamed' genesis – an 'event' – that undermines structure.

(ii) Derrida's 'criticism'

The problem with Husserl's course is thus quite simply that it leads to a notion of history that is false, which is to say 'metaphysical'. Husserl presupposes that the genesis of consciousness itself *has* necessary structures, that we will always be able to deduce its features *logically*. This for Derrida is a mere prejudice that Husserl has inherited from the metaphysical tradition, with its dubious 'philosophies of history'. This prejudice in favour of the existence of structures *even within genesis* excludes in advance the possibility of an 'untamed genesis': in other words, Husserl's thought is a kind of 'structuralism', a prejudgement in favour of finding necessary structures everywhere, even in history, where on the contrary, all could be contingency. This is 'philosophy's most spontaneous gesture' (*GS*, 200/237) and one which Husserl's phenomenology repeats, to elide this opening within any structure, the constant possibility of a new development, a real genesis. Thus, of the two poles of the opposition between structure and genesis, philosophy has always chosen structure, and when it has addressed genesis, it has done so *in relation* to structure.

This is to say that its understanding of history is a teleological one, or an 'arche-teleological' one, in which one begins from something pure and absolute at the origin (or *archē*) that has no need of an actual historical development, which will only ever happen to it accidentally; and if this development actually takes place, one arrives at something similar at the end, to compensate for this detour. Indeed it is this return to self at the end of history that redeems the pure contingency of the route taken and gives it a certain *necessity*, precisely because it will then always have been tending somewhere, it will have had *direction*. History is thus understood by philosophy as destiny or fate. By understanding history in this way himself, Husserl still hopes that an *a priori* discourse will be able to describe consciousness exhaustively, in its necessary structures and in the structures of their genesis.

What is Derrida's solution? While we cannot go into it in sufficient detail here, we can say this: the very idea of a closed structure or a 'finite totality' is contradictory. Deconstruction wishes to show that the only way in which one thing can individuate itself, set itself apart from another, is by relating to that other and differentiating itself from it. In other words, the absolute can only be relative, relative to that which it deems non-absolute, 'other' than it. Thus for its very identity it depends on the other, and is itself characterized by a certain kind of relativity. And what is more, any finite totality always retain *marks* of this detachment and suturing of itself, something like a navel, which marks both the relation of the child to the mother and its severing. This analogy is particularly pertinent because what the structure cannot conceal, what this openness of a totality indicates, is its *genesis*. A structure, in order to maintain itself, in order for it to have a stable meaning, must *ignore* its genesis. Nevertheless, it will contain marks, certain kinds of self-contradiction, ambiguities, or lacunae, which will testify – in a complex way that we cannot investigate here – to the foreclosure of its genesis. It is precisely these marks that Derrida wishes to draw attention to, for in the end, it is this impossibility of ever forming a closed structure that allows there to be a genuine history, it is this that allows a structure to take account of the possibility of a genesis that would be absolutely 'untamed', beyond the jurisdiction of *a priori* structures. And it is this genuine co-dependence of genesis and structure that for Derrida is ultimately elided by Husserl's phenomenology.

For Derrida, Husserl seems to say that while the enumeration of structures – and hence the work of phenomenology – is *de facto* incompletable, infinite, it is nevertheless *de jure* completable and finite. Husserl still believes that the opening of structure is a *contingent fact*. But, as Derrida says at the very beginning of 'Genesis and Structure', 'the opening of the structure is "*structural*"', in a word, *essential* (*GS*, 194/230, my italics). The lack of closure in structural phenomenology is thus not contingent, but a *necessary* characteristic of structure itself. Hence, Derrida speaks of 'the structural impossibility of closing a structural phenomenology' (*GS*, 204/242).

History indeed exists because of an essential fissure in the totality's supposed self-presence, an openness of structure that is unclosable, and hence eternal. Thus Derrida describes the *telos* of history, paradoxically, as *opening and precisely not closure* (cf. *GS*, 210/250). If there never was a moment of purity in the beginning, then there is no reason why genesis should return to any form of closure at the *end*.

For Derrida, particularly in his early works, history is neither purely empirical nor purely necessary. It is precisely the always unclosed nature of any totality, any set of structures, that *allows* history to exist. One cannot have history without structure, but one cannot have structure without history, because by definition structure cannot be closed, and this is what Derrida's deconstruction sets itself to show in each and every case.

As we have seen, deconstruction demonstrates the presence of at least two competing strands in the philosophical texts that it reads, and here once again we find an alternative reading of the Husserlian text *in* the text itself. In response to the first 'criticism', Husserl's texts on the other and on time presented the possibility of an alternative reading that would contradict the dominant interpretation. In this case, the alternative is opened up by his notion of *hylē* or the 'matter' of perception – and Derrida explicitly relates this to the themes of time and the other. This is the moment at which, for Derrida, consciousness opens onto something outside consciousness, which cannot be subsumed by its structures. It is a moment of passivity or pure receptivity, and hence the means by which consciousness could in principle encounter something absolutely new.

It is precisely the passivity of consciousness in its hyletic moment that is developed by at least two other post-Husserlian thinkers, whom we shall come to in the following chapters: Jean-Luc Marion and Michel Henry. First of all, we shall examine in more detail the great thinker of time and the other with whom Derrida shared so much, Emmanuel Levinas.

Emmanuel Levinas (Kovno, Lithuania, 1906–Paris, France, 1995)

18

Levinas has a truly ambivalent relationship to phenomenology. Having closely studied the texts of Husserl and Heidegger, Levinas comes to be convinced that traditional phenomenology not only neglects the Other (*Autrui*), but actually creates a methodological framework which makes it impossible for us properly to understand the Other. At the same time, Levinas's philosophy is very much influenced by his engagement with Husserl and Heidegger, and many of the resources for solving this problem are taken from them.

Concerning Husserl, Levinas criticizes the way in which the Other is approached in the *Fifth Cartesian Meditation* in terms of perception, and in a way that begins from my own consciousness and tries then to infer the presence of the Other's consciousness by way of an analogy with my own. At the same time, he agrees with Husserl about the fundamental inaccessibility of the Other; yet for Levinas, this inaccessibility has an ethical dimension while Husserl conceives of it initially in purely epistemic terms. Levinas's notion of 'ethics' is, however, rather far removed from its traditional conception: 'We name this calling into question of my spontaneity by the presence of the Other ethics' (*TI*, 43/13). The Other is the being who radically calls my conscious freedom into question and puts me in a position of passivity and response. This ontological subordination of my subjectivity assumes ethical dimensions when it becomes clear that the need to respond to the Other which my consciousness cannot itself contain places a responsibility on me which is infinite; it is impossible to draw any line that might delimit this responsibility. The impossibility of 'having fulfilled one's responsibility' applies in principle and by rights; on the empirical level, we often conclude that we have done all we could, but this does not diminish our obligation which remains infinite and unfulfilled.

The more substantial reason as to why the Other places an infinite responsibility on me stems from the Other's own 'infinity' which Levinas explains by recalling the Cartesian idea of infinity: Descartes uses the idea to demonstrate the existence of an 'Other', one whose powers transcend my own: in this case, God. While this idea is not immediately rooted in the realm of ethics, Descartes' insight is nevertheless essential for Levinas insofar as it demonstrates that the presence of such an impossible idea as the idea of the infinite forces us to rethink the very nature of subjectivity: what must a subject be if it is capable of entertaining this idea? My powers are transcended by this idea; my mind contains something that it was not capable of generating by itself: therefore, something beyond me must have implanted the idea in me. According to Levinas, this is exactly the experience that I undergo when I encounter the *human* Other who exceeds any idea of him or her in me. Since this idea is beyond my capacity to conceive and yet I nevertheless have it, this demonstrates that my subjectivity has been in some way affected by the Other prior to its own active, spontaneous ability to form ideas. In other words, my relation to the Other does not take place by way of an analogy with my own experience of my own consciousness or by way of an idea that I myself form of the Other that would limit him to the dimensions of my own finite concepts.

Unlike Heidegger, who starts his ontological investigation from the being that is concerned about its *own* Being, Levinas begins from the 'existent that expresses himself' (*TI*, 201/175). In other words, I do not start from myself and my concerns, but from the expression that I encounter, the self-expression of the Other in their very singularity, which would be betrayed if we attempted to encapsulate it in a concept or constellation of concepts that were already in our possession. This fact *obliges* us not to attempt to reduce the Other to the measure of myself or the 'Same', as Levinas puts it. This expression is a fact for Levinas: the expression and the question it poses to my expectations and assumptions *is there*, and there is no need to provide a proof of its existence – the only question is how I will respond.

Levinas is quite willing, however, to give examples of how the Other expresses him- or herself, from the Other who calls on me to hold open the door for him or her to the Other who requires me to welcome him or her into my home without conditions, to host, feed and ultimately die for him or her, if necessary. The Other expresses him- or herself mainly through what Levinas calls 'the face', of which the face in the literal sense is just one instance. More precisely, Levinas explains that '[t]he way in which the other presents himself, exceeding the idea of the other in me, we here name face' (*TI*, 50/21). 'Face' is thus the way or mode in which the Other comes to appearance in his irreplaceable uniqueness, a singularity which makes demands on me and indeed in a way looks at me, as the literal face does in its speaking and looking.

Even if I only see the shoulders or hear the voice of the Other, it is still the face (in Levinas's sense) of the Other that affects me, and to which I must respond.

Levinas emphasizes that the face of the Other is not something that I perceive or experience in the way perception and experience are grasped by traditional philosophy and even by phenomenology. It therefore cannot be treated with the means supplied by classic phenomenology. The face of the Other is not a perceptual object with eyes, nose and mouth; Levinas points out that the perceptual attributes of the Other are entirely irrelevant to the expression of the Other. Accordingly, Levinas can only call his philosophy a 'phenomenology' if the primacy of perception is not essential to the phenomenological method; we have seen with Heidegger, and even with the late Husserl, that this primacy indeed only holds for certain phenomena.

Levinas defines his relation to phenomenology when he writes: 'if phenomenology is only a method of radical experience, we will find ourselves beyond phenomenology' (*TO*, 54/35). If phenomenology only speaks about that which can be experienced and takes perception as the paradigm case of experience, then Levinas will need to go beyond the phenomenological method to provide an adequate treatment of the Other. However, it seems that the antecedent of the above conditional statement need not necessarily be true of phenomenology, leaving open the possibility that phenomenology is not only a method of experience. Accordingly, Levinas announces elsewhere: 'I have attempted a "phenomenology" of sociality starting from the face of the other person – from proximity – by understanding in its rectitude a voice that commands before all mimicry and verbal expression, in the mortality of the face, from the bottom of this weakness' (*TO*, 109). And also: 'I think that, in spite of everything, what I do is phenomenology, even if there is no reduction, here, according to the rules required by Husserl, even if all of the Husserlian methodology is not respected' (*GCM*, 87/140).

In one of his major works, *Totality and Infinity*, Levinas provides a detailed 'Phenomenology of Eros'. This phenomenology focuses on the '*way* [*manière*] of the tender' (*TI*, 256/233), which he describes as the fragility and vulnerability of the Other whom we encounter in love. Levinas is thus clearly returning to the phenomenological emphasis on the 'how', the way or mode of a phenomenon's givenness, rather than the 'what', or the object as such. But the extraordinary feature of Eros is that the phenomenon itself demands such a treatment, since Eros is not an encounter with an object, but is defined by specific ways or modes, like the mode of tenderness. The caress, for example, is not a touch which aims at an object, but a particular way of aiming at the other person. It involves sensibility, and at the same time, transcends it because erotic desire aims at the Other in his or her infinity, not merely as a physical being.

In Levinas's phenomenology, a new sense of the phenomenon emerges. For him, the phenomenon is the being that 'appears, but remains absent' (*TI*, 181/156). Being on the border between visibility and invisibility, being present in absence and absent in presence is what Levinas calls 'phenomenality', he later describes it as a 'trace': we have seen an example of such an impossible experience with the idea of the infinite, thanks to which something (God, or the Other) can appear to us that we are unable to understand: 'otherness' or 'alterity'. Phenomena in the emphatic sense are those which must be situated on the threshold between visibility and invisibility, being and non-being, presence and absence. A phenomenology of such inapparent phenomena reveals the extreme possibilities as well as the limits of phenomenology, and the need to transform it into a 'phenomenology of sociality'.

Contemporary Phenomenology

19 Michel Henry (Haiphong, Vietnam, 1922–Albi, France, 2002)

Michel Henry wishes to attempt nothing less than 'a redefinition of the concept of the phenomenon and so of phenomenology itself' (*MP*, 79/109). The concept he wishes to supplant is that of intentionality, and this includes Heidegger's notion of 'ekstasis', Dasein's being-outside-of-itself, which is described as its 'being-in-the-world'. This passage beyond oneself creates an open space, a 'world', a sphere enringed by a horizon, in which entities can appear. Thus it would be as a result of the subject's *transcending* itself, or relating to something *outside* of it, that 'phenomenality' is created, in the cleared space opened up by this relation.

This is, for Henry, the way in which the origin of phenomenality has been understood from the Ancient Greeks onwards: 'Philosophy, since its Greek origin at any rate, is confined to this phenomenality of thought [. . .] the horizon of being' (*MP*, 81/111). Henry accepts that this 'Greek' notion of 'transcendence', which leads philosophy to understand the phenomenon in terms of light and visibility, must form *part* of the explanation for the way in which phenomenality comes about, but it is not *sufficient*, it does not capture the most original form of phenomenality, and 'the fundamental insufficiency of such a determination has dominated almost the entire history of human thought' (*EM*, 40/51).

We need to understand the phenomenon as '*a revelation which owes nothing to the work of transcendence*. The clarification of the concept of phenomenon will be the first task of our enquiry [. . .] the determination of the "phenomenon" as something which shows itself within the horizon of light interior to which all things can themselves become visible, remains in fact one-sided' (*EM*, 40/51). Thus Henry wishes to understand the most original form of phenomenality as owing nothing to the subject's transcendence; but this also means that the phenomenon will not be *transcendental* either, since it will not be the result of the *transcendental subject's* activity:

> Philosophy will build on a new foundation when it is capable of circumscribing an absolutely original 'phenomenon' so that *the very mode in conformity to which the phenomenon reveals itself is irreducible to the 'how' of the manifestation of a transcendental phenomenon.* (EM, 40/51)

What is wrong with this 'transcendent' and 'transcendental' understanding of the phenomenon as an entity that appears within the illuminated, visible space of a horizon? For Henry it is a kind of idealism, insofar as, hereby, 'reality is reduced to the knowledge that we can have of it in language and thought' (*MP*, 87/118). This is what allows Henry to extend Heidegger's critique of the primacy of epistemology to *Heidegger himself*. For there is a fundamental structure, still modelled upon the knowing consciousness, that Heidegger himself employs, and that is precisely the notion of visibility, along with light, horizonality and the transcendence which tears this horizon open, which for Heidegger are the very conditions of possibility for the phenomenon. These conditions of possibility are encapsulated in the word, 'Being', and Henry wishes to show that there is in fact a more primordial 'condition' or 'essence of manifestation', a more basic way in which 'appearance' can occur.

Henry wants to show that the notion of intentionality, the subject's exteriority within the confines of a finite horizon, is precisely *not* the most original condition of possibility for appearance. Indeed, he wants to show that far from appearing in the first place by way of transcendence and the production of a horizon surrounding an open space of visibility, the phenomenon emerges originally within an absolute immanence (the opposite of transcendence), and takes the form of a self-relation that precisely does not leave itself and relate to anything outside of it, an *interiority* that is precisely *in*visible or inapparent, closed in upon itself, yet nevertheless *manifest* to itself, phenomenal.

If manifestation originated in an *open* space of visibility, what appeared within this space would always be restricted and *conditioned* by the structures of this space and ultimately by the transcending subject, whose situated, finite perspective caused there to *be* a horizon in the first place. But in fact, the phenomenon 'erupts' from the darkness of a self-enclosure, an inside rather than an outside, an inwardness rather than an outwardness.

Conditions of possibility and the 'event'

Like many phenomenologists and post-phenomenologists, after Heidegger, Henry comes to suspect that the notion of a 'condition of possibility' is inadequate when it comes to explaining the nature of manifestation, and indeed what Henry, Marion, and, in his own way, Derrida wish to broach is the possibility of a phenomenon that is *unconditioned*: 'even though it be *that which realizes* the condition for the possibility of every phenomenon in general, the *mode* whereby the ego *becomes a phenomenon* is something so *fundamental* that it cannot be subordinated to any condition' (*EM*, 37/47). For is it not possible that some things come to appear which are unprecedented and unanticipated, which are not *made* possible and hence are not *to be expected* on the *basis* of a prior state of things? In other words, what of the *im*possible, or the *new*? This is why a number of contemporary philosophers use the term 'event' to describe this unheard-of phenomenon (which would precisely return us to the *colloquial* denotation of the term, 'phenomenon'). 'The event' is something that appears without first being made possible by a prior condition. There is *prima facie* at least a certain resemblance between this event and a 'miracle', and so it is no surprise that a great many post-phenomenologists and contemporary phenomenologists, from Levinas to Derrida, from Henry to Marion, and many others, turn their phenomenological gaze to *religious* phenomena.

Henry names this most primordial 'condition' for phenomenality, '*life*' (cf. *MP*, 94/127). Life is that which is radically immanent to itself and this means that it is in an immediate relation *with* itself. Henry's name for this relation is 'auto-affection' or 'self-affection': 'the theme of radical immanence as transcendental affectivity' (*MP*, 81/111). It is the most basic way in which an appearance is *given*: 'this auto-affection is the original phenomenality, the original givenness as a self-givenness' (*MP*, 81/111). 'This self-givenness, however, is structurally different from "relating-to" but insurmountably excludes it from itself. It is not outside of itself but in itself, not transcendence but radical immanence. And it is only on the basis of such radical immanence that something like transcendence is possible' (*MP*, 81/111). Life *feels* itself to be alive, and this primitive sense of itself is, for Henry, the most basic form of phenomenality as such, the very beginning of appearance.

We should be careful not to understand affectivity along the lines of the usual meaning of the word 'affect', as a certain kind of feeling, but rather as the latter's 'transcendental condition': 'not the simple interplay of our empirical feelings, but their very possibility', their effectiveness (*EM*, xii). Can we then identify affectivity with the mere *possibility*, as yet unspecified, that every living thing has of sensing *itself*, not being indifferent to what impinges upon it, or even to what is occurring within it, its awareness *of* its sensible awareness?

We are limited in what we can say about this life *itself*, for, as Henry puts it, 'absolute transcendental life – this life that is ours for each one of us – slips away from the regard and thus from [. . .] everything that we call knowledge, speech, and *logos*' (MP, 92/125). It is precisely that which will be betrayed by every attempt to express it in language, whose very referential structure can only come to exist on the basis of this, the very earliest form of relation, *after* life has already been affected by itself.

We must however be careful to differentiate this self-*affection* from the relation that *thought* has to itself, which is self-*consciousness*: in the case of the latter, a space of light and visibility is created in the interior of the subject by means of intentionality. Self-affection is in fact the more primordial origin of self-consciousness. What is crucial is that, in consciousness, the bestowal of meaning and the emergence of significant phenomena is a product of *activity*. Henry's idea is that the first condition of phenomenality is rather *passivity*. But this is not the suffering of impacts from the *outside* (this happens even to the *non*-living: things impinge even upon a stone), but the suffering of *oneself*. Life is *defined* by the capacity to touch itself, in the way that one hand can feel the other's grasping it *and* feel itself grasping the other at the same time.

Henry speaks of life's passively *suffering* from itself, being burdened with itself; in other words, it always finds itself lumbered with its own life as a fact which it did not choose or actively create. This goes further than Heidegger's 'facticity', which is also encountered in moods (*Stimmungen*), because for Henry it is precisely this feeling that is the earliest inchoate beginning of the phenomenon: phenomenality does not originate in the understanding, as it does for Heidegger. For Heidegger, moods disclose Dasein's own factitious situation in a world *outside* of itself, but for Henry there is a prior moment, when affectivity feels *only itself*.

Henry's theory of auto-affection is also a rehabilitation of the notion of the ego, which Heidegger had supposedly dislodged with his concept of 'Dasein'. This immediate self-affection of life creates a certain individuality, an 'I' or *ego*. As a result, at the beginning of his colossal tome, *The Essence of Manifestation* (1963), Henry identifies affectivity with the ego, an entity which has the capacity to refer to or at least relate to itself in its individuality, and ultimately, in more advanced forms, to say 'I' (*ego*). So, strictly speaking, it seems that he is describing the process *whereby* the ego *becomes* an ego, and this would be the very starting point of the phenomenon.

How can the ego become a 'phenomenon'? Is it not on the condition of submitting itself to a horizon of visibility in and whereby every thing can become 'visible'? Is not the power which unfolds such a horizon, namely *transcendence, the condition of*

the Being of the ego? The present inquiry has been undertaken in order to show
the need for answering these fundamental questions in the negative. (*EM*, 37/47)

Henry thus speaks of the way in which Life itself (*la Vie*) exists only and
always in the form of particular, individual, living *beings* (*les vivants*). Life as
such is always already *individuated*.

Although Henry began his work before Derrida's intervention was well
known, we can see how he avoids the Derridean critique of the subject's self-
proximity by asserting that, in fact, in the subject's ipseity there is *no difference*:
'life is immediately auto-affected without the separation of any difference'
(*MP*, 123/166). There is in life an immediate self-relation, and it is more primitive even than Sartre's pre-reflective self-consciousness, for this relation does
not make a detour through the world: it does not venture beyond itself even
to that extent. There is simply no distance between itself and its own life which
Derrida could describe as implicitly invoking a signifying referral: there is no
reference here, only absolute self-immanence.

In a way then, we can say that at the most primordial ground of consciousness, prior even to that level whose self-proximity Derrida deconstructs, there
is life and its self-affection, its absolutely immediate self-relation or immanence. We have seen that Derrida himself wishes to engineer a new concept of
life, but this appears to be one in which difference and the trace are inherent,
and hence it cannot be compared with Henry's absolute immanence.

Like Derrida, Henry also finds his reinvention of phenomenology to have
been anticipated in certain neglected corners of Husserl's own work, and specifically in his focus on the living present and the way in which the subject passively
receives impressions, these comprising the material or '*hylē*' of its perceptions,
as opposed to their actively imposed 'form' (*morphē*), and in particular in the
notion of a 'primal impression' which occurs in the experience of time. Thus,
in many ways, Henry picks up on just the same strands in Husserl that Derrida
and Levinas found to be so productive, and yet he takes them in his own highly
original direction. Indeed, perhaps one can ultimately understand Henry to be
addressing Derrida's question – which was also Heidegger's, in another way – of
a 'life' that pre-exists phenomenology's attempts at 'reduction', although he inter-
prets it as lacking all difference rather than being intimately structured by it.

In the rest of his profuse and highly variegated work, Henry investigates the
way in which this radically immanent life can be seen to function in an extraordinary variety of spheres, in particularly brilliant fashion in his work on
Marx, but also in his texts on psychoanalysis and Christianity, among others.

Jean-Luc Marion (Paris, 1946–) 20

For Marion, phenomenology has failed to live up to its initially avowed aim, which is to return to the things themselves, or in Heidegger's terms, to let the phenomenon show itself as it is in itself. Why? Because phenomenologists have made certain *presuppositions* about the nature of the phenomenon. With the two greatest representatives of phenomenology, Husserl and Heidegger, the basic characteristic of all phenomena is taken to be, respectively, *objectivity* and *beingness* (the quality of being an entity or 'a being'). For Marion, the aim of phenomenology must be to let phenomena show themselves without the one's who are experiencing them imposing any *restrictions* on this appearance. Not only does this distort their manner of appearance (perhaps leaving some aspects in abeyance), but it can also leave out entire regions of phenomena, which are not accounted for because they do not *conform* to these restrictions. This is precisely Heidegger's criticism of Husserl, that there are certain phenomena and certain fundamental aspects of phenomena which cannot be understood as 'objects'. Marion applies the same logic to Heidegger, by suggesting that there are certain phenomena which could appear but which cannot even be understood as 'beings', let alone 'objects', and that indeed the most basic form of appearance for *all* phenomena is neither objectivity nor beingness, but *givenness*.

Phenomenologists, and we may presume many other philosophers, particularly after Kant, have failed to understand experience in this way and thus have not allowed phenomena simply to give themselves without restriction, because they have imposed *conditions* on the way in which phenomena show themselves to us. As soon as one filters appearance in this way, allowing only *some* aspects of an entity to appear and only certain entities *tout court*, one is not allowing them to appear as they are, and one is therefore failing in phenomenology's task.

In Kant and especially in Husserl, but, in a certain way, also in Heidegger, the way in which phenomena give themselves to us has been subjected to two limitations: they are admitted into appearance only *on condition* of their appearing within a horizon, and their being constituted by a transcendental 'I' (*BG*, 4/9, cf. *BG*, 27–39/42–60). For Marion, if we remove these conditions, we allow these phenomena to give themselves unconditionally, and thus open ourselves to phenomena in their most basic sense, without imposing conditions.

Thus, Marion completes the sequence that runs from objectness to beingness with *givenness*; and in parallel, this means to replace all notions of conditioning with an *unconditionedness*: the phenomenon must be allowed to give itself unconditionally. The most basic feature of the phenomenon, which must characterize it if it is to be given in any way at all (as a being or as an object), is givenness. Phenomena are *given* before it is even decided what kind of thing, if any, they are to be.

If phenomena at the most basic level are not *constituted* by the subject, they must be received as one receives a *gift*. A gift is not conditioned by the receiver in the sense that he is presented with it without having done anything to deserve it and without having expected it, and in particular without being obliged to give anything back – otherwise it would not be a gift but an object of exchange, an economic object, expected in advance and provoking expectations in return.[5]

The exemplary phenomenon, the 'given par excellence' (*BG*, x) is precisely a special kind of phenomenon which does indeed give itself unconditionally: Marion calls it the 'saturated phenomenon' (ibid.). This is to be contrasted with the 'poor' or 'impoverished phenomenon' that is the phenomenon as it has been understood by Kant and Husserl. In both of these cases Marion believes that the concepts of the understanding have been given priority over the receptivity of *intuition*, the faculty which allows phenomena to be *given* to us immediately. In other words, the pure receptivity of the intuition has been subordinated to the active spontaneity of the understanding.

This has resulted in the following understanding of our encounter with phenomenal things: first we have a concept of that thing, and then we attempt to achieve an intuition of the thing *adequate* to this concept. In both Kant and Husserl, this intuition almost always falls short and remains inadequate, resulting in the experience of the impoverished phenomenon, one that is *incompletely* 'given'. In place of this, Marion wishes to assert the phenomenal rights (the right to appear, the possibility of appearing) of those entities whose intuitive givenness would precisely *exceed* any possible concept. Marion believes that both Kant and Husserl, and perhaps all of phenomenology, have left out a region of phenomena in which what is given to us in intuition overflows any concept, and hence cannot be contained by any notion that we might have in advance of its revelation *to* us. All we can do in the event of such a revelation is to passively receive the phenomenon as a gift, which will always be unexpected, and utterly new. Marion indeed uses the word we have already encountered in Michel Henry: an 'event' (*BG*, 159ff./225ff.).

Thus it is clear that in contrast to almost all of the critics of phenomenology, including Derrida and Adorno (who began his career as a scholar of Husserl), and – arguably – to phenomenologists such as Heidegger and his descendants, Marion does *not* wish to do away with Husserl's notion of intuition, but rather to remain true to the insights contained within it.

Marion broaches the idea of the saturated phenomenon – though not for the first time – in his most famous work, *God Without Being* (1982), by way of the contrast between the notion of the 'idol' and the 'icon'. In the simplest possible terms, every previous phenomenologist has understood the phenomenon in the way of an idol, which reduces the given to the measure of our concepts, while Marion wishes to demonstrate that our experience in fact extends to the icon, where we experience a revelation that cannot be accommodated within any of our concepts. Precisely what appears through the idol and the icon is God, and Marion wants to show that God cannot properly be understood as an object, but in addition he cannot even be understood as a *being*, and yet, at the very least in the appearance of Christ and Christ's crucifixion, whereby God's love for man was *manifested* in the world, God is nevertheless capable of *appearing*. And this 'theological' possibility should advert us to the fact that our previous notions of phenomenality have been too restrictive to allow of this possibility and hence need to be expanded, indeed unconditionally so. The icon is thus a forerunner of Marion's notion of the saturated phenomenon, which receives its most pellucid account in Book IV of *Being Given* (1997) and is then the subject of its own monograph, *In Excess: Studies of Saturated Phenomena* (2001), which completes a phenomenological trilogy begun with *Reduction and Givenness: Investigations of Husserl, Heidegger, and Phenomenology* (1989). *Reduction and Givenness* gives a superb account of Husserl and Heidegger, their differences, as well as Derrida's criticism of Husserl, all of which Marion reconstructs (and adjusts) in a very illuminating way, before showing how they all culminate in his own account of the primacy of givenness (*donation*).

In its basic thrust, Marion's work has certain fundamental – and explicitly avowed – similarities with that of Levinas, whom he acknowledges as one of his masters, but at the same time, he is influenced perhaps even more strongly by a certain Heideggerian gesture, which feeds into his work on negative ('apophatic' or 'mystical') theology. Negative theology is broadly speaking the attempt to speak about that which cannot be spoken of, and hence the attempt to use language to describe the *limits* of language, with a view to ensuring that the nature of God is not assimilated to that of human beings and their concepts. In his philosophical work, as in his historical studies, Marion displays an exceptional erudition, of a kind that is not similarly evident in Levinas's less 'scholarly' works. At the same time, Marion's work indirectly demonstrates the curious fact that Levinas's work, while appearing to be innately Judaic, can be shown to be compatible with Catholic thought, particularly in its negative theological tradition.

Ultimately the relation between theology and phenomenology in Marion's work is a complicated one and has caused consternation among more avowedly 'atheistic' phenomenologists (while proving to phenomenology's opponents that it was always a misguided school of thought). This has given rise to a particularly intemperate and rather over-exposed polemic with Dominique Janicaud (otherwise an exemplary writer on Heideggerian politics and other post-Heideggerian matters) – published in English as *Phenomenology and the 'Theological Turn'* and *Phenomenology Wide Open*. At the very least, Marion believes that religious phenomena remain a possibility, and therefore, if phenomenology wishes to account for the entirety of the phenomenal realm – as phenomenology always has – we must take these into account, but without in any way presuming or believing in their *actuality*, a belief which characterizes theology and not philosophy. No doubt, then, a certain theological if not straightforwardly religious background was the source of the questions which Marion puts to phenomenology, but this does not mean that his phenomenology is necessarily a 'religious' one, at least in the sense of presupposing anything like 'faith'. One of the great virtues of Marion's *God Without Being* (and his earlier book, *The Idol and Distance*) is its demonstration of how complex the notions of atheism and the 'death of god' are when one eradicates the presupposition that god must above all *be*: the possibility broached here is that god, prior to any form of being, gives himself or manifests himself in another way, in the form of charitable love (*caritas, agapē*), which can be understood neither as an object nor as a being. Any opposition to this kind of phenomenology that proclaims itself atheist must take into account a thinking of god which does not straightforwardly claim that god 'exists'.

Notes

Part I: Edmund Husserl

1. Usually, introductions to Husserl's work start with a treatment of *Logical Investigations* (*LI*). In the current study, *LI* will play almost no role. There are two main reasons for this: First, it is not quite clear whether *LI* is actually a phenomenological investigation; Husserl develops his phenomenological method in *Ideas I*, and since our book is an Introduction to Phenomenology, Husserl's explicitly phenomenological work will be the main focus. Second, the *Logical Investigations* are very difficult, partly because of certain inconsistencies in terminology and partly because they respond to debates from the turn of the twentieth century which are no longer an issue for us. The significance of *LI* only comes to the fore in light of Husserl's overall project, and they could thus only reasonably be introduced after certain of the main ideas of phenomenology have been explained. Because of stronger connections to the other phenomenologists discussed in the present volume, we have decided rather to rather focus on Husserl's late philosophy and the topics of the lifeworld, history, crisis and intersubjectivity.

2. The fact that, in the natural attitude, I am directed in a straightforward fashion towards the objects does not exclude me from reflecting on my ego. Husserl says explicitly that everybody can engage in reflection, 'but that is not necessarily to effect a phenomenological reflection' (*Ideas I*, 114/119). If I reflect on my ego in the natural attitude, I conceive myself as something occurring in the world, as an object among other objects – even though this object is a particularly peculiar one. As will become clear later, I do not yet reflect on myself as pure consciousness constituting the world by way of its acts.

3. Descartes, for example, had to rely on the ontological proof for the existence of God which Kant then seems to have undermined; the discussions about this issue and about the possibility of such a proof are ongoing.

4. Dan Zahavi describes this important aspect very well: 'The execution of the *epoché* [. . .], when understood correctly, does not imply an eclipse of the world, but a *suspension of the natural attitude's assumption concerning the mode of its existence*' (Zahavi (2001), 9, my italics).

5. Descartes, *Meditation I*, no. 10.

6. These connections are brought out very effectively by Ludwig Landgrebe (1989).

7. This necessary delay is discussed further in Chapter 4 (d) below.

8. This phenomenon is of interest since it reminds us that something which is crossed out enables us to see two things, the original and the new, revised version. For this reason, it is revealing to read a writer's manuscripts. In the age of computers, the usage of the 'Delete' key more or less eliminates this possibility.

9. We cannot undertake an analysis of attention here, but such an investigation yields interesting results regarding the necessity of understanding the perceptual process as an interplay, as a 'constitutive duet' (*ACPAS*, 15/52) of object and subject. Husserl designates the object's 'enticement' or 'call' as an 'affective force'. This affective force does not function in the fashion of a natural causality, but rather as a call coming to me from the side of the object – a call which I can take up, but do not have to. However, there is not just one affective force that calls me in any given situation but rather, several objects exert affective forces and call me to turn towards them. Husserl in this context speaks of a 'rivalry', in which, for example, the 'phenomenon of concealment' (*Verdeckung*) can occur (*ACPAS*, 146 ff./193 ff.). A necessary selection and exclusion takes place. How powerful the affective force of a particular object is in this rivalry might be a matter of the force's intensity (loud noise can drown out or eclipse quiet music), or a contrast might increase the affective force (light colours come into relief before a dark background). A perceptual situation is, of course, much more complex than these examples show; it is influenced by manifold factors such as remembering preceding similar situations, as well as interests, expectations, etc.

10. See Hua XXXI, 25: '"Object" in the full and genuine sense is identical with itself and is originally constituted as a thematic object for an ego in an identifying activity'.

11. See esp. Hua IV, 'Section Two. Chapter Three: The Constitution of Psychic Reality Through the Body;' *ACPAS*, 13ff., *ACPAS*, Supplementary text XXV/25 ('Kinaestheses and Potential Expectations').

12. For example, Hua X, § 11, 12, 24; *ACPAS*, § 18; *EJ*, 122; cf. also Held (1996), 39ff.

13. Bernet (1979).

14. It would be a separate task to examine how Husserl's genetic phenomenology relates to psychoanalysis as a parallel emergence at the beginning of the twentieth century.

15. Similarities and differences with Leibniz' concept of the monad cannot be considered here.

16. For a detailed examination of generative phenomenology, see Steinbock (1995).

17. Cf. the title of the Vienna lecture on which the *Crisis* text is based: 'Philosophy and the Crisis of European Humanity' (*Die Krisis des europäischen Menschentums und die Philosophie*) (*Crisis*, 314/269).

18. Such access is Husserl's goal in the *Crisis* when he suggests first undertaking an *epochē* with regard to all objective sciences, which is 'not merely an abstraction from them', but means to abstain from all participation (*Crisis*, 138/135). Concerning the *epochē*, see Chapter 1.

19. Kern (1979), 71; Kern is citing from the 1927 lecture course 'Nature and Spirit'.

20. That which evades all mathematization might, in fact, be the very essence of the plena which would call for phenomenological rather than scientific analysis. Heidegger describes this evasion in his 'The Origin of the Work of Art' as follows: 'Color shines and wants only to shine. When we analyze it in rational terms by measuring its wavelengths, it is gone' (*OWA*, 45).

21. For example, 'The Anthropological World' (Nr. 28, Hua XXIX).

22. For more detail, see Steinbock (1995), chapter 7.

23. 'Notizen', 27ff. For more detailed considerations on the lived body as Merleau-Ponty pursued them, building on the second volume of Husserl's *Ideas*, see Chapter 13 below.

24. 'Foundational investigations of the phenomenological origin of the spatiality of nature', 118f.

25. It would be interesting to examine the relation between Husserl's reflections on horizon and ground and Heidegger's essay 'The Origin of the Work of Art'. Heidegger shows how artworks set up the world of a historical people and set forth the earth as concealing ground.

26. In Chapter 4, two further invariant structures of the lifeworld will be treated under the headings of 'homeworld' and 'alienworld'.

27. Husserl speaks of 'naiveté on a higher level' (Hua XVII, 353).

28. Cf. Husserl's presentation in the *Crisis*: 'A pure psychology as positive science [. . .] does not exist. [. . .] Thus pure psychology in itself is identical with transcendent philosophy as the science of transcendental subjectivity. This is unassailable' (*Crisis*, 261/257).

29. Hans-Georg Gadamer suggests that understanding a text means understanding the question to which the text gives an answer (Gadamer (1986), 368ff.).

30. Sartre is dissatisfied with Husserl's method in the *Fifth Cartesian Meditation* because it can only provide 'probability' and no certainty regarding the existence of other minds (Sartre (1993), 252f.). Ricoeur is less explicit, yet he misleadingly states that the role of the *Meditation* is equivalent to that of the proof of God's existence in Descartes' philosophy (1967, 11). The case of Habermas is more complicated; he accepts and continues Schütz' criticism which, despite Schütz' impressive familiarity with Husserl's work, is not a justified criticism of the *Fifth Cartesian Meditation* (see Schütz (2004)).

31. Derrida (1999, 71).

32. Carr (1973).

33. For a helpful account of the real and fictive 'there', see Held (2003b), 51f.

34. For a more detailed account of the relation between the two sphere of ownness, see Staehler (2008).

35. Ms. E III 9, S. 84 (1931), quoted from Held (1966), 166, my translation.

36. The following rather condensed comments are based on Klaus Held's important study *Lebendige Gegenwart* (1966).

37. This peculiar dual character of standing and streaming is familiar to us from the dual meaning of the 'now'. 'Now' designates the enduring form of presence, on the one hand, and the manifold of temporal positions in the flow, on the other. This original unity-in-manifold is necessary in order to encounter a thing as identical. Klaus Held presents the complex relation between enduring, unified form and streaming manifold in a helpful image: 'The Now as the standing and enduring form of current presence marks everything that flows through it, puts the stamp of the unified present upon it, as it were, and makes the marked Now immediately turn into a temporal position'. (Held (1966), 32, my translation).

38. In the second volume of his manuscripts on intersubjectivity, Husserl speaks of the 'unity of a supra-personal consciousness' (*Einheit eines überpersonalen Bewusstseins*) (Hua XIV, 199) and of a 'communal person' (*Gemeinschaftsperson*) (203). For a helpful examination of these manuscripts, see Carr (1987).

39. Steinbock (1995), 185.
40. Waldenfels (1991), 38f.
41. Cf. the controversial discussion between Held (1991) and Steinbock (1995), 183ff.
42. Paul Ricoeur has developed this work most extensively, but very important in this context is also the work of David Carr since his phenomenology of narrativity follows the Husserlian project more directly. See Carr (2004).
43. Carr (2004).
44. See Kozin (2009).

Part II: Martin Heidegger

1. We may ignore here the difficult question of whether Heidegger's understanding of Husserl is ultimately just, but also bear in mind that these thoughts were formulated over the 1910s and 1920s, when Husserl's work was still in the process of developing towards its final state, which we have discussed in the previous chapter, and which may indeed respond to Heidegger's criticisms. Ultimately very few philosophers truly understand one another, and respond rather to a phantasm of the philosopher which is used as a point of departure for their own thought. Productive misunderstandings are surely the rule in the history of philosophy.

2. Ultimately, Heidegger later found it necessary to revise many of his early thoughts, and this applies to all three of these characteristics, but most of all to language, which he found to be a unique kind of entity – if it *is* an entity – that *Being and Time* and its 'ontology' could scarcely account for. Heidegger is inconsistent within the space of *Being and Time* itself in that sometimes he includes 'discourse' among the modes of disclosure and at other times not. He here equivocates as to whether *language* is essential to the manifestation of things, as a necessary part of Dasein's existence, which is to say whether man needs to have language in order to be the site in which being appears. Later on, he will come to clarify this, particularly with his work on poetry, which will explain why poetry itself is a particularly important form of *poiēsis* in general, a 'production' that is revelatory.

3. At least this is the threefold that Heidegger considers in *Being and Time*. He openly admits a difficulty in situating animals as well as a certain kind of 'nature' within it (*BT*, 396/346, cf. 100/71).

4. Towards the end of *Being and Time*, Heidegger thinks of this as another form of temporality, *Temporalität*, which is distinct from the temporality that ultimately belongs to individual Daseins, for which Heidegger reserves the word '*Zeitlichkeit*'.

5. Although 'ethics' for Heidegger will ultimately be defined precisely as an attitude that allows being to show itself, which always takes place *by way* of a certain transformation in man's attitude to the world.

6. Heidegger explores this idea with magisterial brilliance in *Fundamental Concepts of Metaphysics*, which is taken up by many future thinkers, sympathetic to Heidegger but also critical with respect to his stance on animality, and particularly well by Giorgio Agamben in *The Open: Man and Animal* (Stanford: Stanford University Press, 2002).

7. This is a distinction we can make more easily in English (and in French) than in German. Heidegger often specifies '*Technik*' as 'modern' or 'machine powered', so we may take it to mean 'industrial' technology in these contexts.

8. *Poiēsis* means 'production' in Greek, but as Heidegger understands it, a production that *reveals* something.

9. Heidegger seems to have had some inkling of this as early as 1928 (cf. *MFL*, 209/270).

10. Being is not *a* being, it cannot be present to us since it is the very condition of possibility *of* presence, so our encounter with it cannot be described according to the metaphor of *vision*, sight, but it can be described, if at all, by means of the 'unheard of' metaphor of *hearing*. Hence Heidegger's constant use of the metaphor of the 'call'.

11. At this point in the original lecture upon which this essay is based one finds the (in)famous and oft-cited remark comparing technological methods of farming with the Nazi extermination.

12. The fact that today we might understand the entire universe as an entropic process adds an extra dimension to this: the universe as a whole would be singular and irreplaceable.

Part III: Jean-Paul Sartre

1. *The Imaginary* is the longest of Sartre's early works, and as tends to be the case with him, the longer the work the more uneven it is. We may conjecture that this is due to the variable strength of Sartre's inspiration from day to day, which is not covered over in the way it is for most writers as a result of his avowed inability to revise and edit his own work (cf. 'The Writer and His Language' in *Politics and Literature*, 117).

2. It is clear that here, in 1936, as Sartre himself admits, he is still Husserlian, since he does not yet understand intentionality as rendering phenomenology and the psyche it examines irremediably worldly: 'phenomenology, the science of pure transcendental consciousness, is a radically different discipline than the psychological sciences, which study consciousness and the being of man indissolubly linked to a body and confronting a world' (*Imagination*, 127/139). Perhaps ultimately this is why the notion of bringing together two separate disciplines more or less disappears from Sartre's work from *Being and Nothingness* onwards, and his attention returns to fiction. It is as if once intentionality is understood to immerse us in the world, phenomenology and the empirical are so intertwined that they can no longer be understood by bringing together two originally *separate* disciplines.

3. A term derived from Plato's word for essence, '*eidos*', the 'idea' or 'form' of a thing.

4. The exceptional French philosopher, Gilles Deleuze (1925–95) has developed this idea of Sartre's (cf. Deleuze 2004, 77–80), although ultimately he takes it beyond phenomenology as such.

5. Although, in this case, he means more precisely the closeness of interrogator and interrogated in the act of asking a *question* which, like Heidegger, he takes to be a distinctive capacity of the human being.

6. Which is to say that the notion of the 'transphenomenal' is to replace that of the noumenal, as phenomenology replaces metaphysics (cf. *BN*, lxii/29).

7. Thus what being-in-itself *really* is would not be defined *with relation to* being-*for*-itself as 'another [kind of] being [*être*]'. Ultimately this shows that the very distinction between being-in-itself and being-for-itself is a *product* of the *for-itself*, of consciousness, for it is after all a *relation* between two different kinds of thing: 'These are the [. . .] characteristics which the preliminary examination of the phenomenon of being allows us to assign to the being of phenomena' (*BN*, lxvi/34). In fact, one is tempted to say that all of the attributes that are assigned to the in-itself are inappropriate, since they all understand it in a merely *oppositional* way, as the opposite of the for-itself and its characteristics. Perhaps one ultimately has to remain mute with regard to what really existed prior to all consciousness, for any discourse on a certain topic presupposes that the entity at least minimally appears. Sartre suggests as much in the following passage: '"Before" consciousness one can *conceive* only of a plenum of being of which *no* element can refer to an absent consciousness' (*BN*, lv/22, my italics).

Part IV: Maurice Merleau-Ponty

1. Waldenfels (1983), 149.
2. See Chapter 1 above.
3. The remainder or excess of the phenomenological account will remain significant for Merleau-Ponty. In his famous essay 'The Philosopher and his Shadow', the remainder comes under the heading of 'shadow'; it is an essential shadow, or a shadow 'which is not simply the factual absence of future light' (*PS*, 178). It is that which resists phenomenology, yet should nevertheless 'have its place within it' (ibid.). Merleau-Ponty deems it an important part of his phenomenological project to approach this shadow indirectly; this is a significant corrective to Husserl's project which he proposes and takes up in his own philosophy under the heading of 'brute being'.
4. On the connection between wonder and the phenomenological reduction, see Chapter 4 (e).
5. I am indebted here to David Smith (2007) who mentions these two features, yet explores them on a higher level of complexity, in discussion with Shaun Gallagher, to determine whether Husserl could have made these discoveries as well. The translation 'body schema' (rather than Colin Smith's 'body image') for '*schéma corporel*' is also taken from Smith (cf. Smith (2007), fn. 24).
6. It should be noted, however, that Merleau-Ponty more often uses the phrase 'body schema' to denote 'body image', which sometimes obscures the nuances and subtleties to be found in his overall account. – I owe the explanation of the difference between these two significations to Timothy Mooney.
7. See Part I, Chapter 2 above for an account of passive synthesis in Husserl.
8. Ambiguity will be examined in Chapter 15. For some interesting connections between sexuality and other dimensions of life, see the long footnote on historical materialism at the end of the chapter on the body in its sexual being.
9. For a discussion of this and other features of style, see Singer (1981).
10. See Heidegger, 'Origin of the Work of Art', 39.

11. See Casey (1998), especially chapter 10. For the connection between art and place or more precisely the representation of place in landscape painting and maps, see Casey (2002).

12. Namely, Alphonse de Waelhens and Bernard Halda. Merleau-Ponty seemed most obviously comfortable with this title around 1949 when he chose to allow de Waelhens to write a preface for the second edition of *The Structure of Behavior*, entitled 'A Philosophy of Ambiguity'.

13. Halda designates ambiguity as a 'Leitmotiv' in Merleau-Ponty's philosophy (Halda (1966), 33); yet he mainly focuses on only one of its meanings in Merleau-Ponty, namely, opacity, and takes it mainly as an existential concept. De Waelhens approaches Merleau-Ponty in the context of existential philosophy. He provides an introduction to Merleau-Ponty's philosophy as a whole without attending specifically to the theme of ambiguity. In his conclusion, he raises interesting questions about an ambiguous location of Merleau-Ponty's philosophy between phenomenology and metaphysics; but this discussion does not elucidate ambiguity as a concept in Merleau-Ponty. My interest lies neither with an existential concept of ambiguity nor with a criticism of Merleau-Ponty's philosophy as ambiguously located, but with a phenomenological concept of ambiguity.

14. Husserl had already pointed to an essential withdrawal at the centre of the transcendental ego when it turns out that my self-reflection always comes too late and can never reach the ego as it is functioning or reflecting. On a different level, Sartre would explain this essential withdrawal by pointing to our ambiguous status as both subjects and objects.

15. Simon Glendinning detects a '*humanistic* prejudice' in this sentence (Glendinning, 'The genius of man' in Baldwin (2007), 104–17). This objection cannot be explored here, but the precise questions to be discussed would be: is not a phenomenology of the animal always a human phenomenology of the animal, and in that sense, is all phenomenology not necessarily humanistic? Also, it would be interesting to explore what definition of the human would emerge if a genius for ambiguity were the defining feature; this would most likely not be a hierarchical definition.

16. See also *Eloge de la philosophie*, 10.

17. See Chapter 14 (a): 'The Paradox of Expression'.

18. See Tilliette (1970), 33–49 and Waldenfels (1987), 174ff.

19. This is as close as we will get to the social and political dimensions of Merleau-Ponty's philosophy which cannot be treated here (for reasons of space and because they are not always necessarily related to his phenomenological thought, but also because they are part of a complex discussion between different thinkers, especially in *Humanism and Terror*).

20. A brief engagement with Levinas should, despite the difficulties of his thought, not be conceived as a detour here, because Levinas is himself an extremely important post-phenomenologist (or even phenomenologist; see Chapter 18).

21. See Chapter 4.

22. Cf. Simone de Beauvoir, *The Ethics of Ambiguity*, chapter I. De Beauvoir introduces the idea of ambiguity after rehearsing how a human being is a subject in the world as well as an object for other humans. This twofold nature is one dimension of our ambiguous condition, and it can be mapped onto the distinction between mind and matter, or thought and extension. We can never finally determine whether we are subject or object, mind or matter – we are both, yet since these two sides do not allow for a synthesis, we remain an ambiguity.

For a comparison between de Beauvoir's concept of ambiguity and Merleau-Ponty's, see Monica Langer (2003). However, Langer does not seriously explore Merleau-Ponty's concept of ambiguity; she mainly argues (to my mind, convincingly) that de Beauvoir's conception appears to be closer to Merleau-Ponty's than to Sartre's notion of ambiguity.

23. That which enables a certain phenomenon is also that which restricts or delimits it; Jacques Derrida reveals and elucidates such contradictory structures as paradoxical. It seems plausible to suggest that 'good ambiguity' in Merleau-Ponty's sense ultimately points to paradoxes, or, to speak more generally, ambiguity in the dynamic sense might amount to paradox in the Derridean sense. This connection can only be proposed but not explored here.

24. This is a formulation suggested by Renaud Barbaras (2004, 173) who draws several helpful connections between Husserl's phenomenology and Merleau-Ponty's concept of flesh.

25. Dillon states that 'the notion of reversibility is modeled on the phenomenon of touch', thus continuing the earlier analyses (Dillon (2004), 297 and 301). Whether Dillon's analysis of reversibility errs slightly too much on the side of mapping *The Visible and the Invisible* onto *The Phenomenology of Perception* is a different question and will be left open here.

26. Especially Waldenfels; see, for example, Waldenfels (2006) and (2008).

27. Barbaras (2004), 169.

28. These ideas are developed in Merleau-Ponty's essay 'The Philosopher and his Shadow' which complements *The Visible and the Invisible* in a number of ways.

29. The claim that there is a monism inherent in Merleau-Ponty's concept of flesh is proposed, for example, by Lawlor (2003), 48 and 57). Arguing against such a monism are Dillon (1998, 223) and Waldenfels (2008, 82).

Part V: Post-phenomenology and the Future of Phenomenology

1. We are simplifying here: in *Speech and Phenomenon*, Derrida deals at great length with two different forms of *sign* in Husserl, the *expressive* sign and the *indicative* sign, roughly synonymous with speech and language: speech as the immediately heard and understood, writing as a message that is always slightly removed from the process of its production and its conscious producer, and so lacking this immediate relation with its meaning. Naturally, Derrida has good reasons for doing so, but to produce as clear an exposition as we can, we have parenthesized this aspect here.

2. This stress on a life prior to such a reduction is clearly at the centre of the early Heidegger's concerns, which are very close to Derrida's, as the latter clearly acknowledges (*SP*, 25–6n.5/27).

3. 'Platonism' is also a term used by philosophers of mathematics to refer to a certain understanding of numbers, which takes them to be essences really existing in themselves.

4. This is the fallacy of 'psychologism', which Husserl had fallen victim to in his first book, *Philosophy of Arithmetic* and refuted in *Logical Investigations*, addressing Frege's concerns.

5. The question of the gift gives rise to a fascinating debate between Marion and Derrida, for whom the notion is also important. After several scattered references in each other's works, the two finally meet in a debate transcribed in *God, the Gift, and Postmodernism*. Eds. M. Scanlon and J. Caputo (Chicago: Chicago University Press, 2000).

Bibliography

Part I: Edmund Husserl

Selected primary literature by Husserl

Hua   *Husserliana. Gesammelte Werke.* The Hague: Kluwer, 1950ff.

ACPAS   *Analyses Concerning Passive and Active Synthesis.* Trans. A. J. Steinbock. Dordrecht: Kluwer, 2001 (*Analysen zur passiven Synthesis. Aus Vorlesungs- und Forschungs-manuskripten 1918–1926.* Ed. M. Fleischer, 1966. (Hua XI) and *Aktive Synthesen: Aus der Vorlesung 'Transzendentale Logik' 1920/21.* Ergänzungsband zu 'Analysen zur Passiven Synthesis'. Ed. R. Breeur, 2000. (Hua XXXI))

CM   *Cartesian Meditations.* Trans. D. Cairns, The Hague: Kluwer, 1977 (*Cartesianische Meditationen und Pariser Vorträge.* Ed. B. Strasser, 1950. (Hua I))

Crisis   *The Crisis of European Sciences and Transcendental Phenomenology.* Trans. D. Carr, Evanston: Northwestern, 1970 (*Die Krisis der europäischen Wissenschaften und die transzendentale Phänomenologie.* Ed. W. Biemel, 1954. (Hua VI))

EJ   *Experience and Judgment. Investigations in a Genealogy of Logic.* Trans. J. S. Churchill and K. Ameriks. Evanston, IL: Northwestern University Press, 1973. (*Erfahrung und Urteil. Untersuchungen zur Genealogie der Logik.* Ed. L. Landgrebe. Hamburg: Meiner, 1948.)

Ideas I   *Ideas Pertaining to a Pure Phenomenology and to a Phenomenological Philosophy, First Book. General Introduction to a Pure Phenomenology.* Trans. Fred Kersten. Dordrecht: Kluwer, 1982 (*Ideen zu einer reinen Phänomenologie und phänomenologischen Philosophie. Erstes Buch: Allgemeine Einführung in die reine Phänomenologie.* Ed. K. Schuhmann, 1976. (Hua III))

Ideas II   *Ideas Pertaining to a Pure Phenomenology and to a Phenomenological Philosophy, Second Book. Studies in the Phenomenology of Constitution.* Trans. R. Rojcewicz and A. Schuwer. Dordrecht: Kluwer, 1989 (*Ideen zu einer reinen Phänomenologie und phänomenologischen Philosophie. Zweites Buch: Phänomenologische Untersuchungen zur Konstitution.* Ed. W. Biemel, 1952. (Hua IV))

PCT   *On the Phenomenology of the Consciousness of Internal Time.* Trans. J. B. Brough. Dordrecht: Kluwer, 1991 (*Zur Phänomenologie des inneren Zeitbewußtseins* (1893–1917). Ed. R. Boehm, 1966. (Hua X))

PhPsy   *Phänomenologische Psychologie.* Vorlesungen Sommersemester 1925. Ed. W. Biemel,
            1962. (Hua IX)

Hua VIII   *Erste Philosophie* (1923/24). Part II. Ed. R. Boehm, 1959.

Hua XIV   *Zur Phänomenologie der Intersubjektivität.* Texte aus dem Nachlaß. Zweiter Teil:
            1921–1928. Ed. I. Kern, 1973.

Hua XV   *Zur Phänomenologie der Intersubjektivität.* Texte aus dem Nachlaß. Dritter Teil:
            1929–1935. Ed. I. Kern, 1973.

Hua XXIX   *Die Krisis der europäischen Wissenschaften und die transzendentale Phänomenologie.*
            Eine Einleitung in die phänomenologische Philosophie. Ergänzungsband: Texte aus dem
            Nachlaß 1934–1937. Ed. R. Smid, 1993.

Logical Investigations. First and Second Volume. Trans. J. N. Findlay. London: Routledge, 2001. (*Logische*
    Untersuchungen. Band I & II. Tübingen: Niemeyer, 1968.)
'Notizen zur Raumkonstitution' (1934). Ed. A. Schütz. In *Philosophy and Phenomenological Research* 1,
    1941, pp. 21–37. [= 'Notizen']
'Foundational investigations of the phenomenological origin of the spatiality of nature: The originary
    ark, the earth, does not move' in Merleau-Ponty, M., *Husserl at the Limits of Phenomenology,* including
    texts by Edmund Husserl. Evanston, IL: Northwestern University Press, 2002, pp. 117–31.

Selected secondary literature

Alweiss, L. (2003), *The World Unclaimed: A Challenge to Heidegger's Critique of Husserl.* Athens:
    Ohio University Press.
Bell, D. (1990), *Husserl.* London: Routledge.
Bernet, R. (1979), 'Perception as a teleological process of cognition'. In *The Teleologies in Husserlian*
    Phenomenology. Analecta Husserliana, vol. IX. Reidel, Dordrecht: Kluwer, pp. 119–32.
—(1997), 'Edmund Husserl'. In S. Critchley and W. R. Schroeder (eds), *A Companion to Continental*
    Philosophy. Oxford: Blackwell, pp. 198–207.
Bernet, R., Kern, I. and Marbach, E. (eds) (1989), *An Introduction to Husserlian Phenomenology.*
    Evanston, IL: Northwestern University Press.
Bernet, R., Welton, D. and Zavota, G. (eds) (2005), *Edmund Husserl: Critical Assessments of Leading*
    Philosophers. London: Routledge.
Carr, D. (1973), 'The "Fifth Meditation" and Husserl's Cartesianism'. In *Philosophy and Phenomeno-*
    logical Research, vol. 34, no. 1, pp. 14–35.
—(1974), *Phenomenology and the Problem of History.* Evanston, IL: Northwestern University Press.
—(1977), 'Husserl's problematic concept of the life-world'. In Elliston, F. A. and McCormick,
    P., *Husserl: Expositions and Appraisals.* Notre Dame: University of Notre Dame Press, pp. 202–12.
—(1986), *Time, Narrative and History.* Indianapolis, IN: Indiana University Press.
—(1987), *Interpreting Husserl: Critical and Comparative Studies.* The Hague: Kluwer.
—(1999), *The Paradox of Subjectivity. The Self in the Transcendental Tradition.* Oxford: New York.
—(2004), 'Phenomenology and historical knowledge'. In Moran and Embree (2004), vol. III,
    pp. 146–57.

Crowell, S. (2001), *Husserl, Heidegger, and the Space of Meaning: Paths Toward Transcendental Phenomenology*. Evanston, IL: Northwestern University Press.

Derrida, J. (1999). 'Hospitality, justice and responsibility. A dialogue with Jacques Derrida'. In Kearney R. and Dooley M. (eds), *Questioning Ethics. Contemporary Debates in Philosophy*. London: Routledge, pp. 65–83.

Dodd, J. (2004), *Crisis and Reflection. An Essay on Husserl's Crisis of the European Sciences*. The Hague: Kluwer.

Drummond, J. (1975). 'Husserl on the ways to the performance of the reduction'. *Man and World*, 8, pp. 47–69.

—(1979). 'On seeing a material thing in space: the role of "kinaesthesis" in visual perception'. In *Philosophy and Phenomenological Research*, vol. 40, no. 1, pp. 19–32.

Embree, L. (1997) (ed.), *Encyclopedia of Phenomenology*. Dordrecht and Boston: Kluwer.

Fink, E. (1970), 'The phenomenological philosophy of Edmund Husserl and contemporary criticism'. In R. O. Elveton (ed. and trans.), *The Phenomenology of Husserl*. Chicago: Quadrangle Books.

—(2004), 'Operative concepts in Husserl's phenomenology'. In Moran and Embree, vol. V, pp. 44–58.

Gadamer, H.-G. (1986), *Wahrheit und Methode*. Tübingen: Mohr.

Held, K. (1966), *Lebendige Gegenwart. Die Frage der Seinsweise des transzendentalen Ich bei Edmund Husserl, entwickelt am Leitfaden der Zeitproblematik*. The Hague: Kluwer.

—(1991), 'Heimwelt, Fremdwelt, die eine Welt'. In *Phänomenologische Forschungen*, vol. 24/25: Perspektiven und Probleme der Husserlschen Phänomenologie. Freiburg: Alber, pp. 305–37.

—(2000), 'The controversy concerning truth: towards a prehistory of phenomenology'. In *Husserl Studies*, vol. 17, no. 1.

—(2003a), 'Husserl's phenomenological method'. In Welton, Donn (ed.), *The New Husserl. A Critical Reader*. Bloomington, IN: Indiana University Press, pp. 3–31.

—(2003b), 'Husserl's phenomenology of the life-world'. In Welton, Donn (ed.), *The New Husserl. A Critical Reader*. Bloomington, IN: Indiana University Press, pp. 32–62.

Holenstein, E. (1972), *Phänomenologie der Assoziation. Zu Struktur und Funktion eines Grundprinzips der passiven Genesis bei E. Husserl*. The Hague: Kluwer.

Kern, I. (1964), *Husserl und Kant. Eine Untersuchung über Husserls Verhältnis zu Kant und zum Neukantianismus*. The Hague: Kluwer.

Kozin, A. (2009), 'Edmund Husserl's contribution to the humanities: the case of translation studies'. *Topos*. Special Issue: Edmund Husserl.

Landgrebe, L. (1981), 'Husserl's departure from Cartesianism'. In Welton, D. (ed.), *The Phenomenology of Edmund Husserl: Six Essays*, Ithaca, NY: Cornell University Press, pp. 66–121. (Reprinted in Moran and Embree (2004))

Luft, S. (1999), 'Dialectics of the absolute. The systematics of the phenomenological system in Husserl's last period'. In *Philosophy Today*. SPEP Supplement 1999, pp. 107–14.

Merleau-Ponty, M. (1964), 'The Philosopher and his Shadow'. In *Signs*. Evanston, IL: Northwestern University Press, pp. 159–81 (cited as *PS*).

Moran, D. and Embree, L. (eds) (2004), *Phenomenology: Critical Concepts*. 5 volumes. Routledge: London.

—(2005), *Husserl*. Polity Press.

O'Murchadha, F. (2008), 'Reduction, externalism and immanence in Husserl and Heidegger'. In *Synthese*, vol. 160, no. 3, pp. 375–95.

Ricoeur, P. (1967), *Husserl: An Analysis of his Phenomenology*. Evanston, IL: Northwestern University Press.

Schütz, A. (2004), 'The problem of transcendental intersubjectivity in Husserl'. In D. Moran and L. Embree (2004), vol. II, pp. 143–78.

Smith, A. D. (2003), *Husserl and the Cartesian Meditations*. London: Routledge.

Smith B. and Smith D. W. (1995). *The Cambridge Companion to Husserl*. Cambridge: Cambridge University Press.

Soffer, G. (1991), *Husserl and the Question of Relativism*. Dordrecht: Kluwer.

Spiegelberg, H. (1982), *The Phenomenological Movement*. The Hague: Kluwer.

Staehler, T. (2008), 'What is the question to which Husserl's *Fifth Cartesian Meditation* is the answer?' In *Husserl Studies*, 2: 2008, pp. 99–117.

Steinbock, A. J. (1995), *Home and Beyond. Generative Phenomenology after Husserl*. Evanston, IL: Northwestern University Press.

—(2001), 'Translator's Introduction to Husserl's *Analyses Concerning Active and Passive Synthesis*'.

Waldenfels, B. (1990), 'Experience of the alien in Husserl's phenomenology', in *Research in Phenomenology*, 20 (1990), pp. 19–33.

—(1991), *Der Stachel des Fremden*. Frankfurt a. M.: Suhrkamp.

—(1998), 'Homeworld and alienworld'. In *Phenomenology and Life-world*, E. W. Orth, Chan-Fai Cheung, (eds) Freiburg/München: Alber 1998 (reprinted Moran and Embree (2004))

Welton, D. (2000), *The Other Husserl: The Horizons of Transcendental Phenomenology*. Bloomington, IN: Indiana University Press.

Zahavi, D. (2001), *Husserl and Transcendental Intersubjectivity. A Response to the Linguistic-Pragmatic Critique*. Athens, OH: Ohio University Press.

—(2003), *Husserl's Phenomenology*. Stanford, CA: Stanford University Press.

Part II: Martin Heidegger

Strangely, *Being and Time*, Heidegger's most famous work, is perhaps the least well written and least suited to those who come to Heidegger for the first time. Much more accessible are the short work, *The Concept of Time*, and the contemporaneous lecture courses, *History of the Concept of Time* and *Basic Problems of Phenomenology*, as well as *Plato's Sophist*. In general, the vast majority of Heidegger's works are lecture courses. They are, as pedagogical texts, much more accessible than his actual monographs and essays (although many of these are extraordinary), and always immensely illuminating to read, opening up vast swathes of the history of philosophy – among many other things – in a quite unique way.

All of Heidegger writings and most of his lectures are either published or scheduled to be published in his '*Gesamtausgabe*' or 'collected works', published by Vittorio Klostermann in Frankfurt-am-Main, Germany.

Primary texts

BPP   (1982), *The Basic Problems of Phenomenology* [1927]. Trans. Albert Hofstadter. Bloomington and Indianapolis, IN: Indiana University Press.

BT   (1962), *Being and Time* [1927]. Trans. John Macquarrie and Edward Robinson. Oxford: Blackwell. Also trans. Joan Stambaugh. Albany: SUNY Press, 1996.

CT   *The Concept of Time* [1924]. Trans. William McNeill. Oxford: Blackwell, 1992.

HCT   *History of the Concept of Time: Prolegomena* [1925]. Trans. Theodore Kisiel. Bloomington and Indianapolis, IN: Indiana University Press, 1985.

L   (1971), 'Language' [1950] in *Poetry, Language, Thought*, pp. 189–210.

LH   (1998), 'Letter on "Humanism"' [1946] in *Pathmarks, op. cit.* Trans. Frank A. Capuzzi, pp. 239–76.

OWA   (1971), 'The Origin of the Work of Art' [1936] in *Poetry, Language, Thought*. Trans. Albert Hofstadter. New York: Harper and Row, 1971/2001, pp. 15–88. From *Holzwege*.

SZ   *Sein und Zeit* [1927]. Tübingen: Max Niemeyer, 1979.

TB   [1972], *On Time and Being* (*Zur Sache des Denkens*). Trans. Joan Stambaugh. New York: Harper and Row.

Th   (1971), 'The Thing' [1950] in *Poetry, Language, Thought*, pp. 163–86.

WM   (1998), 'What is Metaphysics?' [1929] in *Pathmarks*. Edited by William McNeill. Trans. David Farrell Krell. Cambridge: Cambridge University Press, 1998, pp. 82–96.

Towards a Definition of Philosophy [1919]. Trans. Ted Sadler. London: Continuum, 2002/2008.

Der Begriff der Zeit [1924]. Tübingen: Max Niemeyer Verlag, 1989.

Plato's Sophist [1924–5]. Trans. Richard Rojcewicz and André Schuwer. Bloomington and Indianapolis, IN: Indiana University Press, 1997.

Platon: Sophistes [1924–5]. Frankfurt-am-Main: Vittorio Klostermann, 1992.

Prolegomena zur Geschichte des Zeitbegriffs [1925]. Frankfurt-am-Main: Vittorio Klostermann, 1979.

Die Grundprobleme der Phänomenologie [1927b]. Frankfurt am Main: Vittorio Klostermann, 1975.

Beiträge zur Philosophie: Vom Ereignis [1936–8]. Frankfurt am Main: Vittorio Klostermann, 1989.

Contributions to Philosophy: From Enowning [1936–8]. Trans. Parvis Emad and Kenneth Maly. Bloomington and Indianapolis, IN: Indiana University Press, 1999.

Parmenides [1942–3]. Frankfurt am Main: Vittorio Klostermann, 1982.

Parmenides [1942–3]. Trans. André Schuwer and Richard Rojcewicz. Indianapolis and Bloomington, IN: Indiana University Press, 1992.

Holzwege [1950]. Frankfurt am Main: Vittorio Klostermann.

Discourse on Thinking (*Gelassenheit*) [1959]. Trans. John M. Anderson and E. Hans Freud. San Francisco: Harper and Row, 1966.

Gelassenheit [1959]. Pfullingen: Günther Neske.

Unterwegs zur Sprache [1959]. Pfullingen: Günther Neske.

Die Technik und die Kehre [1962]. Pfullingen: Günther Neske.

Wegmarken [1967]. Frankfurt am Main: Vittorio Klostermann.

Zur Sache des Denkens [1969]. Tübingen: Max Niemeyer Verlag.

Introductory works

Beistegui, Miguel de (2005), *The New Heidegger*. London, New York: Continuum.

Greaves, Tom (2010), *Starting With Heidegger*. London, New York: Continuum.

Harman, Graham (2007), *Heidegger Explained: From Phenomenon to Thing*. Chicago and La Salle, IL: Open Court.

Macann, Christopher (1992), *Heidegger: Critical Assessments*. Four volumes. London: Routledge.

Mulhall, Stephen (2005), *Heidegger's* Being and Time. 2nd edn. London: Routledge.

Further reading

Beistegui, Miguel de (1998), *Heidegger and the Political: Dystopias*. London: Routledge.

—(2002), 'Homo Heideggerians' in F. Raffoul and D. Pettigrew (eds), *Heidegger and Practical Philosophy*. Albany: State University of New York Press.

—(2003), 'The transformation of the sense of Dasein in Heidegger's *Beiträge zur Philosophy (Vom Ereignis)*' in *Research in Phenomenology*, vol. 33.

Bernasconi, Robert (1985), *The Question of Language in Heidegger's Thought*. Atlantic Highlands, NJ: Humanities Press.

—(1993), *Heidegger in Question: The Art of Existing*. Atlantic Highlands, NJ: Humanities Press.

Derrida, Jacques (1987), 'Geschlecht' [1985]. Trans. John P. Leavey Jnr in J. Sallis (ed.), *Deconstruction and Philosophy: The Texts of Jacques Derrida*. Chicago and London: University of Chicago Press.

—(1989), *Of Spirit: Heidegger and the Question* [1987]. Trans. Geoffrey Bennington and Rachel Bowlby. Chicago and London: University of Chicago Press.

—(1993) [1989] 'Heidegger's ear: philopolemology (Geschlecht IV)'. Trans. John P. Leavey Jnr. in J. Sallis (ed.), *Reading Heidegger: Commemorations*. Bloomington and Indianapolis, IN: Indiana University Press.

—(1993), *Aporias: Dying-awaiting (one another at) the "limits of truth"* (*Mourir-s'attendre aux "limites de la vérité"*) [1992]. Trans. Thomas Dutoit. Stanford, CA: Stanford University Press.

—(1999), 'Geschlecht II: Heidegger's Hand'. Trans. Ruben Bevezdrun in P. Kamuf (ed.), *A Derrida Reader: Between the Blinds*. New York: Columbia University Press.

Foti, Véronique (1991), *Heidegger and the Poets: Poiesis-Sophia-Techne*. Amherst, NY: Humanity Books.

Fynsk, Christopher (1986), *Heidegger: Thought and Historicity*. Ithaca, NY and London: Cornell University Press.

Gadamer, Hans-Georg (1994), *Heidegger's Ways* [1983]. Trans. John W. Stanley. New York: State University of New York Press.

Haar, Michel (1993), *The Song of the Earth* [1987]. Trans. Reginald Lilly. Bloomington and Indianapolis, IN: Indiana University Press.

—(1993), *Heidegger and the Essence of Man* [1990]. Trans. William McNeill. New York: State University of New York Press.

Harman, Graham (2002), *Tool-Being: Heidegger and the Metaphysics of Objects*. Chicago and La Salle, IL: Open Court.

Janicaud, Dominique (1996), *The Shadow of That Thought: Heidegger and the Question of Politics* [1990]. Trans. Michael Gendre. Evanston, IL: Northwestern University Press.

Kisiel, Theodore (1993), *The Genesis of Heidegger's Being and Time.* Berkeley, CA: University of California Press.

Krell, David Farrell (1982), 'Work sessions with Martin Heidegger' [1979] in *Philosophy Today*, vol. 26 (Summer 1982), pp. 126–38.

—(1986), *Intimations of Mortality: Time, Truth and Finitude in Heidegger's Thinking of Being.* University Park and London: Pennsylvania State University Press.

—(1992), *Daimon Life: Heidegger and Life-Philosophy.* Bloomington and Indianapolis, IN: Indiana University Press.

Lacoue-Labarthe, Philippe (1990), *Heidegger, Art and Politics (La Fiction du Politique)* [1987]. Trans. Chris Turner. Oxford: Basil Blackwell.

—(1990), *Heidegger and 'the jews'* [1988]. Trans. Andreas Michel and Mark Roberts. Minneapolis, MN: University of Minnesota Press.

Marx, Werner (1987), *Is There a Measure on Earth? Foundations for a Non-Metaphysical Ethics* [1983]. Trans. Thomas J. Nenon and Reginald Lilly. Chicago, IL: University of Chicago Press.

McNeill, William (1992), 'Metaphysics, Fundamental Ontology, Metontology 1925–1935' in *Heidegger Studies*, vol. 8.

—(1993b), 'Spirit's living hand' in D. Wood (ed.), *Of Derrida, Heidegger and Spirit.* Evanston, IL: Northwestern University Press.

—(1998), 'Care for the self: originary ethics in Heidegger and Foucault' in *Philosophy Today* (Chicago, IL: De Paul University), vol. 42, Spring.

Polt, Richard (1999), *Heidegger: An Introduction.* London: UCL Press.

Raffoul, François and David Pettigrew (eds) (2002), *Heidegger and Practical Philosophy.* Albany, NY: State University of New York Press.

Richardson, William J. (1963), *Heidegger: Through Phenomenology to Thought.* The Hague: Martinus Nijhoff.

Sallis, John (1986/1995), *Delimitations: Phenomenology and the End of Metaphysics.* Bloomington and Indianapolis, IN: Indiana University Press.

—(1990), *Echoes: After Heidegger.* Bloomington and Indianapolis, IN: Indiana University Press.

—(ed.) (1993), *Reading Heidegger: Commemorations.* Bloomington and Indianapolis, IN: Indiana University Press.

Schürmann, Reiner (1987), *Heidegger on Being and Acting: From Principles to Anarchy (Le principe d'anarchie: Heidegger et la question de l'agir)* [1982]. Trans. Christine-Marie Gros. Bloomington, IN: Indiana University Press.

Scott, Charles E., 'Nonbelonging/Authenticity' [1993] in *Reading Heidegger: Commemorations.* Ed. J. Sallis. Bloomington and Indianapolis, IN: Indiana University Press.

Stiegler, Bernard, *Technics and Time, 1: The Fault of Epimetheus* [1994]. Trans. R. Beardsworth and G. Collins. Stanford, CA: Stanford University Press, 1998.

Taminiaux, Jacques (1991), *Heidegger and the Project of Fundamental Ontology (Lectures de l'ontologie fondamentale)* [1989]. Trans. and ed. Michael Gendre. New York: State University of New York Press.

Vogel, Lawrence (1994), *The Fragile "We": Ethical Implication of Heidegger's 'Being and Time'*. Evanston, IL: Northwestern University Press.

Wood, David (ed.) (1993), *Of Derrida, Heidegger and Spirit*. Evanston, IL: Northwestern University Press.

Part III: Jean-Paul Sartre

[Generally the state of Sartre translation is somewhat shambolic. Many early translators such as Bernard Frechtman and Philip Mairet did noble jobs, but his work is sorely in need of a standard edition. The fact that nothing like it exists is testimony to a disrespect that we have here wished to dispel, and it has exacerbated this disrespect in the English-speaking world, contributing to the picture of Sartre as a rather rhapsodic, perhaps unsystematic thinker. Thankfully, a number of works have recently been re-translated, but uncooperatively.]

BN   *Being and Nothingness: An Essay on Phenomenological Ontology* Trans. Hazel Barnes. New York: Methuen, 1957; London: Methuen, 1958. Routledge, 1989. (Routledge Classics, 2003). Paris: Gallimard, 1943.

EH   'Existentialism is a humanism' [1946]. Trans. Philip Mairet in Walter Kaufmann, *Existentialism From Dostoyevsky to Sartre*. New York: Meridian, 1956. Also in *Existentialism and Humanism*. Trans. Philip Mairet. London: Methuen, 1948/2007. Paris: Editions Nagel, 1963.

Imaginary   *The Imaginary: A Phenomenological Psychology of the Imagination*. Revised with a historical introduction by Arlette Elkaïm-Sartre. Trans. with a philosophical introduction by Jonathan Webber. London and New York: Routledge, 2004. Paris: Éditions Gallimard, 1940/1986.

     (First translated as *Psychology of the Imagination*. Trans. Bernard Frechtman. New York: Citadel, 1948, London: Methuen, 1949. Routledge, 1972.)

Imagination   Sartre, Jean-Paul, *Imagination: A Psychological Critique*. Trans. with an introduction by Forrest Williams. Ann Arbor: University of Michigan Press, 1967, paperback 1972. Paris: Presses Universitaires de France, 1936/1981. (A new translation from London and New York: Routledge, 2011 is forthcoming at the time of writing.)

Intentionality   'Intentionality: A Fundamental Idea of Husserl's Philosophy'. Trans. Joseph P. Fell in Dermot Moran and Timothy Mooney (eds), *The Phenomenology Reader*. London and New York: Routledge, 2002. pp. 382–4. [From *Situations I*. Paris: Gallimard, 1947. First published in *Nouvelle Revue Francaise*, LII, January 1939.]

     (First translated in *Journal of the British Society for Phenomenology*, vol. 1, no. 2 (1970), pp. 4–5.)

STE   *Sketch for a Theory of the Emotions*. Trans. Philip Mairet. Preface by Mary Warnock. Routledge Classics. London and New York: Routledge, 2002. (First published by London: Methuen and Co., 1962, Routledge: 1994.) Paris: Hermann, 1939/1960. (First translated as *Outline of a Theory of the Emotions*. Trans. Bernard Frechtman. New York: Citadel Press, 1948)

TE   *The Transcendence of the Ego: A Sketch for a Phenomenological Description*. Trans. Andrew Brown with an introduction by Sarah Richmond. Routledge Classics. London and New York: Routledge, 2004. [Originally in Recherches philosophiques 6 (1936/7), pp. 85–123. Reprinted as *La Transcendance de l'ego*. Paris: Vrin, 1966.] (First translated by Forrest Williams and Robert Kirkpatrick (New York: Farrar, Straus and Giroux, 1957, reprinted 1972).)

Search for a Method [1960]. Trans. Hazel Barnes. New York: Alfred A. Knopf, 1963; trans. as *The Problem of Method*. London: Methuen, 1964. Also translated as *The Question of Method*. Included in Volume 1 of *Critique of Dialectical Reason*, as a preface ['Question de Méthode'].

Critique of Dialectical Reason: Volume 1. *Theory of Practical Ensembles*. Trans. Alan Sheridan Smith (*Search for a Method*, the introduction, was translated separately in English), 1960. Paris: Gallimard, 1976].

Critique of Dialectical Reason: Volume 2. Op. posth. 1985. Trans. Quintin Hoare. London: Verso, 1991. Paris: Gallimard, 1985.

War Diaries: Notebooks from a Phoney War. November 1939–March 1940. Trans. Quintin Hoare. London: Verso, 1984. (Verso Classics: 1999.) *Les Carnets de la Drôle de Guerre*. Paris: Gallimard, 1983.

Notebooks for an Ethics. Trans. David Pellauer. Chicago: Chicago University Press, 1992. *Cahiers pour une morale*. Paris: Gallimard, 1983.

Other works

Anti-Semite and Jew: An Exploration of the Etiology of Hate. Trans. George J. Becker. Preface by Michael Walzer. New York: Schocken Books, 1948/1995. *Réflexions sur la question juive*. Paris: Editions Morihien, 1946.

Saint Genet: Actor and Martyr. Trans. Bernard Frechtman. New York: George Braziller, 1963. *Saint Genet: Comédien et Martyr*. Paris: Gallimard, 1952.

Baudelaire. Trans. Martin Turnell. New York: New Directions, 1950. Paris: Gallimard, 1947.

Situations I–X (1947–1976) The ten volumes of *Situations* are not always published under that title or in the same form in English: not all are translated, and we shall list only the most immediately salient:

Situations II = *What is Literature?* Trans. Bernard Frechtman. London: Routledge, 1950/1993/2001. [1948].

Situations III = *The Aftermath of War*. Trans. Chris Turner. London: Seagull books, 2008 [2003/1949]), includes the famous 'Black Orpheus' and 'The Republic of Silence', to which we have referred.

Situations IV = *Situations* [without number]. Trans. Benita Eisler. London: Hamish Hamilton, 1965.
[1964]. Includes Sartre's engagement with Camus, and his tribute to Merleau-Ponty, illuminating
what changes in Sartre's thought after *Being and Nothingness*.

Situation V = *Colonialism and Neocolonism*. Trans. T. McWilliams, S. Brewer, A. Haddour. London:
Routledge, 2001 (Routledge Classics, 2006) [1964].

Selections from these volumes, and other essays may be found in *Modern Times: Selected Non-Fiction*.
Ed. Geoffrey Wall. Trans. Robin Buss. London: Penguin, 2000.

Politics and Literature. Trans. J. A. Underwood, John Calder. London: Calder and Boyars, 1973.

Words. Trans. Irene Clephane. London: Hamish Hamilton, 1964. Harmondsworth: Penguin, 1967.
Les Mots. Paris: Gallimard, 1964. A 'biography' of Sartre's childhood.

Sartre also wrote a gigantic three volume life (translated in five volumes) of Flaubert: *The Family Idiot: Gustave Flaubert, 1821–57*. Trans. Hazel Barnes. Chicago: Chicago University Press, 1981–93. Works such as this, essays in what he once called 'existential psychoanalysis' are frequently referenced by the semiologist Roland Barthes, and are very much to be admired. The Flaubert is considered to be a new development of Sartre's philosophical work by contemporary scholars, in particular Christina Howells and her authors in the *Cambridge Companion to Sartre* which admirably attempts to collect together the most advanced examples of recent work on Sartre. Along with his *Critique of Dialectical Reason* it remains perhaps a sleeping masterpiece of twentieth century writing.

There are also a great many letters, particularly those written to Simone de Beavoir, 'the beaver' ('Castor'), who has in turn written many books on Sartre, in fictional and non-fictional forms. Their relationship remains one of the most extraordinary and in the end the most touching of twentieth century thought, but beyond our remit here.

Secondary texts

Aronson, Ronald (1980), *Jean-Paul Sartre: Philosophy in the World*. London: Verso.

Bernasconi, Robert (2006), *How to Read Sartre*. London: Granta.

Farrell Fox, Nik (2003), *The New Sartre*. London: Continuum. A good progressive guide that centres
its reading on the later Sartre and his continuing relevance even in light of later French thinkers.

Howells, Christina (ed.) (1992), *Cambridge Companion to Sartre*. Cambridge: Cambridge University
Press. Excellent and sympathetic, essential for any charitable, modern reading of Sartre.

Other thinkers who discuss or develop Sartre's work

Badiou, Alain (2009 [2008]), *Pocket Pantheon: Figures of Postwar Philosophy*. Trans. David Macey.
London: Verso,

Deleuze, Gilles (2004), *Desert Islands and Other Texts*. Trans. Michael Taormina. Cambridge, MA:
MIT Press.

Derrida, Jacques (1982 [1972]), 'The Ends of Man' in *Margins of Philosophy*. Trans. Alan Bass.
Brighton: Harvester Press, pp. 109–36.

Fanon, Franz (1967), *The Wretched of the Earth*. Trans. Constance Farrington. London: Penguin.

—(1968), *Black Skins, White Masks*. Trans. Charles Markmann. New York: Grove Press.

Heidegger, Martin (2000), 'Letter on "Humanism"' in *Pathmarks*. Ed. William McNeill. Cambridge: Cambridge University Press.

Lacan, Jacques [1964], *Four Fundamental Concepts of Psycho-analysis*. Trans. Alan Sheridan. New York: Norton, 1977.

Levi-Strauss, Claude [1962], *The Savage Mind* (*La pensée sauvage*). London: Weidenfeld, 1966. Oxford: Oxford University Press, 1996.

Merleau-Ponty, Maurice [1948], *Sense and Non-Sense*. Trans. Hubert L. Dreyfus and Patricia Allen Dreyfus. Evanston, IL: Northwestern University Press, 1964.

—[1955], *Adventures of the Dialectic*. Trans. Joseph Bien. Evanston, IL: Northwestern University Press, 1973.

—(1992), *Texts and Dialogues: On Philosophy, Politics, and Culture*. Trans. Michael B. Smith et al. Ed. Hugh J. Silverman and James Barry Jr. Amherst, NY: Humanity Books.

Part IV: Maurice Merleau-Ponty

Selected primary literature by Merleau-Ponty

CD   'Cézanne's doubt' in G. A. Johnson (ed.). *The Merleau-Ponty Aesthetics Reader*. Evanston, IL: Northwestern University Press, 1993, pp. 3–13.

Eloge   *In Praise of Philosophy and Other Essays*. Trans. J. Wild, J. Edie and J. O'Neill. Evanston, IL: Northwestern University Press, 1963. (*Eloge de la philosophie et autre essays*. Paris: Gallimard, 1953).

EM   'Eye and mind' in G. A. Johnson (ed.). *The Merleau-Ponty Aesthetics Reader*. Evanston, IL: Northwestern University Press, 1993, pp. 121–49.

EN   'Everywhere and nowhere' in *Signs*. Trans. R. C. McCleary. Evanston, IL: Northwestern University Press, 1964, pp. 126–58.

IL   'Indirect language and the voices of silence' in G. A. Johnson (ed.). *The Merleau-Ponty Aesthetics Reader*. Evanston, IL: Northwestern University Press, 1993, pp. 76–120.

PP   *Phenomenology of Perception*. Trans. C. Smith. London: Routledge, 1962. (*Phénoménologie de la Perception*. Paris: Gallimard, 1945.)

    A concordance of page numbers for the different editions of the *Phenomenology of Spirit* (Routledge editions prior to 2002, current edition, French editions) is available on the net: http://philpapers.org/archive/MORCOM-3.1.pdf

Prosp.   'An unpublished text by Maurice Merleau-Ponty: a prospectus of his work' in *The Primacy of Perception*. Trans. J. M. Edie. Evanston, IL: Northwestern University Press, 1964, pp. 3–11.

PS   'The Philosopher and his Shadow'. In *Signs*. Evanston, IL: Northwestern University Press, 1964, pp. 159–81.

VI   *The Visible and the Invisible.* Trans. A. Lingis. Evanston, IL: Northwestern University Press, 1968. (*Le Visible et l'Invisible.* Paris: Gallimard, 1964).

Selected secondary literature

Baldwin, T. (2007), *Reading Merleau-Ponty. On* Phenomenology of Perception. London: Routledge.

Barbaras, R. (2004), *The Being of the Phenomenon: Merleau-Ponty's Ontology.* Evanston, IL: Northwestern University Press.

Beauvoir, S. de (2000), *The Ethics of Ambiguity.* New York: Citadel Press.

Casey, E. S. (1984), 'Habitual body and memory in Merleau-Ponty'. *Man and World* 17, pp. 278–97.

—(1998), *The Fate of Place. A Philosophical History.* Berkeley, CA: University of California Press.

—(2002), *Representing Place: Landscape Painting and Maps.* Minneapolis, MN: University of Minnesota Press.

Dillon, M. C. (1983), 'Merleau-Ponty and the Reversibility Thesis'. In *Man and World,* 16, pp. 365–88.

—(1998), *Merleau-Ponty's Ontology.* Evanston, IL: Northwestern University Press.

Evans, F. and Lawlor, L. (eds) (2000), *Chiasms: Merleau-Ponty's Notion of Flesh.* Albany, NY: SUNY Press.

Foti, V. (1995), *Difference Materiality Painting.* Prometheus Books.

Halda, B. (1966), *Merleau-Ponty ou la philosophie de l'ambiguïté.* Paris: Archives des Lettres Modernes, no. 72.

Johnson, G. A. (1993), *The Merleau-Ponty Aesthetics Reader: Philosophy and Painting.* Evanston, IL: Northwestern University Press.

Kwant, R. C. (1963), *The Phenomenological Philosophy of Merleau-Ponty.* Pittsburgh, PA: Duquesne University Press.

Langer, M. (2003), 'Beauvoir and Merleau-Ponty on Ambiguity' in C. Card (ed.), *The Cambridge Companion to Simone de Beauvoir.* Cambridge: Cambridge University Press, pp. 87–106.

Lawlor, L. (2003), *Thinking through French Philosophy. The Being of the Question.* Bloomington and Indianapolis, IN: Indiana University Press.

Levinas, E. (1987), 'Meaning and Sense' in *Collected Philosophical Papers.* Pittsburgh, PA: Duquesne University Press, pp. 75–107 [cited as *MS*].

Sapontzis, S. F. (1978), 'A Note on Merleau-Ponty's "Ambiguity"' in *Philosophy and Phenomenological Research,* vol. 38, no. 4, pp. 538–43.

Singer, L. (1981), 'Merleau-Ponty on the concept of style' in *Man and World,* 14, pp. 153–63.

Waelhens, A. de (1951), *Une philosophie de l'ambiguïté. L'existentialisme de Merleau-Ponty.* Louvain: Publications universitaires de Louvain.

Waldenfels, B. (1983), *Phänomenologie in Frankreich.* Frankfurt a.M.: Suhrkamp.

—(1993), 'Interrogative thinking: reflections on Merleau-Ponty's later philosophy', in P. Burke, J. van der Veken (eds), *Merleau-Ponty in Contemporary Perspectives.* Dordrecht/Boston/London: Kluwer Academic Publishers.

—(1998), 'Merleau-Ponty', in *A Companion to Continental Philosophy.* Ed. S. Critchley and W. R. Schroeder. Malden, MA/Oxford: Blackwell.

—(2000), 'The paradox of expression' in *Chiasms. Merleau-Ponty's Notion of Flesh*. Ed. F. Evans and L. Lawlor. Albany, NY: State University of New York Press.

—(2006), 'Responsivity of the body. Traces of the Other in Merleau-Ponty's theory of body and flesh', in *Interrogating Ethics. Embodying Good in Merleau-Ponty*. Ed. J. Hatley a. o. Pittsburgh, PA: Duquesne University Press.

—(2008), 'The central role of the body in Merleau-Ponty's phenomenology'. *Journal of the British Society for Phenomenology*, vol. 39, no. 1, pp. 76–88.

Part V: Post-phenomenology and the Future of Phenomenology

Derrida's 'foundational' works and his works on Husserl

GS   '"Genesis and Structure" and Husserl's Phenomenology' in *Writing and Difference*. Trans. Alan Bass. London, New York: Routledge, 1959.

OG   *Of Grammatology* [1967]. Trans. Gayatri Chakravorty Spivak. Baltimore, London: The Johns Hopkins University Press, 1974.

SP   *Speech and Phenomena and Other Essays on Husserl's Theory of Signs* [1967]. Trans. David B. Allison. Evanston, IL: Northwestern University Press, 1973.

The Problem of Genesis in Husserl's Philosophy [1953–4, published 1990]. Trans. Marian Hobson. Chicago, IL: University of Chicago Press, 2003.

Edmund Husserl's Origin of Geometry: *An Introduction* [1962]. Trans. John P. Leavey, Jr. Lincoln, NE; London: University of Nebraska Press, 1989 (first published: Stony Brook, NY: N. Hays, 1978).

Writing and Difference [1967]. Trans. Alan Bass. London; New York: Routledge, 2001.

Margins: of Philosophy [1972]. Trans. Alan Bass. New York; London; Hemel Hempstead: Harvester Wheatsheaf, 1982.

Dissemination [1972]. Trans. Barbara Johnson. London: The Athlone Press, 1981.

Positions [1972]. Trans. Alan Bass. London, New York: Continuum, 2002.

Rogues: Two Essays on Reason [2003]. Trans. Michael Naas and Pascale Anne-Brault. Stanford, CA: Stanford University Press, 2005.

Husserlian responses to Derrida

Naturally, in different ways, Derrida's reading of Husserl has been challenged. We shall not decide on the extent to which these counter-critiques are effective, or at least productive. A recent version may be found in

Evans, Joseph Claude (1991), *Strategies of Deconstruction: Derrida and the Myth of the Voice*. Minneapolis, MN: University of Minnesota Press.

Selected primary literature of Levinas

CPP   *Collected Philosophical Papers.* Trans. A. Lingis. Pittsburgh, PA: Duquesne University Press, 1987.

EI   *Ethics and Infinity. Conversations with Philippe Nemo* (1981). Trans. R. A. Cohen. Pittsburgh, PA: Duquesne University Press, 1985.

GCM   *Of God Who Comes to Mind.* Trans. B. Bergo. Stanford, CA: Stanford University Press, 1998.

OB   *Otherwise Than Being or Beyond Essence* (1974). Pittsburgh, PA: Duquesne University Press, 1981. (*Autrement qu'être ou au-delà de l'essence.* The Hague: Nijhoff, 1974).

TI   *Totality and Infinity* (1961). Trans. A. Lingis. Pittsburgh, PA: Duquesne University Press, 1969. (*Totalité et Infini. Essai sur l'extériorité.* La Haye: Nijhoff, 1961).

TO   *Time and the Other* (1947). Trans. R. A. Cohen. Pittsburgh, PA: Duquesne University Press, 1987. (*Le Temps et l'Autre.* Montpelier: Fata Morgana, 1979).

Existence and Existents (1947). Trans. R. Bernasconi and A. Lingis. Pittsburgh, PA: Duquesne University Press, 2001.

Discovering Existence with Husserl. Evanston, IL: Northwestern University Press, 1998.

The Theory of Intuition in Husserl's Phenomenology. Evanston, IL: Northwestern University Press, 2nd edition 1995.

Selected secondary literature on Levinas

Bernasconi, R. and Critchley, S. (eds) (1991), *Re-reading Levinas.* London: Continuum.

Bernasconi, R. (1999), 'The third party. Levinas on the intersection of the ethical and the political' in *Journal of the British Society for Phenomenology*, vol. 30, no. 1, pp. 76–87.

—(2005), 'No exit: Levinas's aporetic account of transcendence' in *Research in Phenomenology*, vol. 35, pp. 101–17.

Bloechl, J. (ed.) (2000), *The Face of the Other and the Trace of God. Essays on the Philosophy of Emmanuel Levinas.* New York: Fordham University Press, pp. 43–61.

Butler, J. (2005), *Giving an Account of Oneself.* New York: Fordham University Press.

Critchley, S. (1999), *The Ethics of Deconstruction. Derrida and Levinas.* 2nd edition. Edinburgh: Edinburgh University Press.

Critchley, S. and Bernasconi, R. (eds) (2002), *The Cambridge Companion to Levinas.* Cambridge: Cambridge University Press.

Derrida, J. (1978), 'Violence and metaphysics' in *Writing and Difference.* Chicago, IL: University of Chicago Press.

Hand, S. (ed.) (1996), *Facing the Other: The Ethics of Emmanuel Levinas.* Richmond, VA: Curzon Press.

Katz, C. (ed.) (2005), *Emmanuel Levinas: Critical Assessments.* 4 volumes. London: Routledge.

Llewelyn, J. (1995), *Emmanuel Levinas. The Genealogy of Ethics.* London: Routledge.

Peperzak, A. T. (1993), *To the Other: An Introduction to the Philosophy of Emmanuel Levinas.* West Lafayette, IN: Purdue University Press.

—(ed.) (1995), *Ethics as First Philosophy: The Significance of Emmanuel Levinas for Philosophy, Literature and Religion*. London: Routledge.

—(1997), *Beyond. The Philosophy of Emmanuel Levinas*. Evanston, IL: Northwestern University Press.

Selected primary literature of Michel Henry

EM   *The Essence of Manifestation*. Trans. Girard Etzkorn. The Hague: Martinus Nijhoff, 1973. Paris: Presses Universitaires de France, 1963/1990.

MP   *Material Phenomenology*. Trans. Scott Davidson. New York: Fordham University Press, 2008. Paris: PUF, 1990.

Philosophy and Phenomenology of the Body. [Towards a Biranian Ontology]. Trans. Girard Etzkorn. The Hague: Martinus Nijhoff, 1975. Paris: PUF, 1965/1997.

I am the Truth: Towards a Philosophy of Christianity. Trans. Susan Emanuel. Stanford, CA: Stanford University Press, 2003. Paris: Seuil, 1996.

Genealogy of Psychoanalysis. Trans. Douglas Brick. Albany, NY: State University of New York Press, 1993. Paris: PUF, 1985.

Marx: A Philosophy of Human Reality. Indianapolis: Indiana University Press, 1983. Trans. Kathleen McLaughlin. [Abbreviated translation of two volumes in French. Paris: Gallimard, 1976].

'Marx' in S. Critchley & W. Schroeder (eds), *The Blackwell Companion to Continental Philosophy*. Oxford: Blackwell, 1998. [An excellent summary of Henry's *Marx* volumes.]

Seeing the Invisible: On Kandinsky. Trans. Scott Davidson. London; New York: Continuum, 2009. Paris: Bourin, 1988.

'Speech and Religion: the Word of God' in *Phenomenology and the 'Theological Turn': The French Debate*. Trans. Jeffrey L. Kosky. New York: Fordham University Press, 2001.

'Critique of the Subject' in *Topoi 7* (1988). Trans. Peter T. Connor.

Suggested further reading on Michel Henry

There is as yet a distinct paucity of work on Michel Henry in English, but with the recent translations of his work, one can justly expect this scholarship to blossom. What is available is of a high quality, however, and some examples of it are listed below.

Alweiss, L. (ed.) (2009), *International Journal of Philosophical Studies*, vol. 17, no. 3. *The Work of Michel Henry*.

Bozga, Adina (2009), *The Exasperating Gift of Singularity: Husserl, Levinas, Henry*. Bucharest: Zeta Books.

Brassier, Ray (2007), *Nihil Unbound: Philosophy in the Light of Extinction*. Basingstoke: Palgrave.

Derrida, Jacques (2005), *On Touching: Jean-Luc Nancy*. Trans. Christine Izirrary. Stanford, CA: Stanford University Press [2000].

Hallward, P. (ed.), 'Phenomenology of Life' in *The One or the Other? French Philosophy Today*. *Angelaki* 8/2 (August 2003).

O'Sullivan, Michael (2006), *Michel Henry: Incarnation, Barbarism and Belief: An Introduction to the Work of Michel Henry*. New York, Oxford: Peter Lang.

Steinbock, A. (ed.), *Continental Philosophy Review* (formerly 'Man and World') (1999), 32/3, Special Edition on Michel Henry.

Primary texts of Jean-Luc Marion

The phenomenological trilogy

BG *Being Given: Toward a Phenomenology of Givenness* (2002). Trans. Jeffrey L. Kosky. Stanford, CA: Stanford University Press. *Etant donné: Essai d'une phénomenologie de la donation.* Paris: PUF, 1997.

RG *Reduction and Givenness: Investigations of Husserl, Heidegger, and Phenomenology* (1998). Trans. Thomas A. Carlson. Evanston, IL: Northwestern University Press. *Reduction et Donation.* Paris: PUF, 1989.

In Excess: Studies of Saturated Phenomena (2002). Trans. Robyn Horner. New York: Fordham University Press. *Du Surcroît: essais sur la phénomème saturée.* Paris: PUF, 2001.

Marion is also the author of five highly respected books on Descartes, and a number of works which he has described, tentatively, as at least partially 'theological', but which are of great interest and of great relevance to his phenomenology of givenness.

'Theological' works

The Idol and Distance (2001). Trans. Thomas A. Carlson. New York: Fordham University Press [1977].

God Without Being: Hors-texte (1995). Trans. Thomas A. Carlson. Chicago, IL: University of Chicago Press [1982].

Prolegomena to Charity (2002). Trans. Jeffrey L. Kosky. New York: Fordham University Press [1986].

'Metaphysics and phenomenology: a relief for theology' in *Critical Inquiry* 20 (Summer 1994) [1993]. [Very useful in understanding the relation between phenomenology and theology in Marion's work.]

'The Other First Philosophy and the Question of Givenness' in *Critical Inquiry* 25 (Summer 1999).

Suggested further reading on Jean-Luc Marion

Gschwandtner, Christina M. (2007), *Reading Jean-Luc Marion: Exceeding Metaphysics.* Indianapolis, IN: Indiana University Press.

Hart, Kevin (ed.) (2007), *Counter-Exprreiences: Reading Jean-Luc Marion.* Notre Dame, IN: University of Notre Dame Press.

Horner, Robyn (2005), *Jean-Luc Marion: A* Theo-*logical Introduction.* Farnham: Ashgate.

Janicaud, Dominique *et al.*, (2001), *Phenomenology and the 'Theological Turn': The French Debate.* New York: Fordham University Press [1991/2].

—(2005), *Phenomenology Wide Open: After the French Debate* (*La Phénomenologie Eclatée*). Trans. Charles N. Cabral. New York: Fordham University Press [1998].

Leask, Ian and Cassidy, Eoin G. (eds) (2005), *Givenness and God: Questions of Jean-Luc Marion.* New York: Fordham University Press.

MacKinlay, Shane (2009), *Interpreting Excess: Jean-Luc Marion, Saturated Phenomena, and Hermeneutics.* New York: Fordham University Press.

Other important phenomenologists

Other important contemporary phenomenologists include Renaud Barbaras, Jean-Louis Chrétien, Jean-François Courtine, Mikkel Dufrenne, and Didier Franck, among many others both inside and outside of France, not to mention various Husserlians in America and northern Europe.

Barbaras, Renaud (2005), *Desire and Distance: Introduction to a Phenomenology of Perception.* Trans. Paul B. Milan. Stanford, CA: Stanford University Press.

Chrétien, Jean-Louis (2004), *The Call and the Response.* Trans. Anne. A. Davenport. New York: Fordham University Press.

Courtine, Jean-François (2007), *La Cause de la Phénoménologie.* Paris: PUF.

Dufrenne, Mikkel (2009), *The Notion of the 'A Priori'.* Trans. Edward S. Casey. Evanston, IL: Northwestern University Press.

Franck, Didier (1981), *Chair et Corps: sur la phénoménologie de Husserl.* Paris: Editions de Minuit.

—(2002), 'Being and Living' [1987] in H. Dreyfus & M. Wrathall (eds), *Heidegger Re-examined.* London: Routledge.

Janicaud, Dominique *et al.,* (2001), *Phenomenology and the 'Theological Turn'.* New York: Fordham University Press, 2001 [1991/2]. A good collection of essays by Janicaud, Courtine, Paul Ricoeur, Chrétien, Marion, and Henry.

Sample questions for essays and discussions

Part I: Edmund Husserl

Chapter 1

What are Husserl's goals in establishing phenomenology?

Explain the idea and procedure of the phenomenological epochē. What does it accomplish?

What is the relation between the natural attitude and the phenomenological attitude?

Chapter 2

What does Husserl mean when he says: 'External perception is a constant pretension to accomplish something that, by its very nature, it is not in a position to accomplish'?

Why and how does Husserl investigate the realm of passivity?

What is the role of time in our perception of an object?

Chapter 3

What are the consequences of the mathematization of nature?

Why is this mathematization an interesting object of philosophical study?

How does the lifeworld relate to the ideal world of the sciences?

Does the ontological way into phenomenology resolve the problems which emerged from the Cartesian way?

Chapter 4

What is the task that Husserl wishes to undertake in the *Fifth Cartesian Meditation*? Is he successful in carrying it out?

What is the relation between transcendental subjectivity and transcendental intersubjectivity?

Assess Husserl's claim that the homeworld/alienworld structure is irreducible.

Part II: Martin Heidegger

Chapter 5

Is Heidegger attempting to criticize Husserl's notion of intentionality with his notion of 'being-in-the-world'?

What is the difference between Dasein and consciousness?

In what way has traditional thought privileged theory over practice? How does Heidegger rectify this?

Chapter 6

Describe the relation between presence-at-hand and readiness-to-hand. Does it have any relevance to the anthropological study of the first apes to take up an entity and use it as a tool? Can certain other animals be said to use tools in Heidegger's sense?

What is the precise relation of the distinction between presence-at-hand and readiness-to-hand to Heidegger's critique of the history of philosophy as privileging an epistemic and theoretical relation to the world?

What does Heidegger mean when he says that authenticity can only be a 'modification' of *in*authenticity?

Chapter 7

What is the motivation for introducing the notion of 'earth' to supplement the notion of 'world'?

How is an artwork different to an ordinary product of human craft? Why is the work of art important to Heidegger's project?

Why does Heidegger consider only 'great' works of art? What is a 'great work' for Heidegger?

Chapter 8

How might the concept of 'renewable energy' be considered by Heidegger? Is it an answer to the exploitative 'en-framing' attitude of technology?

Is there a place for such a notion as the 'thing' in the early Heidegger? Why does Heidegger introduce the notion and in what way can a thing be said to 'bear' a world?

What does Heidegger mean by 'ethics'?

In what way can art be considered as a countermeasure or antidote to technology?

Part III: Jean-Paul Sartre

Chapter 9

Why does Sartre believe that the empirical sciences are important to phenomenology?

Does the notion of a 'phenomenological psychology' constitute the ultimate ambition of Sartre's early work?

What is the relevance of the image and the imagination in Sartre's thought? Does it have any relation to his fictional works?

Chapter 10

In what way is Sartre's understanding of the self-relation of consciousness different from an epistemic relation?

Where might non-human animals fit into Sartre's theory of consciousness, given that they are often traditionally thought to be 'conscious' without being *self*-conscious?

What does Sartre mean by an 'impersonal' field of consciousness? How might we make sense of it?

Chapter 11

Sartre states that man has no universal essence, that there is no human nature, but there *is* a common 'human condition'. Why does he make this distinction and how are we to understand this notion of a 'human condition'?

How does Sartre's existentialism differ from Heidegger's early philosophy in and around *Being and Time*?

Is existentialism individualistic? Can it accommodate a concern for others and for collectivities?

Chapter 12

How might we differentiate Sartre's distinction between being-in-itself and being-for-itself from Descartes' distinction between extension and thought?

How are we to understand sentient animal life in relation to the distinction between being-in-itself and being-for-itself?

Why is being-in-itself said to be 'contingent'? Distinguish being-in-itself from a God who might be said to be 'self-caused' or 'necessary' in his existence?

Why does Sartre replace Heidegger's word 'Dasein' with 'human reality'?

Part IV: Maurice Merleau-Ponty

Chapter 13

How is the lived body different from a mere thing?

What is the 'habit body'?

What does a phenomenological approach contribute to an account of the 'phantom limb' experience?

Why can intellectualism and empiricism not account successfully for our experience of sexuality? Do you find his criticism convincing?

Chapter 14

In what sense do intellectualism and empiricism fall prey to the same mistake when it comes to understanding speech?

Is the paradox of expression really a paradox?

What are the main similarities and differences between phenomenology and painting?

Do linguistic artworks have a substantially different relation to history than painting?

What is the difference between artistic and scientific accounts of space?

Chapter 15

'There is a genius for ambiguity which might serve to define man' (Merleau-Ponty). Discuss.

What is the difference between good and bad ambiguity?

Is Merleau-Ponty's account of cultural ambiguity convincing?

Chapter 16

What is the criticism of traditional accounts of perception that is implied by the concept of reversibility?

What is Merleau-Ponty's concept of flesh? Is it helpful to link it to the ancient notion of the elements?

Is there a monism inherent in the concept of flesh?

Index

400 × 2% = 8

~~600 × ~~

400 × 1 = 4

200 × 2 = 4